I0021257

Migrating Applications to the Cloud with Azure

Re-architect and rebuild your applications using cloud-native technologies

Sjoukje Zaal
Amit Malik
Sander Rossel
Jason Marston
Mohamed Wali
Stefano Demiliani

BIRMINGHAM - MUMBAI

Migrating Applications to the Cloud with Azure

Copyright © 2019 Packt Publishing

All rights reserved. No part of this book may be reproduced, stored in a retrieval system, or transmitted in any form or by any means, without the prior written permission of the publisher, except in the case of brief quotations embedded in critical articles or reviews.

Every effort has been made in the preparation of this book to ensure the accuracy of the information presented. However, the information contained in this book is sold without warranty, either express or implied. Neither the authors, nor Packt Publishing or its dealers and distributors, will be held liable for any damages caused or alleged to have been caused directly or indirectly by this book.

Packt Publishing has endeavored to provide trademark information about all of the companies and products mentioned in this book by the appropriate use of capitals. However, Packt Publishing cannot guarantee the accuracy of this information.

Commissioning Editor: Amey Varangaonkar
Acquisition Editor: Rahul Nair
Content Development Editor: Ronn Kurien
Senior Editor: Richard Brookes-Bland
Technical Editor: Mohd Riyan Khan
Copy Editor: Safis Editing
Project Coordinator: Anish Daniel
Proofreader: Safis Editing
Indexer: Manju Arasan
Production Designer: Joshua Misquitta

First published: December 2019

Production reference: 1061219

Published by Packt Publishing Ltd.
Livery Place
35 Livery Street
Birmingham
B3 2PB, UK.

ISBN 978-1-83921-747-0

www.packt.com

Packt.com

Subscribe to our online digital library for full access to over 7,000 books and videos, as well as industry leading tools to help you plan your personal development and advance your career. For more information, please visit our website.

Why subscribe?

- Spend less time learning and more time coding with practical eBooks and videos from over 4,000 industry professionals.

- Improve your learning with Skill Plans built especially for you.

- Get a free eBook or video every month.

- Fully searchable for easy access to vital information.

- Copy and paste, print, and bookmark content

Did you know that Packt offers eBook versions of every book published, with PDF and ePub files available? You can upgrade to the eBook version at www.packt.com and, as a print book customer, you are entitled to a discount on the eBook copy. Get in touch with us at customercare@packtpub.com for more details.

At www.packt.com, you can also read a collection of free technical articles, sign up for a range of free newsletters, and receive exclusive discounts and offers on Packt books and eBooks.

Contributors

About the authors

Sjoukje Zaal is a managing consultant, Microsoft Cloud Architect, and Microsoft Azure MVP with over 15 years' experience of providing architecture, development, consultancy, and design expertise. She works at Capgemini, a global leader in consulting, technology services, and digital transformation.

She loves to share her knowledge and is active in the Microsoft community as a cofounder of the Dutch user groups, SP&C NL and MixUG, and the Global Mixed Reality Bootcamp. She is also a board member of Global Azure Bootcamp and Azure Thursdays. She is a public speaker and is involved in organizing events. She has written several books, writes blogs on a regular basis, and is active in the Microsoft Tech community. She is also part of the Diversity and Inclusion Advisory Board.

Amit Malik is an IT enthusiast and technology evangelist focused on cloud and emerging technologies. He is currently employed by Spektra Systems as the director of technology, where he helps Microsoft partners grow their cloud businesses by using effective tools and strategies. He specializes in the cloud, DevOps, software-defined infrastructure, application modernization, data platforms, and emerging technologies around AI. Amit holds various industry-admired certifications from all major OEMs in the cloud and data space, including Azure Solutions Architect Expert. He is also a Microsoft Certified Trainer (MCT). Amit is also an active community member for various technology groups and is a regular speaker at industry conferences and events.

Sander Rossel is a Microsoft-certified professional developer and author with experience and expertise in .NET and .NET Core, Azure, Azure DevOps, SQL Server, JavaScript, and other technologies. With his company, JUUN Software, he builds cloud-native applications and brings companies to the cloud.

Jason Marston is a Cloud Solution Architect based in England. He was recruited by Microsoft because of his OSS background. Jason has worked with Java since version 1 and has a long history with open source. He has over 30 years' experience of developing software and now helps organizations migrate and modernize legacy applications to the cloud. Jason was an SME in the Worldwide Communities project at Microsoft and, as part of the leadership team for those communities, helped many people solve their problems by adopting Java on Azure. In his spare time, Jason reads science fiction books and has two children who think he is a geek/nerd.

Mohamed Wali is a Cloud DevOps engineer based in Amsterdam who has been working with Microsoft technologies for around 7 years. He has been working with Azure since 2013. In July 2014, Mohamed was recognized as the youngest Microsoft MVP in the world. He has already authored/coauthored four books about Microsoft Azure and shares his knowledge and experience through blogging, authoring books, and speaking at events.

Stefano Demiliani is a Microsoft MVP on business applications, a Microsoft Certified Solution Developer (MCSD), Azure Certified Architect, and an expert in other Microsoft-related technologies. His main activity is architecting and developing enterprise solutions based on the entire stack of Microsoft technologies (mainly focused on ERP and the cloud). He has worked with Packt Publishing on many IT books related to Azure cloud applications and Dynamics 365 Business Central, and is a speaker at conferences around Europe. You can reach him on Twitter (@demiliani) or LinkedIn.

About the reviewer

Alexey Bokov is an experienced Azure architect and Microsoft technical evangelist since 2011. He works closely with Microsoft's top-tier customers all around the world to develop applications based on the Azure cloud platform. Building cloud-based applications on challenging scenarios is his passion, along with helping the development community to upskill and learn new things through hands-on exercises and hacking. He's a long-time contributor to, and coauthor and reviewer of, many Azure books, and, from time to time, is a speaker at Kubernetes events.

Packt is searching for authors like you

If you're interested in becoming an author for Packt, please visit `authors.packtpub.com` and apply today. We have worked with thousands of developers and tech professionals, just like you, to help them share their insight with the global tech community. You can make a general application, apply for a specific hot topic that we are recruiting an author for, or submit your own idea.

Table of Contents

Preface   1

Section 1: Planning Application Modernization

Chapter 1: Strategies for Application Modernization Using Azure   9
  Introducing application modernization   9
    The value of application modernization   10
  The cloud maturity model   11
  Different migration strategies   12
    Rehost   12
    Refactor   14
    Rearchitect   15
    Rebuild   16
  Summary   18
  Questions   18
  Further reading   19

Chapter 2: Building Your Application Migration Roadmap   21
  Building a migration roadmap   22
    Assess   22
      Creating a cloud migration plan   22
      Involving stakeholders   22
      Calculating your TCO   23
      Discovering and evaluating apps   23
    Migrate   23
    Optimize   24
      Cost management and billing   24
    Secure and manage   25
      Security   25
      Cloud health monitoring   26
      Data protection   27
  Migration tooling   27
    Microsoft Assessment and Planning Toolkit   28
    Azure Migrate   28
    Azure Site Recovery   30
    Azure Database Migration Guide   31
    App Service Migration   32
  Summary   33
  Questions   34
  Further reading   35

Section 2: Implementing Containerization and DevOps in a Development Cycle

Chapter 3: Getting Started with Docker and Kubernetes 39
  Technical requirements 39
  Understanding the Docker ecosystem in Azure 40
    Azure Container Instances 40
    Azure Kubernetes Service 41
    Web Apps for Containers 42
    Azure Batch for Containers 42
    Docker in Azure Marketplace 42
      Docker Enterprise Edition (basic, standard, advanced) 43
    Azure Service Fabric 43
    Red Hat OpenShift on Azure 44
    Docker in Azure IaaS 45
  Containerizing your applications 45
    Planning for containerization 46
    Building a Docker host in Azure 47
    Preparing Docker images 49
      Preparing a Dockerfile 50
      Preparing a sample Dockerfile for a sample app 51
      Building the Docker image 54
        Pushing Docker images to Docker Hub 55
        Pushing Docker images to the Azure Container Registry 56
      Running the application with containers 60
  Kubernetes and Azure 61
    Kubernetes overview 62
    What does Kubernetes do? 63
    Kubernetes architecture 64
    Kubernetes concepts 66
    Building Kubernetes environments on Azure 68
    Azure Kubernetes Service 68
  Why Azure Kubernetes Service? 68
    Top use cases with AKS 70
  Summary 71
  Questions 71
  Further reading 72

Chapter 4: Deploying Highly Scalable Apps with Kubernetes 73
  Technical requirements 73
  Azure makes Kubernetes easy 74
  Deploying an AKS cluster 74
    Deploying with the Azure portal 74
    Deploying with the Azure CLI 79
    Connecting to the AKS cluster 80
  Understanding AKS networking modes 81

Deploying applications on AKS 82
 Planning scalable application deployment on AKS 82
  Frontend 83
  Backend 83
 Building a deployment YAML file 84
  Deployment for the backend pod 84
  Service for the backend pod's deployment 86
  Deployment for the frontend application 86
  Service for the frontend application 88
 Deploying the sample application 88
Scaling applications on AKS 90
 Scaling applications on AKS manually 91
 Autoscaling AKS applications 92
Scaling the AKS cluster 92
 Scaling an AKS cluster manually 93
 Autoscaling the AKS cluster 93
Upgrading applications on AKS 94
Upgrading an AKS cluster 95
Exposing applications outside the Kubernetes cluster 96
Monitoring and logging AKS using OMS 97
 Insights 99
 Metrics 101
 Logs 102
Running highly scalable AKS applications using ACI 103
Using Helm to deploy applications 103
Summary 104
Questions 104
Further reading 105
Chapter 5: Modernizing Apps and Infrastructure with DevOps 107
 Understanding Azure DevOps 107
  Getting Azure DevOps 108
  Signing up for Azure DevOps 109
 Azure boards 110
 Azure Repos 112
 Azure pipelines 113
  Azure pipeline agents 114
 Azure test plans 115
 Azure artifacts 116
 Building a CI/CD pipeline with Azure DevOps 117
  Creating a new Azure DevOps project 117
   Cloning the voting app code to your development machine 118
  Setting up an Azure repo for the voting app and pushing the application code 119
  Setting up a build pipeline 121

Building a release pipeline 129
Simulating an end-to-end CI/CD experience 141
Using Azure pipelines with GitHub 144
Summary 144
Questions 145
Further reading 145

Section 3: Building a Web and Microservices Architecture on Azure

Chapter 6: Designing Web Applications 149
  Technical requirements 149
  Azure Web Apps 150
    App Service Plans 150
    App Service Environment 153
      Creating an App Service Environment 154
  Web Apps for containers 158
    Creating a web app for containers 159
  Designing web apps for high availability, scalability, and performance 162
    High availability and performance 163
      Using a CDN 163
      Using Azure Cache for Redis 163
      Using Azure Traffic Manager 164
    Scalability 165
      Scaling out 165
      Scaling up 168
  Designing and securing custom web APIs 168
    Designing your web API 169
    Securing your web API 175
  Summary 176
  Questions 177
  Further reading 177

Chapter 7: Scalability and Performance 179
  Technical requirements 179
  Working with HPC virtual machines 179
    Virtual machine scale sets 181
  Understanding Microsoft HPC Pack 185
    Cloud-native HPC solutions 185
    Hybrid HPC architecture 187
    Deploying an HPC cluster on-premises 188
  Understanding Azure Batch 189
    Creating an Azure Batch service 191
    Stateless components 195

Containers on Azure Batch 196
Executing a Batch job from code 196
Summary 202
Questions 202
Further reading 203

Chapter 8: Building Microservices with Service Fabric 205
Technical requirements 205
Understanding Azure Service Fabric 206
Stateless and stateful microservices 207
Stateless services 208
Stateful services 208
Azure Service Fabric application scenarios 209
Programming models 209
The Reliable Services programming model 210
The Reliable Actor programming model 211
Life cycle management 212
Azure Service Fabric Mesh 212
Creating an Azure Service Fabric cluster 213
Creating a Service Fabric .NET application 220
Setting up your development environment 221
Creating the application 221
Deploying the application 229
Creating a Service Fabric Java application 231
Setting up your development environment 232
Setting up a local Service Fabric cluster 232
Installing the Eclipse plugin for service fabric 233
Creating the application 236
Deploying the application 241
Summary 242
Questions 243
Further reading 243

Section 4: Going Serverless and Deploying to the Cloud

Chapter 9: Building Scalable Systems with Azure Functions 247
Technical requirements 247
Understanding serverless computing 248
Dynamic scaling 248
Dynamic pricing 248
Disadvantages of serverless computing 249
Creating an Azure function 249
Creating a Function App 250
Creating a function 252
Consuming your HTTP function 253
Function management 254

Working with triggered functions 256
　Creating a triggered function 256
Creating Azure Functions in Visual Studio 259
Deploying Azure Functions 262
　Deploying using Visual Studio 262
　Deploying using Azure DevOps 263
Timer triggered functions 266
　Using the cron syntax 267
　Writing a second function 267
Input and output bindings 269
　Adding bindings in the portal 269
　Adding bindings in Visual Studio 272
　Understanding bindings 273
Azure Functions proxies 274
　Creating a proxy 274
　Proxies for testing 275
Best practices 277
Summary 277
Questions 278
Further reading 279

Chapter 10: Connecting to the Database 281
Technical requirements 281
Working with Azure SQL 282
　Picking your version 282
　Creating an Azure SQL Database 283
　Pricing tiers 286
　Using your database in the portal 287
Connecting to SQL Server Management Studio 289
Connecting to Azure SQL from .NET Core 291
　Connecting using ADO.NET 292
　Connecting using Entity Framework Core 293
　Entity Framework migrations 294
Connecting to Azure SQL from Java 297
　Connecting using JDBC 297
　Connecting using JPA 298
Understanding Cosmos DB 301
　The key-value model/Table API 302
　The document model/MongoDB API 303
　The SQL API 305
　The graph model/Gremlin API 306
　The wide-column model/Cassandra API 308
Working with the MongoDB API 309
　Working with MongoDB in the Azure portal 311
　Working with MongoDB from C# 312

Working with MongoDB from Java 314
Working with the Redis cache database 319
Creating a Redis cache 319
Working with Redis from C# 321
Using the ServiceStack Redis API 323
Working with Redis from Java 324
Summary 328
Questions 328
Further reading 329

Chapter 11: Managing and Deploying Your Code 331
IDEs for Azure 331
Using Visual Studio with Azure 332
Getting Azure tools for Visual Studio 333
Visual Studio in the Azure Marketplace 333
Installing Azure tools for Visual Studio 334
Logging in to Visual Studio with Azure credentials 335
Using Cloud Explorer in Visual Studio 336
Developing and deploying with Visual Studio for Azure 338
Connecting Visual Studio to an existing Azure DevOps project 338
Deploying applications to Azure using Visual Studio 341
Using Eclipse with Azure 349
Installing Azure Toolkit for Eclipse 350
Signing in to Azure and using Azure Explorer within Eclipse 354
Publishing a Java project to Azure using Eclipse 355
Visual Studio Code and Azure 359
IntelliJ and Azure 360
Summary 360
Questions 360
Further reading 361

Chapter 12: Securing Your Azure Services 363
Understanding Azure Key Vault 363
AKV scenarios 364
AKV advantages 364
AKV flavors 365
Creating an Azure Key Vault 365
AKV keys 370
AKV secrets 374
AKV certificates 374
Securing Azure Storage 377
Securing access to storage accounts 377
Granting the Reader role to a user using RBAC 378
Securing access to the storage account data 380
Azure Storage Service Encryption 381
Advanced Threat Protection for Azure Storage 382

Azure Storage firewall   382
Securing Azure SQL databases   383
   Firewall and virtual network access   384
     Controlling access using a firewall   384
     Controlling access using virtual networks   385
   Access control   386
     Security authentication to Azure SQL   387
   Transparent data encryption   387
     How does transparent data encryption work?   387
     Securing your Azure SQL Databases with your own key   388
     Transparent data encryption tips   388
   Advanced data security for Azure SQL services   388
Securing your Azure VMs and network   389
   Azure VM security   389
   Azure network security   390
Azure Security Center   391
   Microsoft Trust Center   392
Summary   393
Questions   393
Further reading   394

Section 5: Planning for Security, Availability, and Monitoring

Chapter 13: Diagnostics and Monitoring   397
   Azure Log Analytics   398
     Creating a Log Analytics workspace   398
   Azure Monitor   405
   Application Insights   407
   Azure Service Health   409
   Azure Advisor   410
     Addressing recommendation from Azure Advisor   411
   Azure Network Watcher   413
   Summary   416
   Questions   416
   Further reading   417

Chapter 14: Designing for High Availability and Disaster Recovery   419
   Introducing high availability and disaster recovery   420
   App Service   421
     Scaling up the App Service plan   421
       Key points regarding scaling up your App Service plan   424
     Scaling out your App Service plan   424
       Scaling out your App Service plan manually   424
       Scaling out your App Service plan automatically   425
       Key points for autoscaling your App Service plan   430
     App Services deployment slots   431

Deployment slots key points   432
Backing up your App Services   433
Key points for backing up your App Service   436
Azure SQL Database   436
Active geo-replication   436
Auto-failover groups   439
Business continuity for Azure SQL Database   440
Hardware failures   440
Point-in-time restore   441
Key points for point-in-time restore   442
Highly available access to apps using Azure Traffic Manager   443
Azure Traffic Manager benefits   444
Azure Traffic Manager endpoints   444
Azure Traffic Manager routing methods   445
Building a Traffic Manager   445
Azure Traffic Manager key points   448
Azure Backup   449
Supported workloads   449
Enabling backups for a virtual machine   450
Azure Site Recovery   453
Supported scenarios – ASR   454
Summary   454
Questions   455
Further reading   456

Assessments   457

Other Books You May Enjoy   463

Index   467

Preface

This book is designed to show developers and architects how to modernize and run their applications effectively on the cloud. It introduces you to modern technologies, including containers, microservices, DevOps, and serverless computing, with a focus on running applications effectively by choosing the right solution. You'll also learn how to architect, develop, and deploy applications using these modern technologies on Azure.

What this book covers

Chapter 1, *Strategies for Application Modernization Using Azure*, introduces app modernization for Azure and different migration strategies.

Chapter 2, *Building Your Application Migration Roadmap*, focuses on defining an app modernization roadmap for your organization or customers.

Chapter 3, *Getting Started with Docker and Kubernetes*, focuses on the modernization and migration of applications to Azure by leveraging the power of containerization.

Chapter 4, *Deploying Highly Scalable Apps with Kubernetes*, covers deploying and managing Kubernetes-based environments on Azure.

Chapter 5, *Modernizing Apps and Infrastructure with DevOps*, goes into detail about Microsoft's new offering, Azure DevOps, which provides various tools and services to facilitate an enterprise-class DevOps culture in organizations of every size.

Chapter 6, *Designing Web Applications*, covers information regarding Azure web apps, the different App Service plans that are available, and the characteristics of the different App Service plans.

Chapter 7, *Scalability and Performance*, introduces compute-intensive applications. It covers how to design **high-performance computing** (**HPC**) and other compute-intensive applications using Azure services, how to determine when to use Azure Batch, and how to design stateless components to accommodate scale and containers with Azure Batch.

Chapter 8, *Building Microservices with Service Fabric*, dives into creating a microservice application from scratch using Azure Service Fabric. We will create an application in .NET and in Java.

`Chapter` 9, *Building Scalable Systems with Azure Functions*, talks about Azure Function apps, which are a great way to write small pieces of code that are highly scalable, reusable, and cheap.

`Chapter` 10, *Connecting to the Database*, talks about the various databases that can be used to connect your application.

`Chapter` 11, *Managing and Deploying Your Code*, covers Azure integrations and plugins for popular IDEs, including Visual Studio, Eclipse, Visual Studio Code, and IntelliJ.

`Chapter` 12, *Securing Your Azure Services*, teaches you how to secure some of the most commonly used Azure services, such as Azure Storage, Azure App Service, and Azure SQL Database.

`Chapter` 13, *Diagnostics and Monitoring*, introduces the design for operations objective by covering application and platform monitoring and alerting strategies, providing an overview of the solutions that Azure has to offer.

`Chapter` 14, *Designing for High Availability and Disaster Recovery*, covers a number of solutions that will keep your solutions highly available so as to avoid downtime as much as possible.

To get the most out of this book

You should have a basic understanding of, and experience in, developing applications using either the .NET or Java programming frameworks. Knowledge of Azure or cloud fundamentals is desirable. You should have an Azure subscription with admin rights to follow the labs alongside the chapters, and you should also explore related Azure services and samples available on GitHub to dig deeper into any specific Azure service or application modernization methodology. Click on the following link to create your Azure account: `https://azure.microsoft.com/enus/free/`.

Download the example code files

You can download the example code files for this book from your account at `www.packt.com`. If you purchased this book elsewhere, you can visit `www.packtpub.com/support` and register to have the files emailed directly to you.

You can download the code files by following these steps:

1. Log in or register at `www.packt.com`.
2. Select the **Support** tab.

3. Click on **Code Downloads**.
4. Enter the name of the book in the **Search** box and follow the onscreen instructions.

Once the file is downloaded, please make sure that you unzip or extract the folder using the latest version of:

- WinRAR/7-Zip for Windows
- Zipeg/iZip/UnRarX for Mac
- 7-Zip/PeaZip for Linux

The code bundle for the book is also hosted on GitHub at `https://github.com/PacktPublishing/Migrating-Apps-to-the-Cloud-with-Azure`. In case there's an update to the code, it will be updated on the existing GitHub repository.

We also have other code bundles from our rich catalog of books and videos available at `https://github.com/PacktPublishing/`. Check them out!

Download the color images

We also provide a PDF file that has color images of the screenshots/diagrams used in this book. You can download it here: `https://static.packt-cdn.com/downloads/9781839217470_ColorImages.pdf`.

Conventions used

There are a number of text conventions used throughout this book.

`CodeInText`: Indicates code words in text, database table names, folder names, filenames, file extensions, pathnames, dummy URLs, user input, and Twitter handles. Here is an example: "Create a new VNet and call it `PacktPubASEVNet` and pick a region."

A block of code is set as follows:

```
namespace PacktPubToDoAPI.Models
{
    public class TodoItem
    {
        public long Id { get; set; }
        public string Name { get; set; }
        public bool IsComplete { get; set; }
    }
}
```

When we wish to draw your attention to a particular part of a code block, the relevant lines or items are set in bold:

```
namespace PacktPubToDoAPI.Models
{
    public class TodoItem
    {
        public long Id { get; set; }
        public string Name { get; set; }
        public bool IsComplete { get; set; }
    }
}
```

Any command-line input or output is written as follows:

```
git clone  https://github.com/amalik99/project-nodejs-express-webapp.git
cd project-nodejs-express-webapp
```

Bold: Indicates a new term, an important word, or words that you see onscreen. For example, words in menus or dialog boxes appear in the text like this. Here is an example: "Choose your **Subscription**, **Resource group**, and the **Location** where you'd want to deploy this."

 Warnings or important notes appear like this.

 Tips and tricks appear like this.

Get in touch

Feedback from our readers is always welcome.

General feedback: If you have questions about any aspect of this book, mention the book title in the subject of your message and email us at customercare@packtpub.com.

Errata: Although we have taken every care to ensure the accuracy of our content, mistakes do happen. If you have found a mistake in this book, we would be grateful if you would report this to us. Please visit www.packtpub.com/support/errata, selecting your book, clicking on the Errata Submission Form link, and entering the details.

Piracy: If you come across any illegal copies of our works in any form on the internet, we would be grateful if you would provide us with the location address or website name. Please contact us at copyright@packt.com with a link to the material.

If you are interested in becoming an author: If there is a topic that you have expertise in and you are interested in either writing or contributing to a book, please visit authors.packtpub.com.

Reviews

Please leave a review. Once you have read and used this book, why not leave a review on the site that you purchased it from? Potential readers can then see and use your unbiased opinion to make purchase decisions, we at Packt can understand what you think about our products, and our authors can see your feedback on their book. Thank you!

For more information about Packt, please visit packt.com.

1
Planning Application Modernization

In this section, we will modernize and move your existing infrastructure to Azure IaaS and PaaS. You will learn strategies for reducing your costs, increasing storage, and increasing your return on investment.

This section contains the following chapters:

- Chapter 1, *Strategies for Application Modernization Using Azure*
- Chapter 2, *Building Your Application Migration Roadmap*

Strategies for Application Modernization Using Azure

1

This book will cover the different migration strategies, services, resources, and functionalities that Microsoft Azure has to offer to migrate your applications to Azure.

This first chapter introduces application modernization for Azure. It describes the different strategies and steps that companies can take to eventually end up with a full cloud-native app that is fully designed for elastic scaling, is cost-effective, can be decomposed into several loosely coupled services, and is easy to deploy, manage, and maintain.

In this chapter, we will cover the following topics:

- Introducing application modernization
- The value of application modernization
- The cloud maturity model
- Different migration strategies

Introducing application modernization

The cloud is rapidly changing the way in which applications are designed and architected. We are shifting from monolithic applications to applications that are designed as loosely coupled services that can either communicate through APIs or are using asynchronous messaging and eventing. These applications need to be designed to easily scale horizontally, and new instances should be added or removed rapidly, and mostly automatically.

This brings big challenges to the underlying architecture of your applications. Operations should be able to be processed in parallel and deployments must be fully automated. The system as a whole, with all the different services included, should be resilient when failures occur.

Monitoring and telemetry must be embedded for the system as a whole as well, to gain insights into the health and performance of the system and all the loosely coupled services that are used for composing the application.

Let's now go on to understand the advantages of having your application modernized to Azure.

The value of application modernization

Moving applications to Azure can bring big value to organizations. Organizations can now fully focus on the business that they are in and focus on the changes they want to make to their IT environments, their businesses, and their products. By undergoing this digital transformation, organizations are able to think differently about their products, and are able to change the way they engage with their customers and support the things they want to do with their customers in a much faster and more agile way. Employees can be empowered using all of these new technologies, and operations can be optimized easily as well.

By bringing more value to an organization's business and customers, costs can be reduced significantly, because organizations don't have to invest in, or think about, the underlying infrastructure anymore.

The benefits that organizations can enjoy by migrating applications from on-premises environments to Azure can be categorized as follows:

- **Agility/time to market**: This refers to how quickly you can get your applications out and deploy updates. You can use **continuous delivery** (**CD**) and **continuous integration** (**CI**) or containerize your applications for rapid deployment.
- **Reducing costs**: By shifting over to cloud-native applications and services, you can significantly reduce costs, since there is no infrastructure that needs to be maintained and there are no licensing costs. For serverless applications and containers, you only pay for the compute power you need.
- **IT simplification**: Using cloud-native technologies, you can simplify your IT environment. There is no infrastructure to manage anymore and there are no monolithic architectures to maintain. Applications can use modern architectures such as microservices, for instance. Additionally, breaking up applications into reusable pieces makes it a lot easier to maintain.

In the next section, we are going to look at the cloud maturity model, a predefined set of steps that will eventually let your applications evolve into a fully cloud-native application.

The cloud maturity model

For an application to eventually become fully cloud-native, it should follow an iterative process called the **cloud maturity model**. The first two steps will either require minimal code or simply the configuration changes necessary to connect to Azure PaaS services or to optimize the application for cloud scale. Applications are moved to the cloud, but are mostly using the same code base as they were using when they were deployed on the on-premises systems. The last step, that is, the step to rebuild the application, will require a complete redesign and refactoring of the application. This step will be the most difficult and most intensive part of the application migration process.

The order of this process can be completely random. Organizations can decide to rebuild their applications from scratch to fully modernized applications immediately that leverage all cloud-native technologies, such as Azure Functions, microservices, Logic Apps, Service Fabric, and much more. They can also decide to start moving **virtual machines** (**VMs**) with the on-premises applications first, and, over time, expand their Azure resources and start refactoring, rearchitecting, and rebuilding their applications. However, following the steps in this flow, from left to right, is how most organizations start their journey of moving and migrating their applications to Azure:

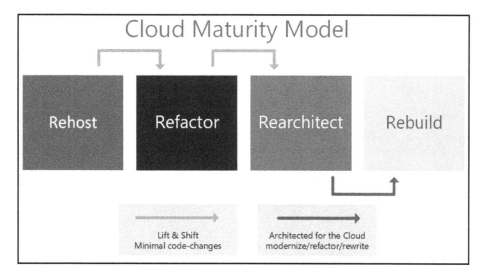

The cloud maturity model

In the upcoming section, we will cover the four different migration strategies.

Different migration strategies

There are four migration strategies that are defined in the cloud maturity model: rehost, refactor, rearchitect, and rebuild. In the upcoming sections, these migration strategies will be explained in more detail.

Rehost

Rehost is often referred to as lift-and-shift migration. When you rehost your applications to the cloud, each application is migrated as-is to the cloud. This technically means that you move the VMs or on-premises servers and put them into the cloud infrastructure. The applications that are installed on the on-premises VMs and servers are then moved in their original state, without any code changes or refactoring of the application.

You can use some of the managed services in the cloud as well. For instance, you can migrate your databases to Azure SQL, PostgreSQL, or MySQL on Azure.

In the following diagram, you can see an illustration of a lift-and-shift migration. On-premises VMs with applications and databases deployed on them are moved as they are to Azure. By using this migration method, the VMs and databases can leverage the Azure IaaS scalability capabilities:

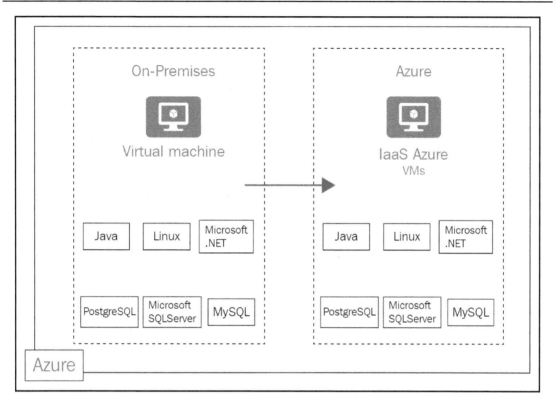

Rehosting applications

The pros of this method include the following:

- You don't have to refactor or rewrite your code.
- You can migrate to Azure quickly. You can just put your VM in the cloud. There could be some minor caveats such as networking issues, for instance, but this is the quickest way of migrating your applications to the cloud.

The cons of this method including the following:

- This method brings the least cloud value to your applications.
- You are still responsible for patching and upgrading the VMs in Azure.
- You can make limited use of horizontal scaling and high availability.
- You are still using a monolithic architecture for your applications.

Refactor

Refactoring is often referred to as repackaging your applications. This is a migration approach that means you only need to make minimal changes to the application code or only apply the necessary configuration changes to connect the application to PaaS services, such as Azure app services or Azure SQL Database managed instances, for example.

In the following diagram, you can see the migration of on-premises applications to PaaS services in Azure. They are deployed in one or more Azure app services and the SQL databases can be moved as-is to Azure SQL Database managed instances:

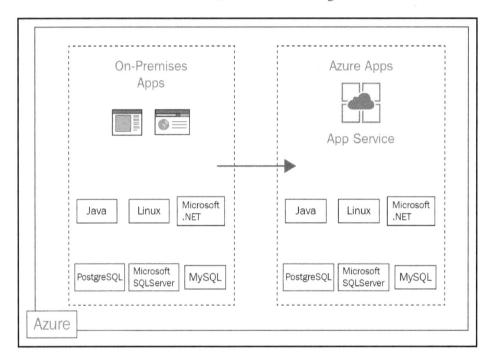

Refactoring applications

The pros of this method include the following:

- You don't have to rearchitect or write new code.
- You can easily repackage your code to deploy in Azure.
- You can start using DevOps practices for your projects.
- You can make use of high availability for your applications.

The cons of this method include the following:

- You can still only make limited use of horizontal scaling and high availability.
- You are still using a monolithic architecture for your applications.

Rearchitect

Using this cloud migration strategy, you are modifying or extending the application's code base to optimize the application architecture for horizontal scale. Your applications will be modernized into a resilient, highly scalable, and independently deployable architecture. You can use Azure services such as containers to speed up the process, scale applications easily, and simplify the management of your applications.

As you can see in the following diagram, on-premises applications are migrated to containers in Azure, such as Azure Kubernetes. Databases are migrated to Azure SQL databases:

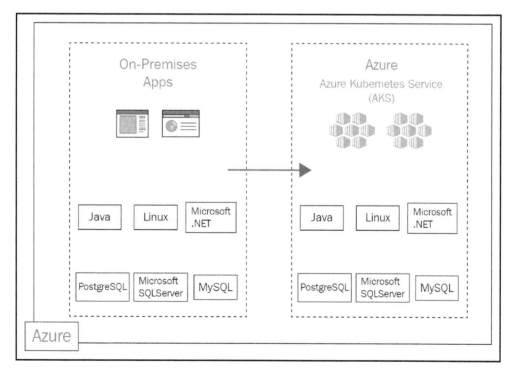

Rearchitecting applications

The pros of this method include the following:

- You can start using horizontal scaling and high availability for your applications in a cost-effective way.
- You can start using DevOps practices for your projects.
- You can lower the deployment costs for your applications.
- You can minimize the use of VMs.

The cons of this method include the following:

- Your applications need major revisions to be rearchitected into applications that can be deployed into containers.
- Your developers need additional skills to start using containerization.

Rebuild

With this migration strategy, the applications are completely rebuilt from scratch using cloud-native technologies. Azure PaaS services and serverless features are used to provide a complete development and deployment environment in the cloud. Such services and features include Azure Functions, Logic Apps, and Azure Service Bus.

In the following diagram, you can see a migration of on-premises applications and databases, which are completely rebuilt from scratch, to cloud-native applications. Databases can be rebuilt and can use Azure SQL databases, or Azure Cosmos DB, for instance. Applications can use the PaaS offering of Azure, such as Logic Apps, Azure Functions, and Cognitive Services:

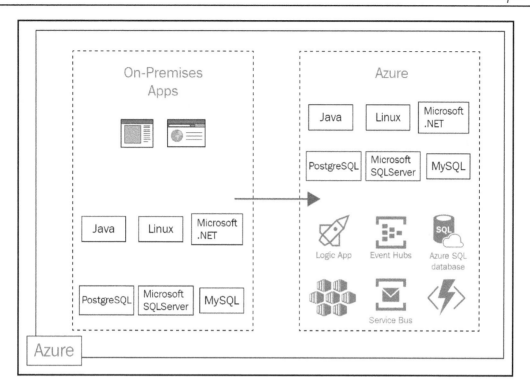

Rebuilding applications

The pros of this method include the following:

- You can make use of rapid development.
- There is no need for managing the underlying infrastructure for your applications.
- Your applications can take advantage of AI, Blockchain, IoT, and more.
- You can fully apply DevOps practices in Azure.
- You can use modern architectures such as microservices.

The cons of this method are the following:

- Your applications need major revisions to be rearchitected into applications that can be deployed into containers.
- Your developers require additional skills to start using all the different cloud-native technologies.
- It requires significant code changes, refactoring, and the rearchitecture of your applications.

Summary

In this chapter, we covered the value that application migration can bring to organizations. We introduced the different migration strategies that are available for migrating your applications to Azure, from a simple lift and shift to a complete rebuild of your application.

In the upcoming chapter, we are going to create a roadmap for application migration to Azure and discuss the different migration strategies.

Questions

Answer the following questions to test your knowledge of the information found in this chapter. You can find the answers in the *Assessments* section at the end of this book.

1. What values can migrating applications to Microsoft Azure bring to your organization?
    1. Reducing costs
    2. No investments in developing the skills of your developers
    3. Faster time to market
    4. IT simplification

2. What are the biggest pros of using the rehost migration strategy for your applications?
    1. No code changes
    2. Migrate quickly to Azure
    3. No infrastructure to manage
    4. Maximum cost reduction

3. Which migration strategy do you need to choose to start making use of the DevOps practices in Azure?
    1. Rehost
    2. Refactor
    3. Rearchitect
    4. Rebuild

Further reading

You can refer to the following links for more information about the topics covered in this chapter:

- **Azure Application Architecture Guide**: `https://docs.microsoft.com/en-us/azure/architecture/guide/`
- **Application Modernization with Microsoft Azure: Build 2018**: `https://www.youtube.com/watch?v=kcHhMjymt_0`
- **Migrate to the cloud**: `https://www.microsoft.com/net/learn/architecture/migrate-to-the-cloud`
- **Azure Migration Center**: `https://azure.microsoft.com/en-us/migration/`
- **Cloud Migration Essentials: A guide to migrating servers and virtual machines:** `https://azure.microsoft.com/en-us/resources/cloud-migration-essentials-e-book/`

2
Building Your Application Migration Roadmap

In the previous chapter, we covered the value for organizations of migrating their applications to Microsoft Azure. We covered the cloud maturity model and different migration strategies.

This chapter focuses on defining an application modernization roadmap for your organization or customers. It covers how to plan your strategy to take advantage of the benefits offered by the cloud by following a couple of predefined steps.

In this chapter, the following topics will be covered:

- Building a migration roadmap
- Migration tooling

Building a migration roadmap

Microsoft defines building a complete road map and strategy for migrating your applications to Azure with the following four steps:

- Assess
- Migrate
- Optimize
- Secure and manage

These are described in more detail in the upcoming sections.

Assess

This is the first phase of the migration journey. In this first step, you take a view of your current environment; you get an overview of all of the virtual machines, applications, and on-premises servers that are deployed inside the environment, and what the migration of all of these different components and features will look like.

This first step—assessing your current environment—consists of the following four steps.

Creating a cloud migration plan

Before you can start planning your migration, you need to set your cloud migration priorities and objectives. By following this approach, a more successful migration is ensured. You can also get insights into the environment and dependencies by using automated cloud migration tools. This way you create the cloud migration project plans.

You can build a template that aligns with individual apps, locations, or groups within your organization for future use by assessing your environment. Start with applications that are expected to have few dependencies to get your migration moving quickly.

Involving stakeholders

Migrating to the cloud is a digital transformation for most businesses. Besides the technical migration, broad organizational change and support are required as well. Involve key people throughout the organization, such as involved business and IT owners. The migration will lead a lot smoother and faster if you get the engagement and support of the stakeholders.

Calculating your TCO

By calculating the **Total Cost of Ownership** (**TCO**), you can evaluate the potential cost savings of migrating to Azure compared to an on-premises deployment. The Azure TCO calculator can be used to build a customized cloud assessment that can help to build a personal business case to support the Azure migration.

Discovering and evaluating apps

The discovery step includes scanning your current environment to create an inventory of all of the physical and virtual servers and all of the applications that are deployed inside your data center. The data obtained by the scan can include profile information and performance metrics about your applications and servers. At the end of this step, you'll have a complete inventory with all of the metadata necessary to build your cloud migration plan.

This inventory can be made using cloud migration assessment tools. One of these tools is Azure Migrate, which is offered by Microsoft and will be covered in more detail later in this chapter. There are other third-party tools available as well.

Using the information from the discovery phase, you can map your servers to represent your on-premises applications. This will help you to identify dependencies between servers, such as communication between applications and servers, for instance. This way, you can include all of the necessary application components in your cloud migration plan. You can group all of the servers logically to represent applications, and then select the best migration strategy for each application based on its requirements and migration objectives.

This is the last step. With all of the application groups mapped, you can use cloud migration assessment tools to evaluate the best way to migrate your on-premises application to the cloud. These tools provide recommendations and migration strategies for your application servers.

Migrate

Step two is to migrate and actually move all of the resources to the cloud. In this step, you pick one or more of the migration strategies that are described in Chapter 1, *Strategies for Application Modernization Using Azure*, in the *Different migration strategies* section.

Just as a recap, the following strategies can be adopted in the migration phase:

- **Rehost**: Also called lift-and-shift migration, this is no-code migration, where each server and application is migrated, as is, using IaaS and Azure networking components. Physical and virtual servers are moved to Azure VMs, and databases can be migrated as is as well, using an Azure SQL Database Managed Instance.
- **Refactor**: Also called repackaging, this involves repackaging your applications, such as web apps and containers, to deploy them to Azure PaaS. This approach involves minimal code changes.
- **Rearchitect**: Using this approach, your application code base is modernized into a resilient, highly scalable, independently deployable architecture. The application is then optimized to scale for the cloud.
- **Rebuild**: Using this approach, the application is completely rebuilt from scratch using cloud-native technologies and design principles. It uses a complete development and deployment environment from the cloud without the need to manage your own infrastructure. All of this is completely handled by Azure.

Optimize

In this third phase, you can use the different Azure Cost Management features to monitor your usage inside Azure. To optimize your cloud usage, you can use the Azure resources mentioned in the upcoming section.

Cost management and billing

Azure Cost Management allows you to track the cloud usage of your Azure resources. It is the process of effectively planning and controlling costs involved in your business. It helps to take action to optimize cloud spending and it helps to analyze costs effectively.

In Azure Cost Management, you can continuously monitor cloud consumption and cost trends using advanced analytics, and track actual spend against your budget to avoid overspending. Reports in Cost Management show the usage-based costs consumed by Azure services and third-party marketplace offerings. You can also use historical data to improve your forecasting accuracy as well. Cost Management uses Azure budgets, management groups, and recommendations on how to reduce costs and how your expenses are organized.

Azure Cost Management can be accessed from the Azure portal. You can also export the cost data to custom applications, external systems, or processes using the various APIs. Scheduled reports and automatic billing data export are also available. You can use Azure Cost Management for free.

Secure and manage

You can use the different Azure security and management features to secure and monitor your applications inside Azure. These services can be used during migration, with Azure Hybrid support, and can be continued after migration for a consistent experience across your (Hybrid) cloud using the products and resources available in the Azure portal.

In the upcoming sections, the different services are explained.

Security

Azure Security Center offers security management and advanced threat protection across (Hybrid) cloud workloads. Security Center gives you insights into—and control over—applications in Azure. You can limit your exposure to threats, and detect and respond to attacks quickly.

You need to make sure that your workloads are secured when you migrate them to the cloud. When you migrate your workloads to **Infrastructure as a Service (IaaS)**, there is more customer responsibility compared to moving to **Platform as a Service (PaaS)**.

Azure Security Center provides the following tools to do the following:

- **Protect against threats**: The workloads in Azure are assessed by Security Center, and it raises threat prevention recommendations and threat detection alerts when needed.
- **Strengthen security posture**: The environment in Azure is also assessed by Security Center, and it enables you to understand the status of your resources, and whether they are secure.
- **Get secured out of the box:** Security Center is natively integrated in Azure and easily deployed.

The following screenshot gives an overview of your Azure and non-Azure workloads from a security perspective inside Azure Security Center. In there, you can discover and assess the security of your environment. The dashboard provides insights into vulnerabilities that require attention:

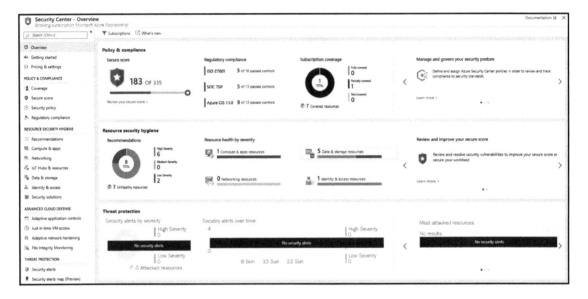

Azure Security Center

Next, we will look at the health and performance of your apps.

Cloud health monitoring

You can use Azure Monitor, Log Analytics, and Application Insights to gain insights into the health and performance of your apps, infrastructure, and data. For instance, you can view application and network dependencies across multiple VMs, or you can track the performance of your applications. You can integrate the monitoring tools with other services' management solutions as well as use the APIs that are provided by Azure.

The following is a screenshot of Azure monitoring in the Azure portal:

Azure Monitor

Next, let's look at data protection.

Data protection

You can back up your applications in Azure, protect your data against human error or ransomware, and meet compliance goals using the backup capabilities of Azure. Azure Backup offers a built-in solution that can be deployed to back up different resources such as VMs, data, databases, and more.

It is easy to set up, and you only pay for what you use. Restoring your data comes with no additional costs.

Migration tooling

When building your application migration roadmap, you can use the guides and tools provided by Microsoft. The possibilities are described in the upcoming sections.

There are third-party migration tools available as well. These tools are provided by the solution partners of Microsoft. You can refer to the following website for an overview of relevant partners and tooling: `https://azure.microsoft.com/en-us/migration/partners/`.

Microsoft Assessment and Planning Toolkit

The **Microsoft Assessment and Planning (MAP)** Toolkit is a free tool with a set of templates that can be used to assess your on-premises environment and current IT infrastructure for a variety of migration projects. It provides a tool that can assess servers and VMs, Office, SharePoint, and Exchange installations, and much more. It can then define whether an application, server, or device is adequately prepared to migrate to a new operating system, server version, or cloud environment. It also offers a reporting tool that simplifies the migration process.

The MAP Toolkit consists of the following components:

- `MAPSetup.exe`: This contains the MAP tool as well as the files that are needed to set up a local SQL database.
- `readme_en.htm file`: This details what administrators need to run MAP Toolkit and known issues.
- `MAP_Sample_Documents.zip`: This provides examples of the types of reports and proposals the MAP Toolkit creates.
- `MAP_Training_Kit.zip`: This explains how to use the MAP Toolkit and provides a sample database of the information that the MAP Toolkit can provide.

You can download the MAP Toolkit from the following website: `https://www.microsoft.com/en-us/download/confirmation.aspx?id=7826`.

Azure Migrate

Azure Migrate assesses on-premises workloads for migration to Azure. It can be used for discovering, mapping, and evaluating your on-premises machines and applications. It provides cost estimations for running your workloads in Azure and it performs performance-based sizing.

You can use it to discover Hyper-V and VMware VMs. It includes CPU and memory utilization, networks, and disk details. You can set up dependency visualization and group machines to view dependencies between groups of VMs.

Azure Migrate offers capabilities of rightsizing your cloud resources to get better control of migration costs based on efficient utilization. If Azure Migrate identifies specific VMs as problematic, it offers step-by-step guidance for overcoming those obstacles to help to keep your migration on track.

Azure Migrate takes the following steps to assess your migration workloads:

1. **Setting up and discovering**: The first step of the migration process is discovering the VMs that are running in your on-premises VMware and Hyper-V environment. You can download the Azure Migrate Collector appliance, which is packaged with all of the prerequisites needed for discovering the on-premises environment. The virtual appliance needs to be configured to start the discovery of the on-premises environment. It collects VM configuration and utilization data to assess the VMs for migration to Azure. After running the Azure Migrate Collector appliance, the discovered VMs will be available for analysis inside the Azure Migrate project in the Azure portal.

2. **Visualizing dependencies**: Inside the Azure Migrate project in the Azure portal, you can view the dependencies of a discovered machine. In there, you can group the discovered machines to plan the migration of an application as a logical unit. By grouping the machines, you can get an in-depth understanding of the application's dependencies and detect additional dependencies to avoid surprises during migration.

3. **Assessing readiness**: You can plan your migration to Azure by customizing the assessment based on your specific needs. You can drill into specific assessment views, including Azure migration readiness and cost estimates. The status of the Azure readiness of each on-premise machine is displayed. Remediation guidance is provided and best practices are offered for the configuration of each Azure VM to meet the needs of the on-premises machine. You get a detailed overview of the costs of running the VMs and Azure, and you can make adjustments to the assessment properties to meet your Azure plan and region requirements. The assessment report can be exported to share with relevant stakeholders as well.

The following is a screenshot of the Azure Migrate service in the Azure portal. It displays the different services that it has to offer:

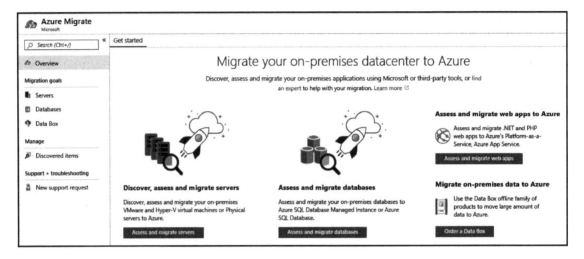

Services in Azure Migrate

After running the cloud assessment with Azure Migrate, you can start migrating your VMs to Azure using Azure Site Recovery and the database migration center. These tools are explained in more detail later in this chapter.

Azure Site Recovery

Azure Site Recovery offers a business continuity and disaster recovery solution by orchestrating and automating the replication of Azure VMs. It can replicate workloads and applications from a primary to a secondary location so that your VMs and applications are still up and running during a disaster. You can easily fall back to the primary location when it is up and running again.

Azure Site Recovery offers the following features and capabilities:

- **Azure VM, on-premises VM, and workload replication**: You can set up the disaster recovery of Azure VMs from a primary region to a secondary region in Azure. You can replicate on-premises VMs and physical servers to Azure or to a secondary on-premises data center. You can replicate any workload from on-premises Hyper-V and VMware VMs, Windows/Linux physical servers, and Azure VMs.
- **Data resilience**: No application data is intercepted during replication. Data is stored in Azure storage and, during failover, the VMs are created using the data that is stored inside Azure Storage.
- **Customized recovery plans**: You can create customized recovery plans, where you can group VMs together or add custom scripts or tasks.
- **BDCR integration**: You can integrate Azure Recovery Services with other BDCR solutions as well.
- **Network integration**: Azure Recovery Services is integrated with networking features in Azure. You can reserve IP addresses, configure load balancers, and integrate Azure Traffic Manager for network switchovers.
- **Consistent apps**: You can keep applications consistent during failovers using recovery points with application-consistent snapshots. These snapshots can capture disk data, all data in memory, and all transactions in process.

Azure Database Migration Guide

The Azure Database Migration Guide offers a set of tools and best practices for migrating multiple database sources to Azure data platform resources with minimal downtime.

You can select a source and a target, and the guide will offer you a detailed plan using the following steps:

1. **Pre-migration**: In this step, the guide provides which database versions are supported as a source, and prerequisites that need to be met before migrating.
2. **Migration**: After all of the prerequisites are met, the schema and database migration can be performed.
3. **Post-migration**: After the migration is finished, a series of post-migration tasks needs to be performed to ensure everything is working. This step provides different tests for your target environment, such as performance and validation tests, for instance.

The following is a screenshot of the Azure Database Migration Guide:

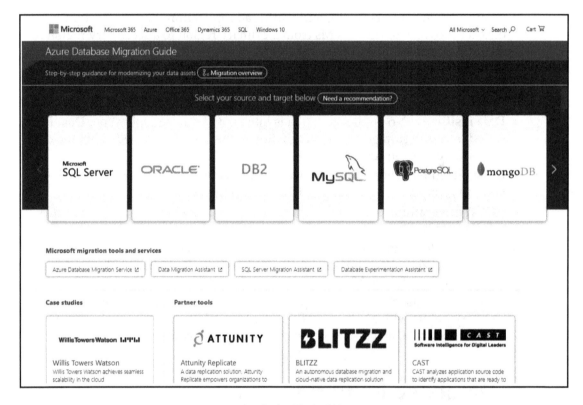

Azure Database Migration Guide

Next, we will be looking at App Service Migration.

App Service Migration

App Service Migration offers two different services. First, you can assess your site and get a detailed report of all of the technologies that are used for your application, and whether the application can be hosted on Azure App Service. You can provide the public endpoint of your application and the service scans the application to create a list of the technologies used.

Next is the Migration Assistant. Once the assessment is finished, you can download this tool, which walks you through the actual migration process and provides a more detailed assessment of your application.

The following is a screenshot of App Service Migration:

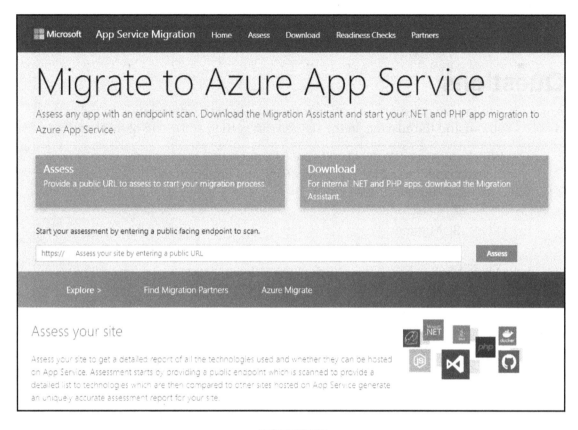

App Service Migration

Summary

In this chapter, we covered the different steps that need to be taken to create an application migration roadmap. We also covered the migration guides and tools that Microsoft provides for assessments, the actual migration process, and post-migration steps.

In the next chapter, we are going to start with refactoring on-premises applications and repackaging them to easily deploy them in Azure. To accomplish this, we are going to look at Docker and Kubernetes to containerize your applications.

Questions

Answer the following questions to test your knowledge of the information found in this chapter. You can find the answers in the *Assessments* section at the end of this book:

1. Which steps need to be taken to create a migration roadmap for your current environment, including VMs, databases, and applications?
    1. Assess
    2. Refactor
    3. Migrate
    4. Optimize

2. Azure Migrate can assess which of the following VMs?
    1. Hyper-V VMs
    2. VMware VMs
    3. Both VMware and Hyper-V VMs
    4. None of the above

3. Azure Migrate uses which of the following tools and services to migrate your workloads to Azure?
    1. Cloud Health Monitoring
    2. Azure Site Recovery
    3. Microsoft Assessment and Planning Toolkit
    4. Azure Database Migration Service

Further reading

You can check the following links for more information about the topics covered in this chapter:

- **Azure Migration Center**: https://azure.microsoft.com/en-us/migration/
- **Azure Cost Management Documentation**: https://docs.microsoft.com/en-us/azure/cost-management/
- **Azure Security Center Documentation**: https://docs.microsoft.com/en-us/azure/security-center/
- **Azure Migrate**: https://docs.microsoft.com/en-us/azure/migrate/
- **Azure Database Migration Guide**: https://datamigration.microsoft.com/
- **App Service Migration**: https://migrate4.azurewebsites.net/

2
Implementing Containerization and DevOps in a Development Cycle

With the advent of containerization, you can take advantage of cloud computing and improve your efficiency. In this section, you will learn techniques for improving the speed of applications and code portability and to ensure faster execution.

This section contains the following chapters:

- Chapter 3, *Getting Started with Docker and Kubernetes*
- Chapter 4, *Deploying Highly Scalable Apps with Kubernetes*
- Chapter 5, *Modernizing Apps and Infrastructure with DevOps*

Getting Started with Docker and Kubernetes

3

This chapter opens the second module of this book, which looks at implementing containerization and DevOps in the development cycle. Here, we'll focus on modernization and migrating applications to Azure by leveraging the power of containerization. Once we've completed the migration process, we'll look at efficient development and release techniques using Microsoft Cloud's DevOps tools and processes.

In this chapter, we'll be talking about running Docker and Kubernetes on Azure.

The following topics will be covered in this chapter:

- Understanding the Docker ecosystem in Azure
- Containerizing your applications
- Kubernetes overview and running Kubernetes on Azure
- Why Azure Kubernetes Service?

 We won't be looking at concepts such as what Docker is in this book. Please refer to the Further reading section if you are interested in digging deeper into that.

Technical requirements

The code files for this chapter can be found at `https://github.com/PacktPublishing/Migrating-Apps-to-the-Cloud-with-Azure/tree/master/Chapter3`. This includes a sample Node.js app that's been built by Microsoft and the code to containerize the application. The original application code can be found here: `https://github.com/microsoft/project-nodejs-express-webapp`.

Understanding the Docker ecosystem in Azure

In January 2015, Microsoft added Docker to the Azure Marketplace, which was a major milestone for Microsoft when it came to integrating containers ecosystems with commercial Azure Cloud. It's been almost 5 years since then and container ecosystems have evolved massively, with support for all the major container engines and container orchestration across a variety of offerings for different business and technological needs.

In this section, we'll list and discuss the various options we have when it comes to running Docker containers in Azure:

- Azure Container Instances
- Azure Kubernetes Service
- Web Apps for Containers
- Docker Enterprise Engine
- Azure Service Fabric
- OpenShift on Azure
- Docker on Azure IaaS
- Azure Batch

Azure Container Instances

Azure Container Instances, also called **ACI**, is a serverless container service from Microsoft. With ACI, you can easily run containers with a couple of clicks and in a matter of a few seconds.

ACI became generally available in April 2018 and is one of a kind in the public cloud market. Simply put, if you want to run a Docker container with ACI, you just supply basic details such as the Docker image, commands, environment variables, compute capacity, networking configuration, and so on and run a container without worrying about the underlying OS or other infrastructure components. Basically, you specify everything you do when you execute a `docker run` command for your container and Microsoft will just launch an ACI instance for you, running the container in exactly the same way.

With its serverless nature, ACI lets you run containers without the need for deploying any underlying container hosts, configuring complex container networking, and persistent storage. It supports both Linux and Windows containers.

It's fairly easy to deploy an ACI cluster. The following Azure CLI command illustrates creating an ACI instance named `nginx` using a `library/nginx` image inside a `packt-aci` resource group that's being published via an Azure public IP:

```
az container create -g packt-aci --name nginx --image library/nginx --ip-
address public
```

You can add more arguments and flags to customize container configuration based on your requirements. Alternatively, you can also use the Azure portal, PowerShell, or Azure APIs for deploying ACI. Refer to the ACI documentation for more details: `https://docs.microsoft.com/en-in/azure/container-instances/`.

ACI is billed per second and charged for the time your container was running (this includes right from the event when ACI starts pulling your image to the stage where the container is terminated/failed). Pricing details for ACI are available here: `https://azure.microsoft.com/en-us/pricing/details/container-instances/`.

Azure Kubernetes Service

Azure Kubernetes Service (**AKS**) provides a managed production-grade Kubernetes environment that allows customers to deploy their containerized workloads. As the name implies, AKS is based on the same open-source version of Kubernetes that's available publicly and provides a consistent experience to customers for deploying their workloads.

This offering simplifies the deployment, management, and operations of Kubernetes-based workloads in Azure by providing a managed service. In a Kubernetes world, there are mainly two kinds of nodes: master nodes and agent nodes. Master nodes are the control planes for the cluster and perform all the management operations for the entire cluster, whereas agent nodes are responsible for running the workload. With AKS, Microsoft takes care of master nodes and provides a managed Kubernetes experience where you only need to worry about your agent nodes and deploying your workload.

We'll talk about Kubernetes and AKS in more detail in further sections and chapters.

Web Apps for Containers

Web Apps for Containers is part of Azure App Service and is a PaaS-based application hosting service in Microsoft Azure. With Web Apps for Containers, you can easily deploy and run containerized web applications on Windows and Linux using the power of Microsoft's Azure App Service capabilities. A good use case for this deployment model would be when you have a Docker-based web application that you want to move to Azure App Service and leverage capabilities such as deployment slots and automated backups without worrying about the underlying infrastructure. For more information about Web Apps for Containers, refer to Chapter 6, *Designing Web Applications*, where we dive deep into deploying web applications on Azure with Azure App Services.

 You can also refer to `https://azure.microsoft.com/en-in/services/app-service/containers/` for more information about Web Apps for Containers.

Azure Batch for Containers

Azure Batch lets you run and scale large numbers of batch computing jobs on Azure.

Batch tasks generally run directly on virtual machines (nodes) in a Batch pool; however, with recent updates to Azure Batch service, you can now run Docker compatible container-based batch processing in Azure Batch as well.

 You can also refer to `https://azure.microsoft.com/en-in/services/app-service/containers/` for more information about Web Apps for Containers.

Docker in Azure Marketplace

If you search for Docker in Azure Marketplace, you'll find various offerings published by Docker, Microsoft, and others. In this section, we'll go through some of the popular Docker offerings in Azure Marketplace.

Docker Enterprise Edition (basic, standard, advanced)

Docker, Inc. has published various deployment options in Azure Marketplace for Docker's commercial product, that is, Docker Enterprise. You can choose to deploy between basic, standard, and advanced editions, as shown in the following screenshot:

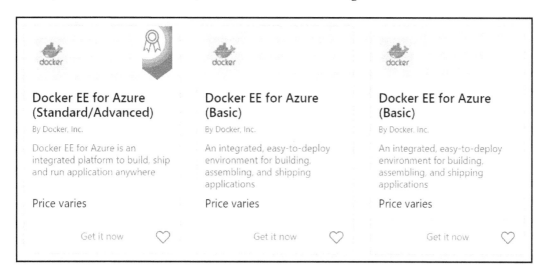

More details about this commercial offering from Docker, Inc. can be found at `https://azuremarketplace.microsoft.com/en-us/marketplace/apps/docker.dockerdatacenter?tab=Overview`.

Azure Service Fabric

Azure Service Fabric is Microsoft's home-grown orchestration and PaaS platform that's used considerably inside various teams at Microsoft for building and deploying cloud-native applications. Microsoft has been using Service Fabric for years internally and it is currently used by Microsoft to host many of the popular cloud services, including Azure SQL databases, Cosmos DB, Cortana, Intune, and Skype for Business, to name a few.

Simply put, Service Fabric allows you to package, deploy, and manage scalable and reliable microservices and containers.

Some of the highlights of Service Fabric include the following:

- Container deployment and orchestration
- Runs on-premises with Azure or on any other cloud
- Supports a wide range of applications, frameworks, and languages

- Runs Docker or Windows containers
- Complete application life cycle management
- Support for stateful and stateless microservices
- Deploys applications in seconds at a high density with hundreds or thousands of applications or containers per machine
- Deploys different versions of the same application side by side and upgrades each application independently
- Effective scaling, upgrades, and monitoring

We'll dig deep into Service Fabric in `Chapter 8`, *Building Microservices with Service Fabric*.

 More details on running Docker containers in Service Fabric clusters can be found at `https://docs.microsoft.com/en-us/azure/service-fabric/service-fabric-containers-overview`.

Red Hat OpenShift on Azure

Microsoft Red Hat OpenShift on Azure is a fully managed PaaS offering that provides managed OpenShift environments in Azure. This service is jointly built, managed, and supported by Microsoft and Red Hat.

Azure Red Hat OpenShift (**ARO**) extends Kubernetes and provides additional tools and resources, such as an image registry, storage management, networking solutions, and logging and monitoring tools, all of which must be versioned and tested together. Along with this, ARO allows you to work with CI/CD pipeline tools, middleware frameworks, and databases for your containerized applications.

Using this service, you can deploy your containerized applications to Kubernetes clusters that are managed by the OpenShift service directly and manage all the aspects of your application development, management, and upgrades using OpenShift.

Similar to AKS, in ARO, the master nodes are managed by Microsoft and Red Hat, where the workload nodes are deployed in your subscription and managed using the ARO service.

 To find out more about Red Hat OpenShift on Azure, please go to `https://docs.microsoft.com/en-us/azure/openshift/`.

Docker in Azure IaaS

Azure IaaS, one of the most widely used and foundational services of Azure Cloud, lets you build your own infrastructure, including servers (VMs), networking, storage, security, and protection on your own terms with full control. IaaS brings complete flexibility, customization, and ownership for your infrastructure in Azure in the same way you had it in your datacenter.

In this deployment option, you design and deploy your own infrastructure on Azure and then use the infrastructure to build a containerized environment. In this model, while you have full control, you also are responsible for a lot of moving parts, starting from OS patching to Docker platform-level components of your application. This increases the deployment time and the time it takes for the production to go live, and also includes management operations overhead.

Containerizing your applications

If we look back at the previous sections, you must have realized that containers are everywhere in Azure, be it IaaS or PaaS. Containers are fundamental when it comes to developing modern-world applications and have transformed the way development and deployment happens in the software world.

Containers allow for faster deployment and, most importantly, easy migration from one place to another. Portability is the key factor in making containers so popular and mainstream, along with many other benefits surrounding agility.

In this section, we'll discuss how we can approach containerizing applications and what it takes to do this by covering the following topics:

- Assessing your application components and defining the components that need to be executed in a different category of containers with their specifications
- Writing a Dockerfile for each type and building Docker images
- Storing Docker images in a Docker registry
- Defining networking and port mappings
- Running your containers and test applications
- Defining a production deployment strategy

With that, let's get started.

Planning for containerization

Before you start preparing Dockerfiles and building Docker images, it is important that you understand how your application components work, how Docker will help them, and, most importantly, whether you need Docker for them. While you can run pretty much every type of application in Docker, that doesn't mean you necessarily have to. Confusing enough? Let's dive in to clarify this.

Before you start containerizing, ask yourself a few questions:

- What's the challenge you're trying to solve by containerizing your application or what feature do you want to utilize most after you move to containers?
- What is the nature of your application components? Divide them into stateful and stateless categories.
- How do you currently handle persistent data for your stateful applications?
- What components are accessible from the public network? How are they secured and exposed to the outside world?
- How do the various moving parts of your applications identify each other or communicate with each other?

Based on the answers you give, you should identify and plan for the following:

- Start with decomposing your application components that can run in independent containers.
- Determine all the independent containers that will need to communicate with each other.
- Define stateless application components with their dependencies on each other, the prerequisites to run applications, and so on.
- Define stateful application specifications. You may also brainstorm if you really need to move your stateful applications to Docker or if they can stay outside the container environment:
    - Where will you store the data? You can choose to store on the host filesystem, network storage, or directly on Azure disks or Azure files when deployed on Azure. In AKS, it is recommended to use Azure Disks to store the application data.
    - Connectivity requirements with other containers.

- List all the containers you'd use independently and their specs. We'll need to prepare Docker images for each of these.
- Identify capacity, compute, and load balancing requirements.
- Define a monitoring and logging strategy.
- Define security specifications based on your current security practices and how they change with containers.
- Define your container orchestration strategy with CI/CD processes.
- Define a **Source Control Management** (**SCM**) strategy for your Docker files and other deployment scripts/tools.
- Define a migration methodology.

Building a Docker host in Azure

In the next couple of sections, we'll learn how to build Docker images and run containers with a hands-on lab. We'll be using an Ubuntu-based Docker host running in Azure. Let's build a lab VM in Azure for this.

We'll be deploying an Ubuntu host in Azure and then installing Docker using Azure VM extensions. We'll use the ARM template that's available in the quickstart repository to do this. Follow these steps to deploy a Docker host in Azure:

1. Launch a modern browser and open `https://github.com/Azure/azure-quickstart-templates/tree/master/docker-simple-on-ubuntu`.

2. Click on the **Deploy to Azure** button. This will launch the Azure portal and will ask you to log in (if you're not logged in already).

3. Enter the required details, that is, **Subscription**, **Resource group**, **Location**, and the credentials for the VM. You can leave **VM Size**, **Ubuntu OS Version**, and **Location** as their defaults unless you intend to use custom configurations here. Choose **password** or **sshkey** as the authentication type, as per your preference.

4. Click **Purchase**; this will start the deployment process:

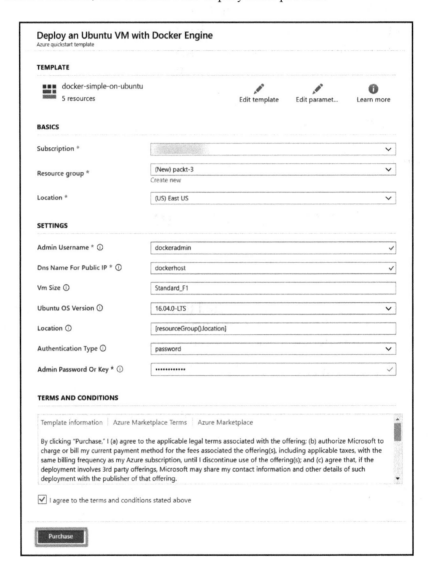

5. Once the deployment has been created, launch an SSH client such as PuTTY (if you're using Windows) or a Terminal (if you're on macOS/Linux). Now, we'll connect to the newly created Docker host. You can find the SSH login details and the public IP on the VM details blade in the Azure portal, as shown in the following screenshot:

6. After connecting to the host, you can use the `docker -v` command to check if Docker has been installed correctly and is working well:

```
dockeradmin@MyDockerVM:~$ docker -v
Docker version 18.06.1-ce, build e68fc7a
dockeradmin@MyDockerVM:~$
```

Your Docker VM is now ready to launch containers and can be used in the rest of this chapter.

Preparing Docker images

In this section, we'll learn about the process and best practices of building Docker images for identified application components.

A Docker image is a file that's used to run Docker containers. In an ideal world, you'd build separate Docker images for the different application components that have been identified. A Docker image includes everything that is needed for the app to run, including the required base OS configuration, packages, frameworks, application files, configurational items, and launch commands or scripts.

Docker images are built using Dockerfiles, which are nothing but plain configuration files that include everything that should be added to the image. We can build images using Dockerfiles and then store them in a private container registry or a public one, such as Docker Hub. In this section, we'll look at writing Dockerfiles, building and storing Docker images, and running containers.

Preparing a Dockerfile

A Dockerfile is a configuration file you write for your application requirements, which in turn produces a Docker image that can be used to run containers.

Let's have a look at some of the common requirements for packaging an application into a container image:

1. **Choose a base image**: Your application will run on some standard OS, such as Ubuntu, CentOS, windowsservercore, and so on. Sometimes, it doesn't have to be an OS and could be a platform image that will contain everything that's needed for the platform to function. **nginx** is one example of this. An nginx image would include everything that's needed to run the nginx web server in a container, and all you would need to do is add your web app files. In the first step of preparing a Dockerfile, you'd choose a base image to start with. We specify the base image with the following syntax:

   ```
   FROM baseimagename:version //For example FROM
   Ubuntu:latest
   ```

2. **Install dependencies**: The base image we selected in the previous step includes a plain vanilla OS image – nothing more. Every application has its own requirements in order to function properly; for example, Java applications would need Java libraries to be installed before the applications can be executed. In this step, we will add all the libraries and packages we need in order to run our application. This may include installing packages, using package managers such as yum, or installing any other RPMs or packages:

   ```
   RUN apt-get install -y sudo wget curl git openssl gnupg //this
   //command will install dependencies such as wget, sudo etc. -y
   is //specified to automatically accept confirmations prompts
   ```

3. **Add application files**: This is where you will add your application code. You may choose to copy it from your localhost while building the image or download from any public/private location on the internet with commands such as `wget`:

```
COPY package*.json /app/ //Copying files to /app/ directory
                         // inside the Image
```

4. **Deploy the application**: Once the application files have been copied, you can choose to install the application using tools such as `mvn` and `npm`, depending on your application type. You can also add any standard Linux/Windows commands such as `mkdir`, `chown`, and so on, to prepare the application for installation:

```
RUN npm install /install NodeJS project dependencies
```

5. **Expose network ports**: Here, you can define the network ports that will be exposed to the world outside your container:

```
EXPOSE 80 443
```

6. **Add volumes**: Containers are ephemeral; they start and die. To store any data that you may need, even when the container is dead, you can define volumes inside a Dockerfile that can map a directory inside the container to a filesystem location on your Docker host or to network storage. This is mainly used for stateful applications:

```
VOLUME /myvol
```

7. **Define the entry point for the container**: Every container needs to have an entry point, that is, a startup command that is executed when the container is launched. You can choose to give a direct command or execute a script as part of the entry point that will launch your application:

```
ENTRYPOINT ["./startapp.sh"]
```

8. **Add a health check probe**: You can add a health check probe inside your Dockerfile, which will include a step to validate whether your application is running well. Docker Engine will continue to monitor the health probe and restart the container if it is found to be unhealthy:

```
HEALTHCHECK --interval=5m --timeout=3s \
CMD Curl -f http://localhost/ || exit 1
```

Next, let's create a sample Dockerfile.

Preparing a sample Dockerfile for a sample app

In this example, we'll look at a Node.js Express-based web application that's been published by Microsoft and we will containerize the application.

Microsoft published this Node.js Express-based web application as a sample that can deploy Node.js apps on Azure App Service and VM. The application code can be found at `https://github.com/Microsoft/project-nodejs-express-webapp`.

While we love Azure Web Apps and VMs, we want to deploy this as a container in order to align this with our app modernization strategy. I've forked this repository in my GitHub account and created a Dockerfile for the application so that I can build a Docker image. Here's the link: `https://github.com/PacktPublishing/Migrating-Apps-to-the-Cloud-with-Azure/tree/master/Chapter3`.

Let's review the Dockerfile that's available at `https://github.com/PacktPublishing/Migrating-Apps-to-the-Cloud-with-Azure/blob/master/Chapter3/Dockerfile`:

```
FROM ubuntu:16.04
MAINTAINER Amit Malik(contact2amitmalik@gmail.com)
#Define Work directory
WORKDIR /app
#Preare Image for NodeJS and Install NodeJS with build tools
RUN apt-get update
RUN apt-get install -y sudo wget curl git openssl gnupg &&\
    curl -sL https://deb.nodesource.com/setup_8.x | sudo -E bash - &&\
    sudo apt-get install -y nodejs &&\
    sudo apt-get install -y build-essential
#Copying only Package file to the image
COPY package*.json /app/
#Install all dependencies etc
RUN npm install
#Copying application content from local app folder inside app folder
COPY . /app/
#Define what will happen when the container will start
CMD npm start
#Expose the port where your application is running
EXPOSE 3000
```

Let's look at each line:

- `FROM ubuntu:16.04`: In this statement, we're defining which base image we want to start with. We can also choose Node.js images directly by specifying `FROM nodejs:8`. We're using a base Ubuntu image here so that we can include examples of installing dependencies.

- `MAINTAINER`: This is just a block of text that's used to define author/maintainer information for the Dockerfile.
- `WORKDIR /app`: Specifies that all further operations and commands will be executed in the `/app` directory. Docker creates a directory if one doesn't exist already.
- `RUN apt-get update`: The standard Ubuntu command to update the list of available packages and their versions.
- Install dependencies and Node.js using the following command:

```
RUN apt-get install -y sudo wget curl git openssl gnupg &&\
    curl -sL https://deb.nodesource.com/setup_8.x |
    sudo -E bash - &&\
    sudo apt-get install -y nodejs &&\
    sudo apt-get install -y build-essential
```

- We can specify the `RUN` command in each line for each command; however, this is not the best way to do this since each command will produce a new layer. The lower the number of layers, the better the Docker images. In the preceding code block, we're installing some standard tools and Node.js with its dependencies. We're clubbing multiple packages to be installed, as well as commands, in a single `RUN` statement by using `&&\` at the end.
- `COPY package*.json /app/`: `package.json` is a standard file in the Node.js world that includes all the dependencies that are required for the application to run. In this step, we're copying the `package.json` file to the `/app` directory inside the Docker image.
- `RUN npm install`: Installs dependencies and node modules based on `package.json` specifications.
- `COPY . /app/`: Copies all the application files in the current application directory to the Docker image inside `/app`.
- `CMD npm start`: Here, we're specifying what will happen on container execution. `npm start` will start the application at launch.
- `EXPOSE 3000`: Configures the container to expose port `3000`. This sample application is configured to use port `3000`.

Now that we have got an understanding of our Dockerfile, let's build Docker images and run containers.

It's good practice to perform `npm install` with `package.json` copied, since the chance of changes in `package.json` is lower than the chance of changes in the overall application code. By copying the application code later, we're trying to minimize the number of layers that will be downloaded by hosts when we make an application upgrade.

Building the Docker image

After preparing a Dockerfile, the next step is to build the Docker image. We'll be using the Docker build command for that.

Let's build the Docker image with the Dockerfile we prepared for the sample Node.js Express-based web application:

1. Log in to the Docker host using SSH.
2. Install Git tools in the VM by running the `sudo apt-get install git` command.
3. Clone the GitHub repository by issuing the following command:

   git clone
   https://github.com/amalik99/project-nodejs-express-webapp.git

4. Change directories to the cloned repo directory by issuing the following command:

   cd project-nodejs-express-webapp

5. You can verify the directory's content by issuing the `ls -l` command. Once verified, issue the following command to build the image. You may have to use `sudo` as a prefix for all the Docker commands if you get a permission denied error:

   docker build -t nodejsexpresssample .

   Let's look at the preceding command in detail:

   - `docker`: Initializes the Docker client daemon for the CLI.
   - `build`: Specifies that you want to build a Docker image.
   - `-t`: Keyword for specifying that the next text is the value to be tagged with the Docker image.

- `nodejsexpresssample`: Name of the image. You may choose to add a version to the name, such as `nodejsexpresssample:1.0.0`. If you do not specify a version, the image is tagged with the latest version by default.
- `"."`: Specifies the path for the Dockerfile. A dot instructs the Docker daemon to look for the Dockerfile in the current working directory where the filename is **Dockerfile**. You may specify the path to a custom file if that's required.

Executing this command will start the build process. It will take a few minutes for the process to finish. Once completed, you'll see that the image has been created, stored locally, and tagged with the value we specified. Now, this image is ready to be used to run containers. You can verify this by running the `docker images` command.

Since the Docker image we just created is only available on the local system, it can only be used to run containers on this host. In order to distribute this image, we need to store it in a container registry that is accessible on the network. There are two types of container registries: public and private. As the name suggests, public registries are open to the public and anyone can use the images stored there. In a production environment, you'd go with the private one since it doesn't make sense to put your images out there on the internet. Let's look at publishing images to the repository.

Pushing Docker images to Docker Hub

Docker Hub is a cloud-based public container registry hosted by Docker, Inc. By default, any Docker host you configure is set to use Docker Hub as the default container registry. Follow these steps to store the image we created in Docker Hub:

1. Create a Docker Hub account if you don't have one already. You can do that by going to `https://hub.docker.com/`.
2. Once your account is ready, you can use the following command on the Docker host to log in. You will be asked for the Docker Hub username and password in the Terminal itself:

   ```
   docker login
   ```

3. Once you've logged in, you need to tag the image we created earlier with your Docker Hub account name and an image name. Look at the following command. The specification of this command is as follows:
   - `docker`: Specifies the Docker daemon.
   - `tag`: Specifies that you want to tag the image.
   - `nodejsexpresssample`: Name of the Docker image that's available locally.
   - `accountname/nodejsexpresssample`: The target Docker Hub account name, where `nodejsexpresssample` is the image name to be used in Docker Hub:

```
docker tag nodejsexpresssample
accountname/nodejsexpresssample
```

4. Once tagged, you can use the following command to push the image to Docker Hub:

```
docker push accountname/nodejsexpresssample
```

5. Your image is now stored in Docker Hub and can be used to create containers on any host. You can pull the image to any other host using the following command:

```
docker pull accountname/nodejsexpresssample
```

Pushing Docker images to the Azure Container Registry

The **Azure Container Registry (ACR)** is a private Docker container registry that's hosted and managed by Microsoft Azure. The ACR is fully compatible with Docker and works in the same way, except that it's managed, hosted, and secured by Microsoft.

Let's create a new ACR and store the image we created to the ACR:

1. Log in to the Azure portal (`https://portal.azure.com`).
2. Click on **Create a resource** | **Containers** | **Container Registry**:

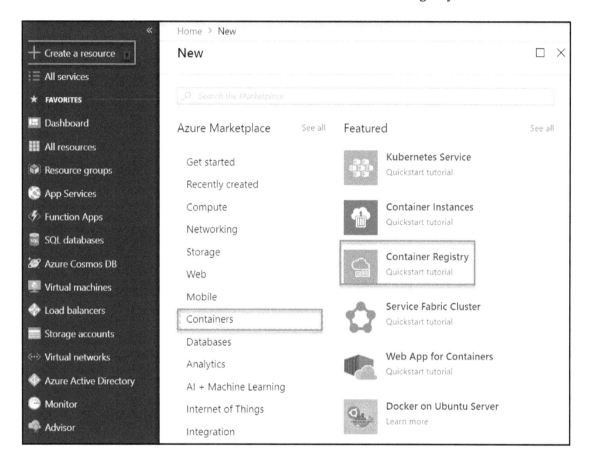

3. Specify the configurations as follows:
   - **Registry name**: Enter a value for the registry name. After this, choose your **Subscription**, **Resource group**, and the **Location** where you'd want to deploy this.
   - **Admin user**: You can choose to enable the registry name as the username and the key as the password to log in to the ACR. Enabling this will allow you to use the ACR as just another Docker registry with a server name, username, and password. If you choose to disable it, you can use AZ CLI commands to interact with the ACR.

- **SKU**: Choose an edition for your ACR, that is, **Basic**, **Standard**, or **Premium**. The major differences between these SKUs are to do with the amount of storage that's available, the number of webhooks you can set up, and whether you want to have ACR replicated across Azure Geo for HA and DR. Pricing differs for each; refer to `https://azure.microsoft.com/en-in/pricing/details/container-registry/` for more information about pricing and features:

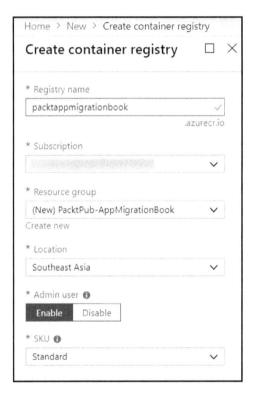

4. You can also create an ACR using the Azure CLI by issuing the following command:

```
az acr create --resource-group myResourceGroup --name
packtappmigrationbook --sku Standard
```

5. Now, we can configure our Docker host so that it uses this ACR repo instead of the default Docker Hub. To log in to the ACR, we can use the following command:

```
docker login myregistry.azurecr.io -u myUsername -p myPassword
```

Let's get the configuration for these items using the Azure portal. Browse through the Azure portal and open the newly created ACR resource. Click on **Access keys**. You will need to enable **Admin user** if it's not enabled already. You'll have everything that you'll need to use the Docker login on this blade:

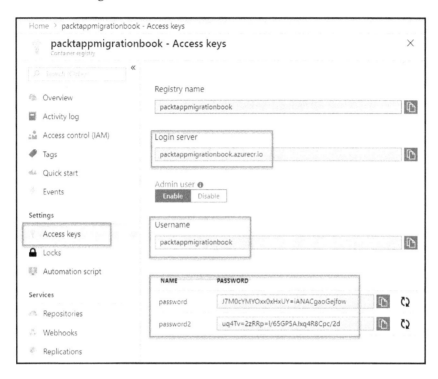

Run the following command to log in to the Docker registry and set it as the default registry for all Docker image-related operations:

```
docker login packtappmigrationbook.azurecr.io -u packtappmigrationbook -p
J7M0cexample0xHxUY=iANACgfow
```

Now, you're logged in to the ACR and can use the regular Docker push and pull commands to work with images in the same way that we did with Docker Hub. Remember to change the Docker Hub account name to your ACR registry name in the preceding commands.

Alternatively, you can use the following Azure CLI command to log in to the ACR and perform the Docker image-related operation:

```
az acr login --name packtappmigrationbook
```

Always specify the fully qualified registry name (all in lowercase, ending with `azurecr.io`) when you use the Docker login and when you tag to push images to your ACR registry. Refer to `https://docs.microsoft.com/en-us/cli/azure/acr?view=azure-cli-latest` to learn more about `az acr` commands.

Running the application with containers

Now that our application is containerized and the Docker image is stored in an accessible registry, we can go ahead and run the application.

Take a look at the following command, which we will use to launch our application:

```
docker run -p 80:3000 amitmalik/nodejsexpresssample
```

Let's take a look at each item in the command:

- `docker`: Initiates the Docker client daemon.
- `run`: Keyword for starting the containers.
- `-p 80:3000`: Does the mapping of host port `80` to port `3000` inside the Docker container. This will redirect all the requests coming from host port `80` to port `3000` inside the container.
- `amitmalik/nodejsexpresssample`: Specifies the Docker image to be used. In this example, we're using Docker Hub to download our image.

Now, your container will be running. You can browse the Docker host IP on port `80` to access the application. If you're running your Docker host in Azure, be sure to configure the **Network Security Group** (**NSG**) to allow port `80` inbound (if it's not allowed already). You should see the following application page up and running, with your browser on the public IP of your Docker host:

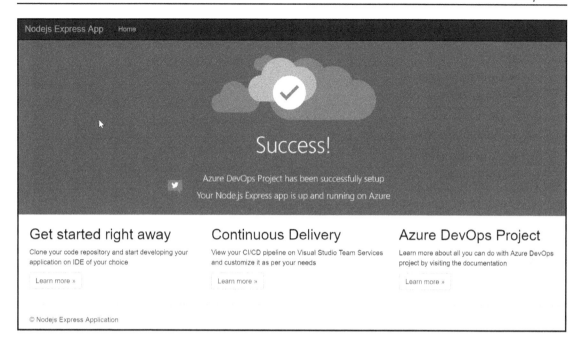

In this section, we looked at preparing Docker images and launching containers; however, this is not production-ready yet. In the upcoming sections, we'll look at how to run production-ready Dockerized applications on Azure.

Kubernetes and Azure

In the previous section, we looked at running applications that have been packaged inside a Docker container. As the number of application components and scale grows, it becomes harder to manage the overall application's deployment and management, while ensuring availability, by just using the Docker commands. This creates a need for a controller that can do all the heavy lifting of running and managing containers for our application and ensuring that our application deployment remains healthy and available. These controllers sit on top of the Docker engine and orchestrate all the Docker operations based on our application requirements. In this scenario, as DevOps personnel, we only talk to the orchestrator, whereas Docker stays in the background.

There are many container orchestrators, such as the following:

- Kubernetes
- Docker Swarm
- Mesosphere
- DC/OS
- HashiCorp Nomad
- Containership
- Many more

This section will focus on Kubernetes and running Kubernetes in Azure.

Kubernetes overview

Kubernetes is one of the most powerful and popular container orchestrators and works with Docker containers, RKT containers, and Windows Containers. Kubernetes was invented by Google in 2003 – 2004 and was made available as an open-source product in 2014. Google had been using Kubernetes internally to run thousands of containers for years; this is a key differentiator when it comes to stability and maturity among container orchestrators.

Kubernetes eliminates the limitations that were introduced by Docker when it was running a production-grade containerized environment, and provides enhancements such as the ability to ensure the application is always up and running by defining a minimum number of containers that should always be running and healthy.

Kubernetes hides the complexity of running a multi-node Docker host cluster in the background and controls the application's deployment and management. Let's find out more about Kubernetes.

Let's look at a couple of Kubernetes' key properties:

- **Portable**: It can be run anywhere – on public, private, hybrid, and multi-cloud environments, as well as on bare-metal servers in data centers.
- **Extensible**: It's modular, pluggable, and hookable. It can easily extend to work with resources outside a Kubernetes cluster.
- **Self-healing**: Auto-placement of the application, auto-restart, auto-replication, and autoscaling.

What does Kubernetes do?

Kubernetes' primary goal is to schedule and run your application's workload on a cluster of nodes while you're running Docker or any other container engine. Kubernetes provides an abstract layer on top of Linux hosts or Windows hosts that are running Docker. You wouldn't deploy a container or application on a host; instead, you'd submit it to Kubernetes and it would deploy it somewhere in the cluster based on various aspects, such as load, health, any user-defined constraints, and so on.

Let's look at what Kubernetes does:

- Controls and manages your workload host's state
- Schedules containers (in the form of pods – more on that later) for your applications
- Replicates application instances to increase their availability and enhance performance
- Exposes an API endpoint so that administrators can perform every operation related to your application infrastructure
- Enhances networking and storage capabilities using its native technologies and extensible architecture
- Load balancing and dynamic DNS discovery
- Autoscaling and downtime-free application upgrades
- Manages both stateless and stateful applications
- Monitoring and enhanced debugging
- Strong authentication and authorization
- Logging across systems and components

Kubernetes is platform-agnostic, so you can run it anywhere on your Linux hosts. You can build your own Kubernetes cluster on bare-metal servers, run it on VMs hosted on Hyper-V or VMware or any other virtualization layer, or run it on any public cloud such as Azure, Google Cloud Platform, or AWS.

Similarly, Kubernetes doesn't restrict any application, framework, or language. If you can run something in Docker containers, you'd be able to run it as is with Kubernetes as well. It's not a PaaS platform – it just controls your application's deployment, which can use any development stack. There are products that have been built on top of Kubernetes or use Kubernetes, such as OpenShift, which are pure PaaS platforms.

Kubernetes architecture

Kubernetes follows the standard master-slave architecture pattern. There are two types of nodes in a Kubernetes cluster:

- Kubernetes master
- Kubernetes nodes

A Kubernetes cluster is a collection of masters and nodes, along with a supporting network and storage infrastructure. You may have many hosts in your Kubernetes cluster and multiple Kubernetes clusters in your overall environment.

The Kubernetes master is the control plane that manages the entire state of the cluster and is responsible for all the Kubernetes management operations.

Kubernetes nodes are the workload servers where your actual application instance will run. Nodes are managed by the Kubernetes master and include a container engine, such as Docker, along with Kubernetes components. Previously, nodes used to be called minions.

Let's look at the architecture in detail:

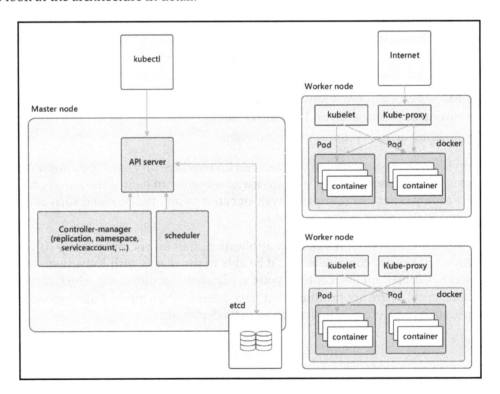

If we look at the master node, it has the following components:

- **API server**: The API server is the only endpoint in the entire cluster and is exposed outside. It exposes a REST endpoint where tools, administrator, and `kubectl` (the command line for working with Kubernetes) submit all the requests using REST calls. The API server processes the requests, validates them, and executes the corresponding operation. This is a stateless component.
- **etcd storage**: etcd is the configuration database of Kubernetes. It is an open-source key-value store. It provides a REST endpoint for CRUD operations, which is accessible only to the master node. Being a distributed key-value store, you can run it outside the master node on a separate cluster and ensure high availability. It stores every configurational aspect of Kubernetes, such as the number of pods running, desired and scheduled, replication information, and so on.
- **Scheduler**: As the name implies, the scheduler is responsible for watching for pods requests and scheduling them in the Kubernetes nodes. Basically, the scheduler is the component that gets the containers running in the form of pods on the nodes. The scheduler keeps an eye on the cluster state, such as which node is healthy or load monitoring, and decides where the deployment should happen.
- **Controller manager**: The Kubernetes master includes various controllers, such as the replication controller, which is responsible for replicating the pods, namespace controllers, and service account controllers. Controllers are responsible for ensuring the desired state of the deployments and clusters based on specified configurations. The controller manager is the daemon containing all the controllers.

Now, let's look at the worker node:

- **Kubelet**: Kubelet is the Kubernetes agent running on the worker nodes. It is responsible for getting the desired configuration from the master by talking to the API server and ensuring that the required containers are up and running.
- **kube-proxy**: Kubernetes has its own networking controller called `kubenet`. On nodes, `kube-proxy` is responsible for getting the networking stack up and running on nodes and performs operations such as load balancing.

- **Container engine**: Kubernetes is just a container orchestrator; it still needs a container engine to run the containers. Kubernetes supports Docker and RKT as container engines; however, Docker is the most widely used option. Kubernetes also supports Windows containers.
- **kubectl**: `kubectl` is the CLI for interacting with Kubernetes. Each node has it by default and it is used to talk to the API and send commands to masters. You may install `kubectl` on your administrator/developer machine as well, so that it can interact with your Kubernetes environment.

Kubernetes concepts

Kubernetes works with a concept called objects. Everything in a Kubernetes cluster is an object. Let's look at some of the popular objects and how they're used:

- **Namespaces**: Namespaces are virtual clusters running in a single physical cluster. Here, you build a large physical cluster and then divide that into multiple logical clusters, also known as namespaces, so that you can run different environments. There is no physical isolation with namespaces; that is, a single node can run resources from multiple namespaces.
- **Pod**: A pod is the fundamental unit of deployment in a Kubernetes cluster. A pod contains one or more similar containers, carries a single IP, and works in a single process namespace. A pod can only be scheduled on a single host. Along with the same IP, all the containers in the pod can communicate using inter-process communication or localhost, and all have access to the same shared storage that's been mapped to the pod. So, essentially, your application instances run inside a pod. You can have multiple components of your application run inside a single pod; however, this is not a recommended practice. This also helps in decoupling the application components and allows you to deploy, upgrade, and scale them independently. Also, as a golden rule in a containerized environment, keep it as small as you can so that it's as fast as it can be.
- **Services**: Unlike Docker containers, a pod cannot be accessed directly from outside by mapping a host port in Kubernetes. There's an element called **service**, which publishes your application over a network. Service load balances the requests and redirects them to one of the pods from the configured backend pool of pods that are responsible for that application. Services can expose your application over the network in many ways, such as the following:
    - **Cluster IP**: Exposes an internal IP (`kubenet`) that your application can be accessed through. It can only be used internally.

- **NodePort**: Exposes the application on a specific port of your hosts, similar to Docker containers.
- **LoadBalancer**: Exposes the application via extensible networking components such as Azure Load Balancer, AWS LBs, or any other third-party load balancers.
- **Headless services**: Used for stateful services where it is required to connect to a specific pod where you have some data being stored and processed.

- **Volumes**: Volumes are persistent storage locations that are used to store persistent data for stateful applications. You can create volume objects in Kubernetes, which may include a path to a specific directory on hosts or other storage solutions. Once volumes have been created, they can be mapped inside pods. Kubernetes storage is extensible and you can use Azure managed disks and Azure files directly inside Kubernetes pods.
- **Replica sets**: A replica set works on top of pods and provides high availability for pods by running multiple copies of them on different nodes. In a replica set configuration, you define a minimum number of instances you'd always want to have running for the pods you added in a replica set.
- **Deployment**: Deployments are another layer of abstraction on replica sets and pods. You can define a complete application configuration inside a deployment, which will include various pod definitions and replica sets definitions, and submit that to the API server. The deployment controller will ensure that the desired state of deployment is deployed and maintained.
- **Stateful sets**: Stateful sets are used to run stateful pods where data is persistent. A stateful set will guarantee uniqueness and the order of the pods for the applications. Similar to deployments, stateful sets also include pods for application configuration; it's just that they are not created to die every now and then. Stateful sets also include a unique identity for each pod.
- **Daemon set**: A daemon set ensures that, for a defined pod, there should be at least one copy of the pod scheduled on each host. An example would be running logging containers or a storage agent.
- **Jobs**: A job is used to perform batch processing, where a pod will perform certain processes and mark itself as complete. Once all the pods have been completed inside a job, the job is marked as completed.

Building Kubernetes environments on Azure

Microsoft Azure considers Kubernetes as a key component when it comes to running containers in production. There are various ways you can run Kubernetes in Azure, such as the following:

- Running an **Azure Container Service** (**ACS**) cluster
- Running an **Azure Kubernetes Service** (**AKS**) cluster
- Running an **Azure Red Hat OpenShift** (**ARO**)-based Kubernetes cluster
- Building your own cluster in Azure IaaS VMs

We looked at these options in brief in the previous sections of this chapter. Building your own cluster in Azure VMs includes setting up your own Azure IaaS infrastructure and installing Kubernetes environments in them manually.

Azure Kubernetes Service

Azure Kubernetes Service (**AKS**), as we mentioned earlier, is a managed Kubernetes offering from Microsoft Azure. Looking back at the Kubernetes architecture, we know that there are two types of hosts in Kubernetes clusters – master and nodes. In the world of AKS, there's no master for end users. Microsoft creates and manages master nodes and hides them away from end-users.

As a user, you only deploy AKS nodes (Kubernetes nodes) in your subscription, whereas the configuration of Kubernetes and the joining of Microsoft-managed Kubernetes masters happens in the background. With AKS, you only pay for the nodes' infrastructure cost; masters are provided for free by Microsoft.

Why Azure Kubernetes Service?

AKS simplifies the deployment, management, and operations of Kubernetes. With AKS, you don't have to worry about managing Kubernetes' control plane, availability, upgrades, and so on. You can focus more on the things that matter to your business: your LOB applications.

Let's look at some of the advantages of using AKS:

- **Easy deployment and management**: Deploying a highly available Kubernetes cluster can be a tedious task, as is upgrading a cluster. With AKS, you can create a production-ready HA Kubernetes cluster within a few minutes by issuing a single command. The same goes for upgrades: AKS handles a Kubernetes version upgrade very efficiently without having any impact on applications.
- **Fully compatible Kubernetes feature parity**: AKS is not a Microsoft flavored Kubernetes or a separate Azure fork from the original Kubernetes codebase. It is exactly the same open-source Kubernetes you've been using and loving.
- **Identity and authorization with AAD**: AKS can be integrated with Azure AD for authentication and authorization so that you can manage access to your Kubernetes cluster by using your same favorite Azure AD user and groups.
- **Scalability**: With AKS, you have access to Azure's vast footprint of datacenter and resources. You can configure the autoscaling of your pods and clusters with confidence.
- **Advanced networking**: You can use Azure CNI networking with AKS to allow your pods to be reachable in your virtual network, thereby enabling various advanced networking topologies.
- **Monitoring and logging with OMS**: You can use Microsoft **Operations Management Suite** (**OMS**) to monitor the health of your overall Kubernetes cluster and analyze logs. You can view your pod state and so on right from the Azure portal itself.
- **Secure**: AKS can be secured using Azure's NSGs or Azure Security Center by storing secrets in the Azure Key Vault. AKS is also compliant with SOC, ISO, and PCI DSS.
- **Integrated CI/CD pipeline**: AKS works very well with Microsoft DevOps products such as DevOps Project, Azure DevOps, and VSTS, thereby allowing you to build an efficient CI/CD pipeline. We'll look at this in more detail in `Chapter 5`, *Modernizing Apps and Infrastructure with DevOps*. You can also continue using tools such as Jenkins if you're using them already.
- **HTTP add-on**: This includes a built-in Nginx-based ingress controller with integration to Azure DNS service. You can publish your application with this add-on annotation and AKS will create an ingress object and DNS record in the public Azure DNS.

- **Support for GPU-enabled VMs**: You can choose to deploy AKS nodes with GPUs and run graphics and compute-intensive workloads.
- **Free control plane**: You don't pay for using an AKS service; you only pay for AKS nodes running in your subscription and related storage and network costs. This helps reduce your overall costs.
- **Burst with ACI**: With AKS, you can use ACI as your target for pod deployment. This allows you to quickly burst your application scale without adding more AKS nodes.
- **Integration with developer tools**: You can work with AKS directly from Visual Studio Code or Azure CLI.
- **Helm support**: Helm, also known as a package manager for Kubernetes, is fully supported with AKS. You can deploy your application packaged with Helm as is with AKS.

In the next chapter, we'll get into the technical details of AKS and deploying the workload on AKS. We'll realize the aforementioned benefits during our hands-on labs.

Top use cases with AKS

Although AKS can be used anywhere where Kubernetes can be used, here are some common use cases where AKS fits the best:

- **Lift-and-shift containers**: If you're running on containers already, you can just lift and shift your application without refactoring. This will allow you to take advantage of the power of AKS and reduce your overall costs.
- **Microservices**: Deploy your microservices with agility, thus enabling faster application development.
- **Machine learning**: Ad hoc, low latency, high-performance processing with AKS GPU-enabled nodes and premium disks.
- **IoT**: Build your containerized application in AKS or anywhere else and run it elsewhere easily.
- **Secure DevOps**: By implementing secure DevOps with Kubernetes on Azure, you can achieve a balance between speed and security and deliver code faster at scale.

Summary

In this chapter, we learned about the Docker ecosystem in Azure and realized that containers are everywhere in the Microsoft Cloud. With so many deployment options with different target workloads, Azure becomes your go-to cloud for running containerized applications.

We also learned about containerizing applications with Docker and tried running an application inside a Docker container. Later, we were introduced to Kubernetes and Kubernetes offerings in Azure and learned about Microsoft's managed Kubernetes offering called **Azure Kubernetes Service**.

In the next chapter, we'll learn how to run Kubernetes on Azure and deploy a highly scalable workload on Azure Kubernetes Service.

Questions

Answer the following questions to test your knowledge of this chapter. You can find the answers in the *Assessments* section at the end of this book:

1. Is it mandatory to build a Linux VM and install Docker within it in order to run containers on Azure?
    1. Yes
    2. No
2. What is the access type of the Azure Container Registry?
    1. Public
    2. Private
    3. Both
3. Where can we store persistent data in an Azure Kubernetes Service cluster?
    1. In a directory on the local filesystem of the Docker host
    2. Azure disks
    3. Azure files
    4. Any other network accessible storage
    5. All of the above

Further reading

Check out the following links to find out more about the topics that were covered in this chapter:

- **Everything about Docker, from the fundamentals to advanced topics**: `https://www.packtpub.com/tech/Docker`
- **Best practices of using Dockerfiles**: `https://docs.docker.com/develop/develop-images/dockerfile_best-practices/`
- **Azure Kubernetes Service documentation**: `https://docs.microsoft.com/en-us/azure/aks/`
- **Azure Container Instances documentation**: `https://docs.microsoft.com/en-us/azure/container-instances/`

4

Deploying Highly Scalable Apps with Kubernetes

In this chapter, we'll dig deep into deploying and managing Kubernetes-based environments on Azure. We'll understand **Azure Kubernetes Service** (**AKS**) deployment options for Kubernetes. Then, we'll deploy an AKS cluster and deploy a highly scalable application on top of it.

Later, we'll look at operational aspects of the Kubernetes environment, such as monitoring and upgrading an AKS cluster.

The following topics will be covered in this chapter:

- Deploying an AKS cluster
- Understanding AKS networking
- Deploying highly scalable applications on AKS
- Exposing applications outside AKS
- Scaling applications and clusters
- Upgrading AKS applications and clusters
- AKS monitoring, operations, and upgrading
- Using Helm to deploy applications

Technical requirements

The code files for this chapter can be found here: https://github.com/PacktPublishing/Migrating-Apps-to-the-Cloud-with-Azure/tree/master/Chapter4.

Azure makes Kubernetes easy

Microsoft Azure gives you the flexibility to deploy Kubernetes on your own terms by leveraging Microsoft Cloud's hyperscale IaaS infrastructure or to deploy a production-grade Kubernetes cluster using an AKS service in a few clicks. It also allows you to run applications directly on managed Kubernetes clusters.

With Azure, you can design, deploy, and manage open source Kubernetes environments using any of the following options:

- **AKS**: A managed Kubernetes service that lets you quickly deploy your containerized application with less management overhead and reduced costs.
- **Build on your own**: Leverage Azure's infrastructure to design and build your Kubernetes cluster using Azure VMs.

Deploying an AKS cluster

In this section, we'll look at deploying an AKS cluster. As part of cluster deployment, Microsoft Azure performs the following actions:

- Deploys infrastructure components for Kubernetes nodes
- Registers nodes with Microsoft's managed Kubernetes master nodes
- Deploys any optional add-ons, such as HTTP routing, RBAC, monitoring, and Azure DNS

Deploying with the Azure portal

To deploy an AKS cluster using the Azure portal, follow these steps:

1. Launch `https//portal.azure.com` in a modern browser and log in with your Azure subscription credentials.

2. Click on **Create a resource** | **Containers** | **Kubernetes Service**:

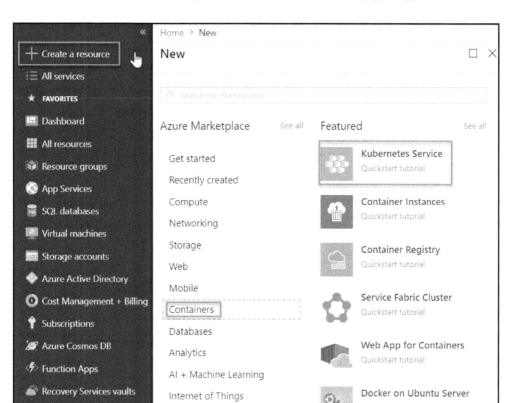

3. Provide the following details on the **Basics** page. Click the **Next: Scale** button once you're done:

- **Subscription and Resource group**: Choose the subscription and the resource group that you want to deploy your AKS cluster to.
- **Kubernetes cluster name**: Set the identifier for your AKS cluster.
- **Region**: Mark your Azure region.
- **Kubernetes version**: Select the version you want to install. It is recommended you choose the default one for better stability.

- **DNS name prefix**: This is the DNS name prefix you will use with the hosted Kubernetes API server FQDN. You will use this to connect to the Kubernetes API when managing containers after creating the cluster.
- **Primary node pool**: Choose the VM size for AKS agent nodes and the node count you want:

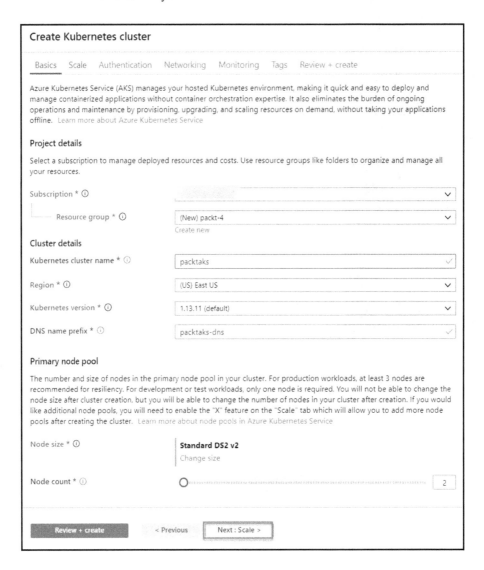

4. On the **Scale** page, you can choose to enable virtual nodes (ACI as AKS deployment targets for pods) and VM scale sets (auto-scaling for AKS nodes).

5. On the **Authentication** page, apply the following settings:
   - **Service principal**: The AKS cluster needs to authenticate against your Azure subscription for various tasks, such as creating Azure Load Balancers and public IPs. AKS uses the service principal in your AAD to perform this authentication programmatically. You can choose to let the wizard create a new SPN for you (you need to have the required permissions on your AAD and subscription to do this) or you can use an existing SPN.
   - **Enable RBAC**: This enables Kubernetes **role-based access control (RBAC)**, which provides fine-grained control over cluster resources. It is recommended you enable RBAC for any production cluster if you're considering security best practices:

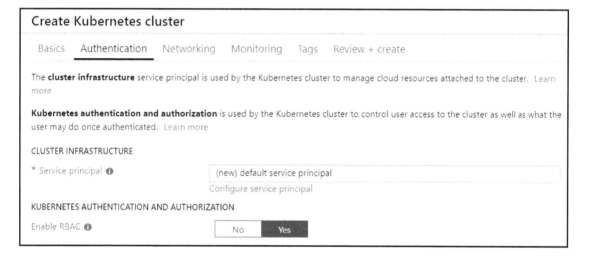

Create Kubernetes cluster

Basics   Authentication   Networking   Monitoring   Tags   Review + create

The **cluster infrastructure** service principal is used by the Kubernetes cluster to manage cloud resources attached to the cluster. Learn more

Kubernetes authentication and authorization is used by the Kubernetes cluster to control user access to the cluster as well as what the user may do once authenticated. Learn more

CLUSTER INFRASTRUCTURE

* Service principal ❶   (new) default service principal
                              Configure service principal

KUBERNETES AUTHENTICATION AND AUTHORIZATION

Enable RBAC ❶   No   Yes

 Take a look at the following link to find out more about using SPN with AKS and creating an SPN in advance: https://docs.microsoft.com/en-us/azure/aks/Kubernetes -service-principal.

6. On the **Networking** page, choose whether you wish to enable HTTP application routing and which networking mode you want. AKS supports two networking modes: **basic**, which is also called kubenet, and **advanced**, which is an Azure CNI implementation for Kubernetes networking (more on this in the next section). You can also choose to create a new virtual network to be used with AKS. You can select an existing virtual network if you select the **Advanced** network type:

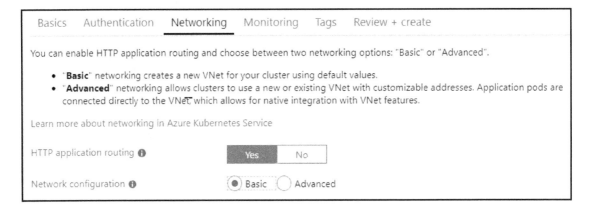

7. On the **Monitoring** page, you can choose to **Enable container monitoring** using the **Operations Management Suite** (**OMS**). At the time of writing, you can use an existing OMS workspace or create a new OMS workspace so that you can monitor your AKS workload:

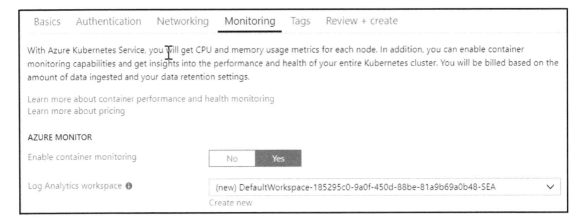

8. Add any key-value pair as tags for your billing-related consolidation and click **Next**.

Tags are name/value pairs that allow you to categorize resources and view consolidated billing by applying the same tag to multiple resources and resource groups. You can find out more about tags at `https://docs.microsoft.com/en-us/azure/azure-resource-manager/resource-group-using-tags`.

9. Review all of the configuration settings and click **Create**. You can also choose to download an ARM template for the configuration. The portal will try to create an SPN for AKS at this point; if you see an error, review your permissions on your AAD and subscription.

Now, the deployment will start. Typically, it takes about 12 to 15 minutes for provisioning to finish.

Deploying with the Azure CLI

In the previous section, we looked at deploying a Kubernetes cluster via the portal. Using the Azure CLI, you can launch an AKS cluster using just a single command. Follow these steps to learn how to deploy using the CLI:

1. Launch the Azure CLI on your computer or launch Azure Cloud Shell. You can use `az login` to log in to your subscription (not required if you're using Cloud Shell).

2. Create a resource group using the following command:

```
az group create --name packt-4thchapter --location eastus
```

You can skip this step if you want to use an existing resource group for AKS deployment.

3. Create an AKS cluster using the following command:

```
az aks create --resource-group packt-aks --name packt-4thchapter --node-count 3 --enable-addons monitoring --generate-ssh-keys
```

Let's look at this command in detail:

- `az aks create`: The syntax for creating an AKS cluster
- `--resource-group` & `--name`: The resource group's name and AKS cluster node
- `--node-count`: The number of AKS nodes you're creating

- `--enable-addons`: This specifies add-ons such as monitoring and HTTP routing
- `--generate-ssh-keys`: This is a flag that lets `az cli` create SSH keys to be used for agent nodes

Connecting to the AKS cluster

As AKS cluster should be ready by now, you can connect to the AKS cluster and deploy applications. You can connect to a Kubernetes cluster using any of the following methods:

- **kubectl**: CLI for communicating with Kubernetes. This is the go-to tool for Kubernetes professionals.
- **Kubernetes dashboard**: GUI-based admin interface.
- **Kubernetes API**: The Kubernetes cluster exposes REST APIs so that your application can be integrated with Kubernetes.

`kubectl` is the primary tool that's used by Kubernetes administrators. `kubectl` supports various OSes, including Windows, Mac, and Linux. You can install `kubectl` on your administration endpoint using the Azure CLI as well. Run the following command to install `kubectl` using the Azure CLI:

```
az aks install-cli
```

kubectl can also be installed manually using the installers available at `https://Kubernetes .io/docs/tasks/tools/install-kubectl/`.

After installing `kubectl`, you need to log in to your Azure subscription using `az cli`. To connect with the AKS cluster, you need to download the `credentials` file, which contains your Kubernetes cluster endpoint details and authentication keys. This file needs to be stored in a config file under the `.kube` directory in your user's home directory. **AZ CLI** takes does this for you using a single command:

```
az aks get-credentials --resource-group Packt-AKS --name packtaks
```

The following screenshot shows the output of the preceding command:

```
amit@Azure:~$ az aks get-credentials --resource-group Packt-AKS --name packtaks
Merged "packtaks" as current context in /home/amit/.kube/config
amit@Azure:~$ ▮
```

You can now use `kubectl` to communicate with the AKS cluster. You need to run a couple of basic commands to verify your connectivity.

The `kubectl cluster-info` command shows basic details about your AKS cluster, such as your Kubernetes master API endpoint URI for a few other Kubernetes service components:

You can use `kubectl get nodes` to get information about the number of nodes in your AKS cluster. In the following screenshot, we can only see agent nodes; in an ACS-based cluster or manually deployed Kubernetes cluster, you'd also see master nodes when running this command:

 Take a look at the following link to find out more about using Kubernetes Dashboard with AKS: `https://docs.microsoft.com/en-us/azure/aks/Kubernetes-dashboard`. If you've deployed an RBAC-enabled AKS cluster, you also need to explicitly give permissions to the Dashboard service account if you want to use Dashboard in your Kubernetes cluster.

Understanding AKS networking modes

In the previous section, while deploying the AKS cluster, you must have noticed two network modes – basic and advanced.

The basic networking mode is based on kubenet, a plugin based on Kubernetes' native networking functionality that provides the ability to extend networking features to cloud providers and support integration with capabilities such as Azure route tables. With the basic networking mode, each pod in a Kubernetes cluster gets an internal IP address that is non-routable on an Azure Virtual Network and must be published outside the network using Kubernetes services.

You can read more about Kubenet here: `https://Kubernetes .io/docs/ concepts/extend-Kubernetes/compute-storage-net/network-plugins/ #kubenet`.

The advanced networking mode uses Microsoft's Azure container networking plugin, developed by Microsoft, to provide advanced network capabilities in containerized solutions. This means that your pods can be placed inside an Azure Virtual Network, which makes them routable on VNet.

Advanced networking enables all kinds of hybrid integration, such as the ability to reach your pod directly from your on-premise network via a site-to-site VPN connection to the Azure VNet where the AKS cluster is running. You can also use native Azure networking capabilities, such as NSGs, route tables, and NVAs, in order to control and secure your pod networking.

Deploying applications on AKS

In this section, we'll look at deploying applications on AKS. We'll be using an example app called Azure Voting App, which is a standard multi-container-based application that uses the following components:

- **Azure Voting App backend**: This will be running on Redis
- **Azure Voting App frontend**: Web application built with Python

The application's original source code can be found at `https://github. com/Azure-Samples/azure-voting-app-redis`. For the purposes of this book, we've modified the original code, which is maintained at `https:// github.com/PacktPublishing/Migrating-Apps-to-the-Cloud-with- Azure/tree/master/Chapter4`.

In this section, we'll look at deploying this application on an AKS cluster.

Planning scalable application deployment on AKS

Looking at its specifications, it's a simple two-tier application. Let's look at the requirements and plan for each of these components.

Frontend

The requirements and specifications are as follows:

- It is a standard web-based application, published over HTTP.
- The application must always be available.
- The application needs to be exposed outside the internal network; users should be able to access the application over the internet.
- The application should be highly scalable based on utilization.
- The application is regularly updated with new features and fixes; deployment should provide a seamless upgrade experience without any downtime and a minimal maintenance window.

Let's look at the solution:

- While we can use a pod or StatefulSet to deploy the frontend, it is best to use deployments, which include the following:
    - Standard pod specifications to run the application containers
    - Using StatefulSets to ensure the pod is replicated to various nodes and that the application is always available
    - Using Kubernetes deployments for easy upgrades
- We can expose the application to the outside world using Kubernetes services. We can choose to publish the application directly using Azure Load Balancer and public IPs or use an Ingress Controller. We'll look at these options in upcoming sections.
- We will configure autoscaling for the deployment process so that we can automatically increase/decrease the number of pods based on utilization.

Backend

The requirements and specifications for the backend are as follows:

- A Redis-based backend data store that's used to store the voting data.
- Must be highly secure and not exposed outside the Kubernetes network; only the frontend application should be able to access the data.
- Scalable and always available.
- In the case of non-cache databases such as MySQL, another requirement could be having persistent storage.

Let's look at the solution:

- Similar to the frontend, we'll use deployment to deploy pods to provide the same benefits.
- We'll use a Kubernetes service to expose the application; however, this will be configured so that it's only accessible inside the AKS cluster.
- The deployment will ensure that it is always available and easily scalable.

Building a deployment YAML file

Kubernetes provides us with a declarative way to deploy and manage objects inside the cluster. You can define a configuration in YAML or JSON format and submit it to the Kubernetes master for processing. You can also deploy the application using the `kubectl` command option (similar to `docker run`); however, that's only recommended for `dev` environments where you want to run some containers quickly.

In this section, we'll look at a YAML configuration manifest so that we can deploy the voting app on AKS. We'll be creating the following objects in the Kubernetes cluster:

- Deployment object for the backend Redis pod
- Service object for the backend Redis pod
- Deployment object for frontend pods
- Service object for frontend application pods

Let's look at the code for each of these. The configuration files for this can be found at `https://github.com/PacktPublishing/Migrating-Apps-to-the-Cloud-with-Azure/blob/master/Chapter4/azure-vote-all-in-one-redis.yaml`.

You can clone the repository in Azure Cloud Shell or in your Terminal.

Deployment for the backend pod

Here's the code for the deployment object for the backend Redis pod:

```
apiVersion: apps/v1beta1
kind: Deployment
metadata:
  name: azure-vote-back
spec:
  replicas: 1
  template:
```

```
metadata:
  labels:
    app: azure-vote-back
spec:
  containers:
  - name: azure-vote-back
    image: redis
    ports:
    - containerPort: 6379
      name: redis
```

Let's go over the preceding code:

- apiVersion: Every Kubernetes resource definition needs to start with the API version, which basically defines the schema and object definition you're allowed to use as part of the manifest (you can find out more about the Kubernetes API at https://Kubernetes .io/docs/concepts/overview/Kubernetes –api/).
- kind: This defines the Kubernetes object you're creating or managing with this manifest. In our case, this object is Deployment.
- metadata: This is the key-value pair information that we use to identify the object in the cluster. It is also very useful while selecting certain components based on certain conditions, such as environment type (prod/dev/test).
- spec: The deployment specifications start here:
    - replica: The minimum number of pods that should always be running. We'll start with 1 and upgrade later if required.
    - template: Template of the pod definition.
    - metadata: Metadata for the pod (the previous metadata was for deployment).
    - spec: This provides the container's specifications. You can add multiple container definitions here if you have a multi-container pod application:
        - name: Name of the container.
        - image: Which Docker image is going to be used. Here, we're using the official Redis image.
        - ports: The network ports your pod will be exposed to. You can define a name against each network port.

Service for the backend pod's deployment

Here's the code for the service object for the backend Redis pod:

```
---
apiVersion: v1
kind: Service
metadata:
  name: azure-vote-back
spec:
  ports:
  - port: 6379
  selector:
    app: azure-vote-back
```

Let's go over the preceding code:

- `kind`: We're using `Service` here, which is used to expose the pods to other resources inside and outside the network.
- `metadata`: This is the metadata for `Service`.
- `spec`: Port specification about the service, which includes the port numbers where it'll be listening:
  - `- port: 6379`: Tells the service to listen on `6379`.
  - `Selector`: Defines details about the pods that the service will be load-balancing requests between. Here, we're specifying the `app: azure-vote-back` condition. This condition will filter pods with the `app` key and `azure-vote-back` value. If you look at the backend deployment manifest, you'll see that we defined this label in the pod template. This is how the service identifies the pods that are responsible for a particular application's requests.

Deployment for the frontend application

In this section, we'll talk about a few new options that we haven't discussed regarding the deployment object's definition for the backend service. Here's the code for the deployment object for frontend pods:

```
---
apiVersion: apps/v1beta1
kind: Deployment
metadata:
  name: azure-vote-front
spec:
```

```
replicas: 1
strategy:
  rollingUpdate:
    maxSurge: 1
    maxUnavailable: 1
minReadySeconds: 5
template:
  metadata:
    labels:
      app: azure-vote-front
  spec:
    containers:
    - name: azure-vote-front
      image: microsoft/azure-vote-front:v1
      ports:
      - containerPort: 80
      resources:
        requests:
          cpu: 250m
        limits:
          cpu: 500m
      env:
      - name: REDIS
        value: "azure-vote-back"
```

Let's go over the preceding code:

- `strategy`: Under `strategy`, you define your deployment and upgrade strategy with a configuration, such as the maximum number of pods that can be available at a given time during the upgrade rollout and the maximum number of pods we can have during any deployment or upgrade. We can also define the deployment strategy, that is, how the rollout will be handled and distributed, which is a rolling update in our case. We'll talk about this in more detail later in this chapter.
- `minReadySeconds`: Defines the number of seconds Kubernetes will wait for the application to go live before marking the pod as healthy so that it can receive application requests. This could be useful in scenarios where the application startup time is a bit high.

- `resources`: Under resources, you define the minimum amount of memory (in MB) and the CPU time slice in milliseconds assigned to your pod.
- `env`: These are your environment variable values; in this case, our application is configured to connect to the backend Redis cache by using the `REDIS` environment value. Here, we're specifying the value of `REDIS`, which is the name of the service that's responsible for accepting requests for backend Redis pods. Every service can be reached using the DNS name (which is the service name) inside the Kubernetes cluster.

Service for the frontend application

Here's the code for the service object for frontend application pods:

```
---
apiVersion: v1
kind: Service
metadata:
  name: azure-vote-front
spec:
  type: LoadBalancer
  ports:
  - port: 80
  selector:
    app: azure-vote-front
```

Let's go over the preceding code:

- `type: LoadBalancer`: This specifies how the service is exposed. If we select a Load Balancer, this means Kubernetes will create a Load Balancer in our cloud environment using the `configure default` class and authentication credentials for the cloud account.

Now that we have our manifest ready for deployment, we can deploy the application.

Deploying the sample application

You can deploy the application using either the Kubernetes Dashboard or `kubectl`. We'll be using `kubectl` in our example. Let's look at the steps for deploying the application:

1. Launch an Azure Cloud Shell or Azure CLI Command Prompt. Connect to your AKS cluster (see the previous sections if you need to find out more about how to connect to the AKS cluster).

2. Download the YAML configuration to your local filesystem or Cloud Shell:

```
wget
https://raw.githubusercontent.com/PacktPublishing/Migrating-App
s-to-the-Cloud-with-Azure/master/Chapter4/azure-vote-all-in-
one-redis.yaml
# or you can clone the entire repo
git clone
https://github.com/PacktPublishing/Migrating-Apps-to-the-Cloud-
with-Azure.git
```

3. Running the following command will start the deployment based on the configuration defined in the file (ensure that you have the **credentials** downloaded so that you can connect to an AKS cluster (`az aks get-credentials`) before running this command):

```
kubectl apply -f azure-vote-all-in-one-redis.yaml
```

The `-f` flag notifies the Kubernetes master that the deployment manifest is a YAML or JSON file, as shown in the following screenshot:

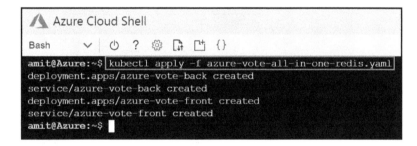

4. As we can see in the preceding screenshot, Kubernetes objects are created. Let's look at the status by issuing the `kubectl get deployment` and `kubectl get pods` commands:

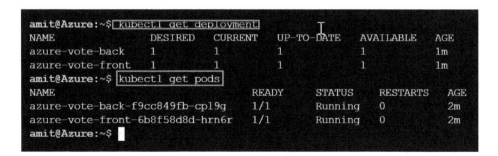

5. Looking at the preceding screenshot, it looks like our deployments are ready for use. Let's look at the service details to see whether we have an IP for our frontend application yet. Let's run the `kubectl get service` command:

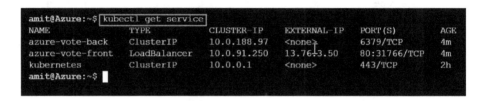

6. Browse to `azure-vote-front` on the external IP. This IP has an Azure public IP assigned to the Azure Load Balancer. We can use this to verify that our application is running on an AKS cluster and has been published via the Azure Load Balancer:

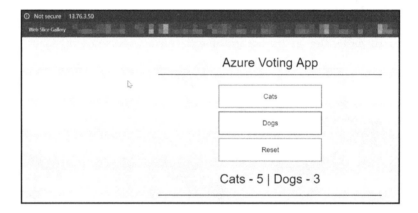

Now that our deployment has been successful, we'll take a look at the operational aspects of the application, such as scaling and updating.

Scaling applications on AKS

Scaling in terms of AKS simply means increasing or decreasing the number of pods (replicas) for each application instance. You can choose to manually scale the number of replicas up or down, or you can configure autoscaling based on utilization.

Before you scale your deployments, you should also ensure that you have sufficient capacity on the AKS nodes so that they can take that much load. If not, you should add new nodes first and then scale the application.

Manually scaling a deployment is very easy; you just need to modify the number of replicas in the YAML deployment file and submit the updated configuration using `kubectl apply -f filename.yaml`. This doesn't have an impact on any existing deployment and provisions the new pods based on the numbers defined.

Kubernetes services watch new pods that meet their label requirements and ensure they are healthy; any new healthy pod will automatically be added to the load balancing backend pool for the service, while any unhealthy pods will be removed automatically. So, in order to scale your application, you only need to increase the number of pods; the rest will be taken care of automatically.

Scaling applications on AKS manually

In this section, instead of modifying the YAML manifest file and resubmitting it, we'll use the `kubectl` command-line option to scale out the frontend application:

1. In the previous section, we executed `kubectl get deployment`. Here, we'll scale out the `azure-vote-front` deployment. Now, run `kubectl get deployments`.

2. Run the following command to increase the replica count to 4. You should see a response containing `deployment scaled`:

   ```
   kubectl scale deployments/azure-vote-front --replicas 4
   ```

3. Let's look at `kubectl get deployments` and `kubectl get pods` to see the status again. In the following screenshot, we can see that 2 pods are ready for `azure-vote-front` and that the desired number is 4.

4. The `kubectl get pods` command also shows that 2 containers are in the creation stage:

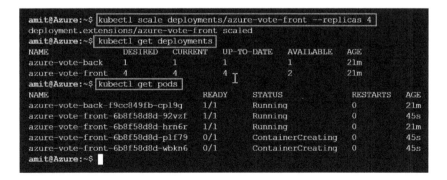

This is how we can scale pods up or down using `kubectl`. Now, let's look at how to autoscale deployments.

Autoscaling AKS applications

When autoscaling applications, the cloud computing platform itself has to have the ability to automatically increase or decrease the number of application instances based on the utilization and load.

In Kubernetes, the **Horizontal Pod Autoscaler (HPA)**, a component of Kubernetes, is responsible for performing autoscale-related operations. It is implemented as a control loop that watches the utilization and increases or decreases the number for pods for an application instance.

You can define a threshold such as a percentage of CPU utilization to watch for and then increase/decrease the pods to a maximum/minimum number. Let's use the `kubectl` command to configure autoscaling for `azure-vote-front` deployment:

```
kubectl autoscale deployment azure-vote-front --cpu-percent=50 --min=4 --
max=10
```

In the preceding code, we're configuring HPA so that it watches for `azure-vote-front` CPU utilization and autoscale pods to a maximum of `10` and a minimum of `4`.

The initial version of HPA only supported CPU utilization as a threshold; now, there are lots of other parameters available, such as memory. You can check the status of HPA by issuing the `kubectl get hpa` command. More information about HPA is available in the Kubernetes documentation at `https://Kubernetes.io/docs/tasks/run-application/horizontal-pod-autoscale/`.

Scaling the AKS cluster

In the previous section, we configured our Azure voting application so that it can autoscale based on utilization. However, we didn't consider the underlying capacity of Kubernetes nodes. To ensure that our application scales well when necessary, we also need to make sure we've got enough capacity available on our Kubernetes nodes to be able to run the required pods.

Similar to scaling applications, AKS also allows you to scale manually or configure autoscaling.

Scaling an AKS cluster manually

A single Azure CLI command or a couple of clicks in the Azure portal can increase or decrease the number of Kubernetes nodes in your AKS cluster. While scaling the cluster, you should keep your deployment strategy in mind to ensure that decreasing the number of nodes doesn't endanger your application's availability.

Let's look at the Azure CLI command to learn how to scale an AKS cluster. The following command will increase our AKS cluster node count to 4:

```
az aks scale --name packtaks--resource-group Packt-AKS --node-count 4
```

Using the Azure portal, go to **AKS Cluster resource and Scaling**. Slide the slider to increase the count and click **Save.** This will start the deployment process for new nodes. Note that this may take a few minutes to complete:

Next, we'll learn how to autoscale the cluster.

Autoscaling the AKS cluster

You can use the **Cluster Autoscaler (CA)** extension of Kubernetes to configure autoscaling for agent nodes in your AKS cluster. CA is a tool that automatically adjusts the number of Kubernetes nodes in a cluster based on the following specifications:

- There are pods that failed to run in the cluster due to insufficient resources.
- There are nodes in the cluster that have been underutilized for an extended period of time, and their pods can be placed on other existing nodes.

By default, CA scans for pending pods every 10 seconds and removes a node if it's not needed for more than 10 minutes. We can use CA in conjunction with HPA to ensure autoscaling capabilities across cluster infrastructure and application pods. In this case, HPA will update pod replicas and resources in line with demand. If there aren't enough nodes or unnecessary nodes afterward, CA will respond and schedule the pods on the new set of nodes.

 Please note that CA for AKS is in preview at the time of writing. Here is the documentation and configuration steps for autoscaling AKS clusters: `https://docs.microsoft.com/en-us/azure/aks/autoscaler`.

Upgrading applications on AKS

One of the key reasons for container adaption is the ability to release and deploy applications faster and release them every week, if not every day.

In Kubernetes, there are multiple ways to release an update to existing applications. Let's look at them now:

- **Recreate**: In this strategy, you delete your existing deployment and perform a new deployment with the new version. As we can see, downtime will be involved in this approach. One use case where you'd want to go with this approach would be a scenario where your application doesn't support running multiple versions of the application at the same time.
- **Rolling upgrade**: This is the default upgrade approach in Kubernetes. Here, you'll roll out an update by introducing pods with newer versions one at a time and take down the old ones. This approach ensures outage-free upgrades, but it takes time for the upgrade to be available for all users.

Upgrading an application in an AKS cluster requires you to define a deployment strategy and define conditions such as the minimum number of pods that should always be available during the upgrade process to avoid any outages.

Let's look at an example of performing a rolling upgrade. You can do the following with a rolling update:

- Roll out a new version of the application.
- Roll back to a previous version; if something goes wrong, you can easily roll back to the previous working configuration state.
- DevOps process with a CI/CD pipeline.

We can easily upgrade our `azure-vote-front` application Docker image using the following command:

```
kubectl set image deployments/azure-vote-front azure-vote-
front=Microsoft/azure-vote-front:v2
```

You can check the status of the rollout using the following command:

```
kubectl rollout status deployments/azure-vote-front
```

In the next section, we'll learn how to upgrade the AKS cluster.

Upgrading an AKS cluster

Kubernetes is the most popular open source project out there on GitHub and is updated frequently. Kubernetes cluster upgrades aren't that easy and often involve extensive planning and testing before they're rolled out.

AKS simplifies this by providing managed upgrade functionalities to your Kubernetes nodes/masters using a single command. Microsoft keeps on adding new supported Kubernetes versions regularly in AKS.

Let's try upgrading an AKS cluster. First, you need to determine what versions are available for you to upgrade. You can do that by using the following command:

```
az aks get-upgrades --name packtaks--resource-group Packt-AKS--output table
```

This will display the available version upgrade that's available for you. Note that once you've upgraded, you can not downgrade an AKS cluster. Since there's an upgraded AKS version, we can start the upgrade process by issuing the following command:

```
amit@Azure:~$ az aks get-upgrades --name packtaks --resource-group Packt-AKS --output table
Name     ResourceGroup    MasterVersion    NodePoolVersion    Upgrades
-------  ---------------  ---------------  -----------------  ----------
default  Packt-AKS        1.11.1           1.11.1             1.11.2
```

Please note that Kubernetes may be unavailable during a cluster upgrade and this should be planned carefully based on your business needs. It will take a few minutes for the upgrade to finish, depending upon the size of your cluster:

```
az aks upgrade --name packtaks --resource-group Packt-AKS --Kubernetes -
version 1.11.2
```

Once upgraded, you can verify the version using the `az aks show` command and start using the functionalities of the latest release.

Exposing applications outside the Kubernetes cluster

When we deployed the voting app, we published the frontend web interface via a Kubernetes service type; that is, we used a Load Balancer. In this section, we'll look at the various ways in which we can expose applications outside the Kubernetes cluster:

- **Kubernetes service type – Cluster IP**: This is used when you want to assign a Kubernetes internal IP to the service and the service is supposed to only be reachable inside the Kubernetes network and usually only communicates with other pods. In our voting app example, we're deploying the backend of Redis as a Cluster IP since the backend datastore should only be reachable inside the Kubernetes network.
- **Kubernetes service type – NodePort**: Specifying NodePort requires you to specify a port number for the AKS agent nodes that will be mapped to the exposed port in the pod configuration. Once you have a NodePort service, you can connect to the pod using any of the Kubernetes agent nodes on the same port.
- **Kubernetes service type – Load Balancer**: Load Balancer is used by Cloud providers to expose Kubernetes applications outside the internet. Specifying the Load Balancer type creates an Azure Load Balancer (if one doesn't already exist), adds the backend nodes to the pool, and configures load balancing for the service. You also get a public IP for each service.

- **Expose via ingress controller**: In this scenario, you deploy an ingress controller on Kubernetes pods (nginx is a well-known one) that will act as a reverse proxy. Once the ingress controller is ready, you'll create an ingress route for each URL you're planning to expose outside. In this case, the public IP that's assigned to the ingress controller will be a public interface for all the configured pods and will route requests to the appropriate pods based on the DNS name in the URL.
- **Expose via Azure HTTP routing**: Microsoft provides a built-in add-on for AKS where you can publish your applications outside AKS using Microsoft-managed nginx-based controllers and public IPs. HTTP add-on-based publishing also includes an Azure DNS service, which is used to create DNS records for ingress routes automatically based on specified names.

> **Additional hands-on labs**: Additional AKS Kubernetes files are available at `https://github.com/PacktPublishing/Migrating-Apps-to-the-Cloud-with-Azure/tree/master/Chapter4`. You can delete the published application using `kubectl delete -f filename.yaml` and try using these methods to expose your applications securely:
>
> - `azure-vote-all-in-one-redis-http-addon.yaml`: Uses Azure Kubernetes service's native HTTP route add-on-based publishing
> - `azure-vote-all-in-one-redis-ingress.yaml`: Uses nginx-based ingress to expose applications

You can try deploying the application again with these config files, and you can even create your own manifest for the NodePort service type if you want to try that out.

Monitoring and logging AKS using OMS

Microsoft contains native container monitoring and health analysis solutions that can be accessed through the OMS. When we created our AKS cluster, we had the option to enable monitoring. This option creates a new OMS log analytics workspace (or uses an existing one, if specified) and configures AKS monitoring using OMS's container monitoring solution.

Let's have a look at some of the monitoring capabilities we have inside the Azure portal itself:

1. Launch the Azure portal and browse to your Kubernetes resource.
2. Under **Monitoring**, you'll see three settings options:
   - **Insights**
   - **Metrics**
   - **Logs**:

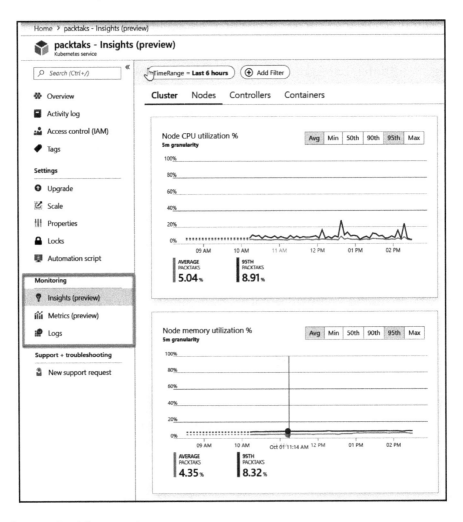

Let's explore each of these options.

Insights

Insights provides you with a detailed view of the following:

- Your cluster utilization and historical utilization trend across CPU and memory counters.
- Detailed information about the status of the Kubernetes node processes, including how they're mapped to Kubernetes components:

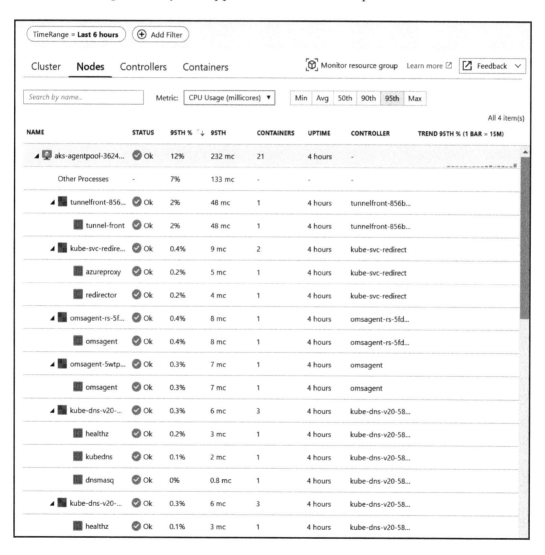

- The health and utilization trends of all the Kubernetes controllers:

TimeRange = **Last 6 hours**	(+) Add Filter							

Cluster   Nodes   **Controllers**   Containers   [◻] Monitor resource group   Learn

Search by name...	Metric:	CPU Usage (millicores) ▼	Min	Avg	50th	90th	95th	Max

NAME	STATUS	95TH %↓	95TH	CONTAIN...	RESTA...	UPTIME	NODE
▷ ▦ omsagent (DaemonSet)	1 ⚠ 4 ✓	7%	10 mc	5	1	5 mins	-
▷ ▦ omsagent-rs-5fdd5db598...	1 ✓	5%	8 mc	1	0	4 hours	-
▷ ▦ tunnelfront-856b4bc554 (...	1 ✓	2%	48 mc	1	0	4 hours	-
▷ ▦ heapster-d58cb46f9 (Repl...	1 ✓	2%	1 mc	2	0	25 mins	-
▷ ▦ heapster-d6489f7fd (Repli...	1 ✓	1%	0.8 mc	2	0	4 hours	-
▷ ▦ addon-http-application-r...	1 ✓	1%	0.1 mc	1	0	4 hours	-
▷ ▦ kubernetes-dashboard-79...	1 ✓	0.5%	0.5 mc	1	0	4 hours	-
▷ ▦ kube-proxy (DaemonSet)	1 ⚠ 7 ✓	0.2%	4 mc	8	0	6 mins	-
▷ ▦ addon-http-application-r...	1 ✓	0.2%	3 mc	1	0	4 hours	-
▷ ▦ kube-svc-redirect (Daemo...	1 ⚠ 4 ✓	0.1%	3 mc	10	0	6 mins	-
▷ ▦ kube-dns-v20-585487cbb...	2 ✓	0.1%	2 mc	6	0	4 hours	-
▷ ▦ metrics-server-789c47657...	1 ✓	0.1%	1 mc	1	0	4 hours	-
▷ ▦ azure-vote-front-6b8f58d...	6 ✓	0.1%	0.3 mc	6	0	14 mins	-
▷ ▦ addon-http-application-r...	1 ✓	0%	0.7 mc	1	0	4 hours	-
▷ ▦ azure-vote-back-f9cc849f...	1 ✓	0%	0.6 mc	1	0	1 hour	-

- Details about the health and configuration of all the containers running in the cluster:

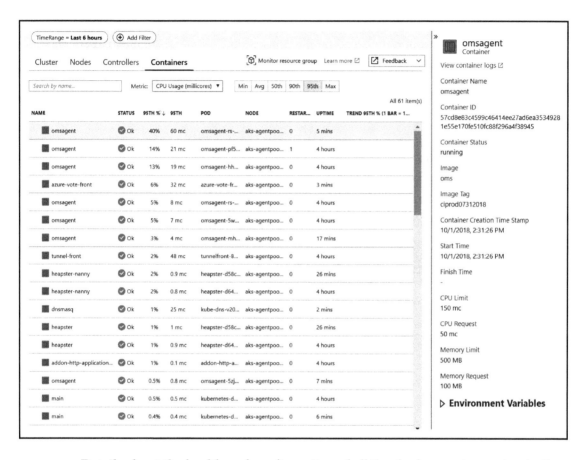

- Details about the health and configuration of all the deployments running in the cluster. This is currently in preview.

Metrics

Metrics provides you with detailed information regarding the number of pods, the number of ready pods, the available memory, and so on in a graph. You can configure **Metrics** to display a graph for the following values and configure alerts for any of them:

- The number of pods by phase
- The number of pods in the ready state

- The status of various node conditions and availabilities
- The total amount of available memory in the cluster
- The total amount of available CPU in the cluster

You can also choose to split data based on the phase, the Kubernetes namespace, or the name of the pod.

Logs

Logs use OMS log analytics to store all logs that are received from AKS. Here, you can use Log Analytics to get meaningful insights out of logs and use them in troubleshooting. You can use Query Explorer to write search queries for logs:

Here's some further reading on monitoring:

- https://docs.microsoft.com/en-us/azure/monitoring/
  monitoring-container-insights-overview
- https://docs.microsoft.com/en-us/azure/aks/view-master-
  logs
- https://docs.microsoft.com/en-us/azure/aks/kubelet-
  logs
- https://docs.microsoft.com/en-us/azure/container-
  service/Kubernetes /container-service-Kubernetes-oms

Running highly scalable AKS applications using ACI

Previously, we talked about scaling applications using a pod autoscaler, a cluster autoscaler, and so on. Sometimes, we may not have clarity about the required scale and it could be very dynamic in nature. In this case, it could be a pretty costly affair to run AKS nodes all the time.

Azure container instances can be integrated with AKS. AKS can schedule pods on ACI. Here, you can define your regular Kubernetes manifest and Azure will take care of any underlying infrastructure resources and will use ACI to run the pods. This is also known as virtual kubelet; this will be where your Kubernetes nodes will be backed up by cloud provider services such as ACI.

You can use virtual kubelet to deploy both Windows- and Linux-based containers. Check out the following link for more information on how to use ACI with AKS: https://docs.microsoft.com/en-us/azure/aks/virtual-kubelet.

Using Helm to deploy applications

Helm is an open source tool for packaging and deploying Kubernetes-based applications. Simply put, Helm is a package manager for Kubernetes, just like we have yum in Linux.

The Helm repository includes a wide variety of charts that you can download, modify, and deploy on your AKS cluster. Helm is getting very popular among Kubernetes professionals and is becoming the de facto standard for deploying AKS applications. AKS supports Helm just like any regular Kubernetes cluster would.

More information about deploying Helm-based applications on AKS is available here: `https://docs.microsoft.com/en-us/azure/aks/Kubernetes-helm`.

Summary

In this chapter, we got hands-on with Kubernetes and used it to run scalable applications. We deployed Kubernetes clusters and highly scalable applications, and looked at autoscaling and auto-upgrading.

In the next chapter, we'll go a step further and integrate what we've learned in this chapter with Azure DevOps and establish enterprise-wide development best practices using Azure DevOps and Kubernetes.

Questions

Answer the following questions to test your knowledge of the information that was covered in this chapter. You can find the answers in the *Assessments* section at the end of this book:

1. What managed Kubernetes services are offering Azure?
   1. **Azure Kubernetes Service (AKS)**
   2. Containers on web app
   3. All of the above

2. How do we run persistent storage applications in Kubernetes?
   1. This doesn't work in Kubernetes
   2. Create a persistent storage claim to create the Azure disk and map the disks inside the pods using the storage claim in the pod definition

3. How can we deploy applications on Kubernetes?
   1. Kubernetes manifest files (YAML/JSON)
   2. Helm charts
   3. kubectl
   4. All of the above

Further reading

Check out the following links for more information about the topics that were covered in this chapter:

- **Azure Kubernetes Service**: https://azure.microsoft.com/en-in/services/Kubernetes -service/
- **Azure Container Service**: https://docs.microsoft.com/en-us/azure/container-service/
- **Kubernetes documentation**: https://Kubernetes.io/docs/home/
- **Scaling your applications on Kubernetes**: https://Kubernetes.io/docs/tutorials/Kubernetes-basics/scale/scale-interactive/
- **Helm**: https://helm.sh/
- **Stateful applications on Kubernetes**: https://Kubernetes.io/docs/tasks/run-application/run-replicated-stateful-application/
- **Kubernetes networking**: https://Kubernetes.io/docs/concepts/cluster-administration/networking/

5
Modernizing Apps and Infrastructure with DevOps

In this chapter, we'll discuss modern application and infrastructure deployment using **Azure DevOps**. We'll go into detail about Microsoft's new offering called Azure DevOps, which provides various tools and services that we can use to facilitate an enterprise-class DevOps culture in organizations of every size.

The following topics will be covered in this chapter:

- Azure DevOps overview
- **Continuous integration** (**CI**) and **continuous delivery** (**CD**)
- Azure boards
- Azure pipelines
- Azure Repos
- Azure test plans
- Azure artifacts
- Building a CI/CD pipeline with Azure DevOps
- GitHub integration with Azure DevOps

Understanding Azure DevOps

DevOps is a culture an organization forms with a set of tools and processes that allows it to quickly and effectively build and deliver software applications. DevOps brings the development and operations teams together to build a mechanism that optimizes the application life cycle.

According to Microsoft, DevOps is a compound of **development** (**Dev**) and **operations** (**Ops**) and is the union of people, processes, and technology so that value can be provided continually to customers. Azure DevOps, Microsoft latest's offering in the DevOps space, allows organizations to plan smarter, collaborate better, and ship faster with a set of modern Dev services.

Azure DevOps is a transformation of **Visual Studio Team Services** (**VSTS**). VSTS has been the flagship offering in cloud-based DevOps products from Microsoft for the last 7 years (at the time of writing). Azure DevOps is more than just a rebranding exercise and brings a completely new experience and capabilities to VSTS.

Along with Azure DevOps, **Team Foundation Server** (**TFS**) has been transformed into Azure DevOps Server. TFS was a popular on-premises hosted DevOps solution.

Azure DevOps includes the following toolset (at the time of writing):

- Azure boards
- Azure pipelines
- Azure Repos
- Azure test plans
- Azure artifacts

Along with these core offerings, Azure DevOps is also extensible and there are over 1,000 extensions available for integration with Azure DevOps.

Getting Azure DevOps

You can purchase Azure DevOps as an entire suite, which includes all the services that we mentioned in the previous section, but you can purchase each service separately. At the time of writing, only Azure pipelines and Azure Artifacts can be purchased independently; however, Microsoft has announced that you'll have the flexibility to buy any service of Azure DevOps independently.

Azure DevOps has the following variants:

- **Free for open source projects**: A completely free service with access to Azure boards, pipelines, and repos. You get unlimited users and build minutes, along with 10 parallel jobs.

- **Free for small teams**: This includes teams of up to five members. You get Azure boards, pipelines, repos, and artifacts with one hosted pipeline job of 1,800 minutes per month. You also get to bring one self-hosted job (you'd have your own build server).
- **User license – basic plan**: A paid version including Azure pipelines, Azure Boards, Azure Repos, Azure Artifacts, and Load Testing. The pricing model is per user per month, depending on the number of users you have, with the first five users being free.
- **User license – basic and test plan**: This includes all the features of the Basic Plan and the Azure Test Plans.
- **Individual services**: You can purchase Azure pipelines and/or Azure Artifacts separately.

More information about pricing is available here: `https://azure.microsoft.com/en-in/pricing/details/devops/azure-devops-services/`.

If you're interested in only purchasing an Azure pipeline, please refer to the following link: `https://azure.microsoft.com/en-in/pricing/details/devops/azure-pipelines/`.

Signing up for Azure DevOps

You can sign up for a free account with Azure DevOps using a Microsoft account or an Azure AD account. Let's look at the signup process:

1. Visit `https://azure.microsoft.com/en-in/services/devops/` in a modern browser.
2. Click on **Start Free**. Here, you can log in with a work account or Microsoft account. You can also choose to create a new Microsoft account if you don't have one already.
3. Accept the terms and conditions; now, you can start creating your Azure DevOps organization.
4. Create a project to get started. You can give it any name.

5. Select **Private** for now; choosing **Public** will allow anyone on the internet to view the project. This may be appropriate for open source projects:

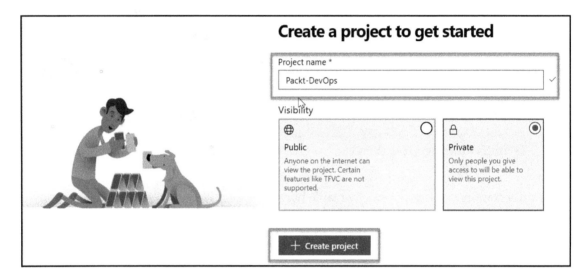

6. You can now use this project for your application DevOps process. We'll come back to this later in this chapter.

In the next section, we will look at Azure boards.

Azure boards

Azure boards allow you to plan, discuss, and track tasks across teams and team members. Task management and tracking is a crucial component of the DevOps practice since it starts from conceptualizing the work and is linked until the release.

Azure boards are based on standard Kanban boards and provide capabilities such as the following:

- **Work items**: Create and assign work items to your team. Team members can also use work items to track their items and update statuses against work progress in the work item itself. There are multiple categories of work items available out of the box, such as the following:
    - Bug
    - Epic
    - Feature

- Issue
- Task
- Test case
- User story

Each type of work item has different properties. Team members can track their efforts in hours with work items.

- **Boards**: Create boards with various buckets and move the work items across buckets toward completion. This helps teams and management get a quick and clear view of the overall progress of the project. It's a visual interface for teams to plan their work and priorities easily, and show progress.
- **Backlogs**: Backlogs are work items that are categorized based on sprints and displayed as a list. Using backlogs, you can move items across iterations. You will also get to plan sprints here and allocate tasks to sprints with visibility on efforts. Your project comes with predefined sprints, such as iteration 1 and iteration 2. You can customize them or define new sprints.

> Boards are work items in the visual interface that look like cards; backlogs are work items in list format.

- **Sprints**: Sprints allow you to get a holistic view of all the tasks and their statuses for various sprints. You can choose to view the tasks for a sprint and move them through different stages (developing, ready, delivered, and so on). You can also view and assess team capacity here, based on the planned efforts in work items and team availability.
- **Queries**: Queries allow you to filter out specific tasks/bugs based on the various parameters you can choose from, such as *the work item is of the bug type, has been open for the last five days*, and *does not have any updates*. Queries are very useful with large teams where there is an enormous number of tasks and processes to manage.

In our example hands-on lab in this chapter, we'll use Azure boards to create feature requests and address them through the Azure DevOps process.

For more information, read the Azure boards documentation at `https://docs.microsoft.com/en-in/azure/devops/boards/index?view=vsts`.

Azure Repos

Azure Repos, as part of Azure DevOps, give you unlimited cloud-hosted private repositories so that you can store and control your project code. Simply put, it's a set of version control tools for software projects.

Version control tools are critical for any software project, whether you're a single developer or part of a large team of developers. It helps you centrally store and track code changes so that you can refer to them later on and roll back if required.

Some of the features of Azure Repos are as follows:

- Support for standard Git tools, which means you can integrate and use it with any Git tools, IDEs, and so on.
- Integrated WebHooks and API. This is a fully extensible service, and you can use WebHooks/APIs for further automation.
- Simplified and intelligent search capabilities with semantic code search.
- Effective collaboration with standard PR and review process.
- Automate build, test, and deployment with natively integrated Azure pipelines.
- Use branch policies to ensure code quality is the best by including required controls and reviews.

Azure Repos provide two types of source control:

- **Git**: Distributed version control
- **Team Foundation Version Control (TFVC)**: Centralized version control

Git is the most popular source control version control system; that's the reason Microsoft has adapted Git as a standard when it comes to SCM over and above Microsoft's own TFVC.

Azure Repos are standard Git-based repos, similar to GitHub. This means you can use your existing toolset, processes, and knowledge with Azure Repos as well. It includes standard features such as code commit, pull requests, and branches.

You can find out more about Git concepts here: `https://docs.microsoft.com/en-us/azure/devops/repos/git/overview?view=vsts`.

In the example in this chapter, we'll use Azure Repos to store our code. For more information, read the Azure Repos documentation at `https://docs.microsoft.com/en-in/azure/devops/boards/index?view=vsts`.

Azure pipelines

Azure pipelines is the core DevOps service and is responsible for continuous integration and continuous delivery. Pipelines allow you to continuously build, test, and deploy your application to any platform and any cloud.

Azure pipelines work with the code that's stored in your standard Git providers, such as GitHub, GitLab, Bitbucket, and Azure Repos, and perform deployment across cloud platforms such as Azure, AWS, and Google Cloud. Along with that, they work with any language and any platform. Simply put, pipelines are the automation services that will watch for your code changes, build them to ensure there are no errors, perform test cases, deploy them to staging, and finally deploy them to production. All of this is done in a fully automated fashion with no intervention required unless it's been configured explicitly.

Azure pipelines offer a free version for open source projects with unlimited build minutes and up to 10 parallel jobs. Let's look at the key features of Azure pipelines:

- **Any language/platform**: You can use Azure pipelines with many languages and platforms, which offers you full flexibility for the development environment of your choice.
- **Integrated containers and Kubernetes operations**: You can use these to build and deploy your modern world applications.
- **Extensible**: You can integrate with various third-party products such as SonarCloud in order to enhance capabilities and further integration.
- **Deploy to any cloud**: Pipelines don't only work with Azure; they also work with AWS, Google Cloud, or your private clouds.
- **GitHub integration for source code and CI/CD**: Available on the GitHub marketplace.

You can build an Azure pipeline using the Azure DevOps portal designer or using YAML-based configuration files. Let's look at what you can build with pipelines.

The languages that are supported for out of the box build integration are ASP.NET, .NET Core, Android, C/C++/C#, Docker, Go, Java, JavaScript, Node.js, PHP, Python, Ruby, **Universal Windows Applications** (**UWP**), Xamarin, and Xcode.

Along with these, you can choose to code in other languages as well.

The supported deployment platforms for out of the box release integration are as follows:

- Azure Kubernetes services or any other Kubernetes cluster using Helm charts or the Kubernetes manifest
- Azure stack
- Azure app service (including web apps and container apps)
- Azure SQL, MySQL, and PostgreSQL
- Linux VMs and Windows VMs, either on the cloud or physically
- Azure service fabric
- VM scale sets
- Azure functions
- VMware
- **System Center Virtual Machine Manager** (SCVMM)
- Publish NPM/NuGet packages

Along with these, you can choose to deploy to other platforms using any scripting language.

With Azure pipelines, you can also integrate your test cases into your CI pipeline. You can leverage test capabilities such as the following:

- Run tests with Selenium for the UI or any other automated unit tests.
- Run various tests in parallel.
- View and analyze your test results in your CI job.
- Test analytics.

For more information, read the documentation of the Azure pipeline at `https://docs.microsoft.com/en-in/azure/devops/pipelines/index?view=vsts`.

Azure pipeline agents

Every Azure pipeline operation runs on an agent. Microsoft provides hosted agents; you can also use your own agents if you have specific requirements or if you only want to keep your code in your servers. An agent is a VM with an Azure pipeline agent installed. You can have separate agents for build and release operations. You can have agents with one of the following platforms:

- Windows
- Ubuntu 14.04/16.04

- macOS
- Red Hat Linux
- Linux Docker containers

Azure test plans

Azure test plans help you improve your code quality using planned and exploratory testing services for your apps. You can also use Azure test plans with Azure pipelines for your overall CI/CD cycle. It's a simple browser-based tool that can be used to test your web or desktop applications.

With Azure test plans, you can do the following:

- **Manual and exploratory testing**:
    - **Planned manual testing**: Regular testing activities by your testers and test leads. You can organize tests into categories and assign them.
    - **User acceptance testing**: Generally, these are actual users who have agreed to test the product before launch to verify that the requirements have been met.
    - **Exploratory testing**: Testing is carried out by the core engineering team that comprises developers, testers, product management, user experience designers, and so on, by exploring the software systems without using test plans or test suites.
    - **Stakeholder feedback**: Generally, this is done by non-engineering teams that test out products from a sales and marketing standpoint.
- **Load testing**: You can use this to perform load testing on your websites, apps, and APIs using standard load testing techniques such as JMeter.

With that, let's look at the tools we can use for various kinds of testing:

- **Automated testing**: Use Azure pipelines and the build and release configuration to perform automated application testing. Automate testing using build-deploy-test workflows and make sure your app still works after every check-in.
- **Manual testing**: Use the Azure test plan and create test plans to track manual testing for sprints or milestones. Run tests, log defects, and quickly view the status using lightweight charts.

- **Load testing**: Use Azure test plans to understand and fix performance issues before they impact your business. Scale your tests to hundreds of thousands of concurrent users:

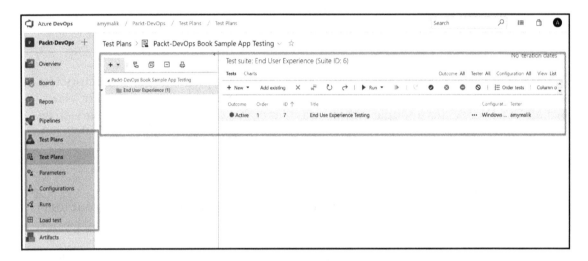

For more information, read the Azure test plans documentation at `https://docs.microsoft.com/en-us/azure/devops/test/index-tp?view=vsts`.

Azure artifacts

Azure artifacts is a package repository where you can create, host, and share packages with your teams. This includes package support such as Maven, NPM, and NuGet. Azure artifacts can watch public and private package repositories and integrate them with package management practices in your CI/CD pipelines.

In Azure artifacts, you create feeds where you can store packages that can be used in your applications by developers. You can also define an upstream repository on your feed, such as a public `npmjs` repository, where you can choose to update packages.

Azure artifacts help you do the following:

- **Keep your artifacts organized**: You can store and manage all your packages together and ensure that consistent packages are used across your applications.

- **Protect your packages**: Keep every public source package you use – including packages from `npmjs` and `nuget.org` – safe in your feed where only you can delete them and where they're backed by the enterprise-grade Azure SLA.
- **Integrate with your CI/CD pipeline**: Your Azure DevOps CI/CD pipeline resources can access your packages and other artifacts easily with native integration.

Building a CI/CD pipeline with Azure DevOps

In this section, we'll take our sample application, that is, Azure Voting App, that we used in the previous exercise for AKS deployments and use that to demonstrate an end-to-end CI/CD process. We'll be using the following components of Azure DevOps:

- **Azure Repos**: To store our application code and version control
- **Azure boards**: For work items related to new feature requests in the application
- **Azure pipeline along with Azure test plans**: To automatically build, test, and deploy the application

Let's get started!

Creating a new Azure DevOps project

In this section, we'll create a new Azure DevOps project for the purposes of our lab:

1. Log in to your Azure DevOps account. See the previous sections if you don't have one already.
2. Click on **Create Project**. Create a project with the following specifications:
   - **Project name** and **Description**: `Voting App` or similar; whatever you want
   - **Visibility**: **Private**

- **Advanced**:
  - **Version control: Git**
  - **Work item process**: This choice is up to you (**Agile, Scrum**, or **CMII**):

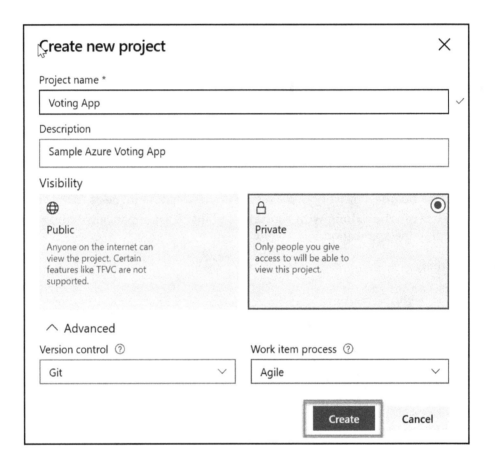

Cloning the voting app code to your development machine

You need Git to be installed on your local development machine for this exercise. You can install Git from the following sources:

- **Git for Windows:** `https://git-scm.com/download/win`
- **Git for macOS:** `https://git-scm.com/download/mac`

- Git for Linux: `https://git-scm.com/download/linux`

Once Git has been installed, launch a PowerShell or Terminal window, depending on your operating system. Run the following command to copy the sample voting app code into your local system. You can also `cd` into a different directory before cloning the repository:

```
git clone
https://github.com/PacktPublishing/Migrating-Apps-to-the-Cloud-with-Azure.g
it
```

Setting up an Azure repo for the voting app and pushing the application code

Now, let's set up an Azure repo for our project and push the voting app code into it. In this exercise, we'll set up an Azure repo in our local endpoint and then push the code using regular Git commands:

1. Log in to your Azure DevOps account and open the `Voting App` project.
2. Click on **Repos** and copy the Git repo URL:

3. Launch a Git command window on your laptop and enter the following command. This will launch the Microsoft authentication window. Sign in with your Azure DevOps credentials:

```
git clone yourcopiedurl
```

4. Now, you can browse the directory in any file browser and copy the code you cloned earlier into the new directory. Copy all the files in the `Chapter5` folder to the newly cloned directory:

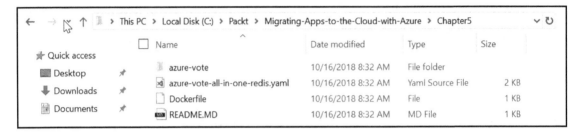

5. Once you've copied the data, issue the following commands:

```
git add .
git commit -m "Adding Initial Code"
git push origin master
```

6. Now, refresh your Azure Repos file page. You should see the updated files:

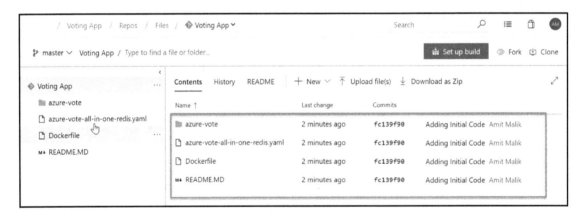

Your code is now in Azure Repos. You can use the standard Git process to create a branch, perform pull requests, and more.

Refer to `https://www.codecademy.com/learn/learn-git` to learn more about Git.

Setting up a build pipeline

Now that we have our application code in Azure Repos, we can set up a build pipeline to perform the application build.

The Azure Voting App is a simple Python-based Docker app, so, in our case, the build operation should be generating a Docker image with the updated app code. We'll automate this process with an Azure pipeline. Let's set up a build pipeline:

1. Launch a modern browser and log in to Azure DevOps.
2. Open the `Voting App` project.
3. Click on **Pipelines** and click **New pipeline**:

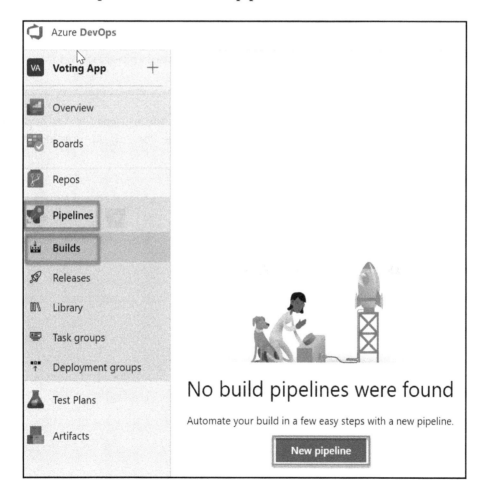

4. On the **New pipeline** page, click on **Use the visual designer**:

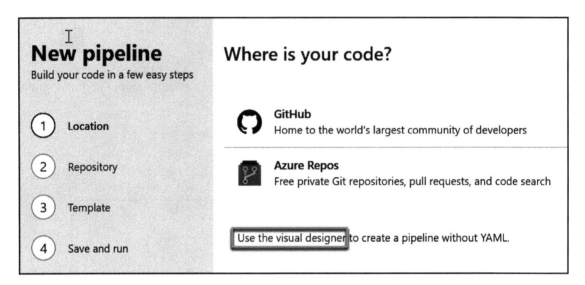

5. On the next page, you will see various support code sources for Azure pipelines. We'll choose **Azure Repos Git** here and select the `Voting App` project and repo:

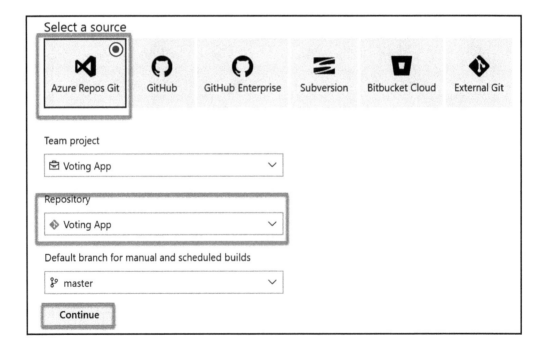

6. Select **Docker container** as the template:

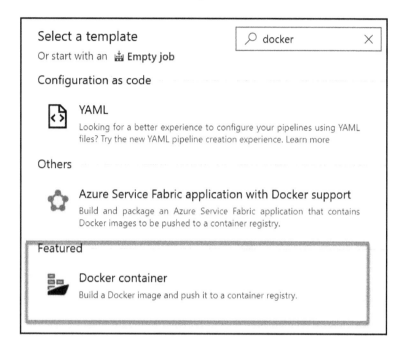

7. This will open the build configuration page. Let's set up some basic configuration, such as build agents. In the following screenshot, we've given the build a name and selected **Azure Pipelines** as **Agent pool** with Ubuntu-16.04-based agents:

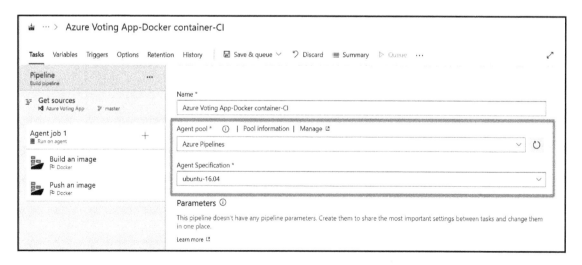

8. Give the step a name and set **Container Registry Type** as **Azure Container Registry.**
   1. Select your **Azure subscription** and authorize this (you'll need to log in again).
   2. Choose the ACR from the dropdown list. Let's configure the **Build an image** step. Here, we'll use an **Azure Container Registry (ACR)** to build and store the image. Azure pipelines integrates with ACR directly, so we'll need to choose the subscription and ACR to be used here:
   3. Set **Action** to **Build an image**.
   4. Select **Include Latest Tags.**
   5. Leave the other options as their defaults:

9. Similarly, configure the ACR settings for the **Push an image** step. This is where we'll be storing the image. Ensure that you check **Include Latest Tag**:

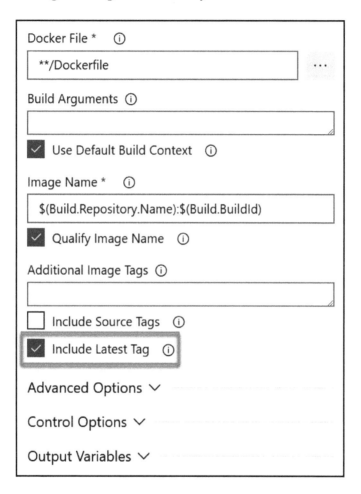

10. Click on **Save & queue** to save the build definition and start a test build:

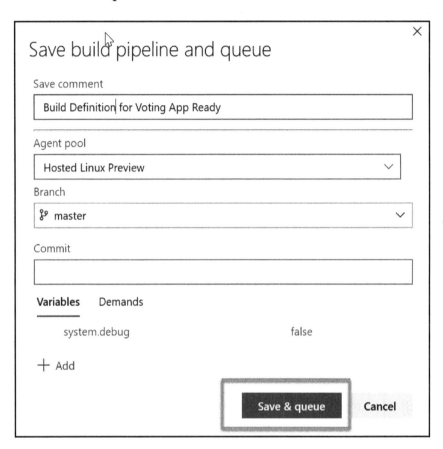

11. This will start the build operation. You can click on the **Build Job** link and see a real-time update for the build operation.

12. Once the build is successful, you should see all the steps passing successfully and a new Docker image should be stored inside the ACR. You can click on any step and see a detailed log of every operation:

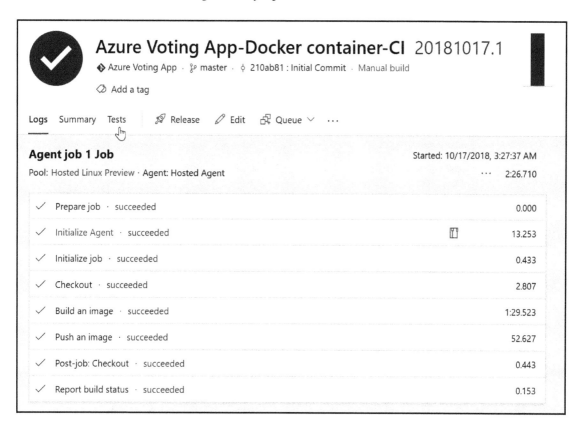

13. The ACR should show that a new image has been pushed, along with its tag version and **latest**. We're tagging with **latest** because we're using that in our deployment configuration in the Kubernetes YAML file:

14. Now, let's enable CI; that is, the build should start as soon as there's a commit to the configured branches in the repo. We can configure the CI settings in **Build configuration** | **Edit** | **Triggers** and check the **Enable continuous integration** button. You can configure which Git branches you want to include here. Click **Save** to save this configuration:

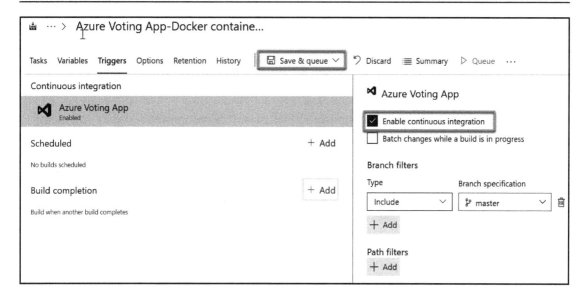

In the following subsection, we will be looking at building the release pipeline.

Building a release pipeline

In the previous section, we defined a build definition for our application. As we saw, this is a Docker-based app. In this section, we'll configure a release definition so that we can deploy this app on a Kubernetes cluster.

There are three ways to deploy applications to a Kubernetes cluster with Azure pipelines:

- Deploy to AKS using Helm charts using Azure integrated authentication.
- Deploy to any Kubernetes cluster anywhere using `kubeconfig` native authentication.
- Deploy to AKS using `kubectl` using Azure Integrated authentication.

Our application manifest is a YAML-based Kubernetes deployment, so we'll choose the second method here. This will also help you understand that Azure DevOps can be used for any platform, not just Azure components.

To authenticate against the Kubernetes cluster, we need to get `kubeconfig`, which includes Kubernetes endpoints and authentication keys. We can get this information by connecting to the AKS cluster and copying the `kubeconfig` data from the user's home directory.

Let's get the `kubeconfig` data for our AKS cluster:

1. Ensure that you have a running AKS cluster. It is recommended that you clean up the previous voting app deployments using `kubectl delete -f filename.yaml`.

2. Launch the Cloud Shell or any other Terminal and connect to the AKS cluster using the following command:

   ```
   az aks get-credentials -g <RGName> -n <AKSClusterName>
   ```

3. View the config file by issuing the `cat kubeconfig` command under `/home/username/.kube/config`. In my case, I'd issue `cat /home/amit/.kube/config` in Cloud Shell.

4. Copy the entire file into a Notepad file and store it for future use.

Now that we've got the Kubernetes cluster authentication information, let's ensure that our application deployment manifest has the right image mapping and that the Kubernetes cluster has access to the container registry:

1. Browse to **Azure repos** | **Files** and open `azure-vote-all-in-one-redis.yaml`. Browse to the `azure-vote-front` deployment resource and ensure that the image value has been updated to the one for your ACR repo. It should be in `reponame.azurecr.io/imagename` format. Note that you'll need to click on **Edit** to modify the file:

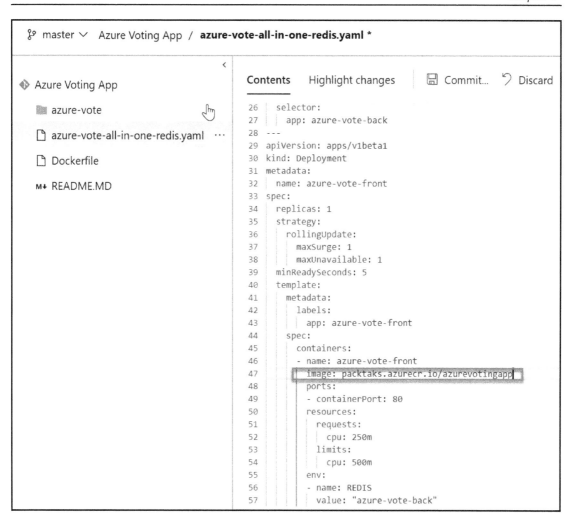

2. Now, our AKS cluster should have access to the container registry so that we can download the images. We can do this by using one of two methods:

   - Integrate using native Kubernetes methods and create a Docker registry secret in AKS with the configuration and authentication details of ACR, similar to just another Docker registry.

   - Integrate using native AKS and ACR integration. In this case, we just need to assign access to ACR to the Azure SPN that's used by AKS for Azure interaction.

3. We'll be using the second method here. Update the AKS and ACR resource names and resource groups names given in the following code snippet and run this script to configure AKS SPN access for your ACR:

```bash
#!/bin/bash

AKS_RESOURCE_GROUP=myAKSResourceGroup
AKS_CLUSTER_NAME=myAKSCluster
ACR_RESOURCE_GROUP=myACRResourceGroup
ACR_NAME=myACRRegistry

# Get the id of the service principal configured for AKS
CLIENT_ID=$(az aks show --resource-group $AKS_RESOURCE_GROUP --name $AKS_CLUSTER_NAME --query "servicePrincipalProfile.clientId" --output tsv)

# Get the ACR registry resource id
ACR_ID=$(az acr show --name $ACR_NAME --resource-group $ACR_RESOURCE_GROUP --query "id" --output tsv)

# Create role assignment
az role assignment create --assignee $CLIENT_ID --role Reader --scope $ACR_ID
```

More information about authentication with ACR can be found at `https:/
/docs.microsoft.com/en-us/azure/container-registry/container-
registry-auth-aks`.

Now, we're ready to build a release pipeline so that we can deploy the solution to AKS with CD:

1. Log in to Azure DevOps and browse through the pipelines in your project.
2. Click on **Release** | **Create a new release pipeline**.
3. Select **Deploy to a Kubernetes cluster** when selecting a template:

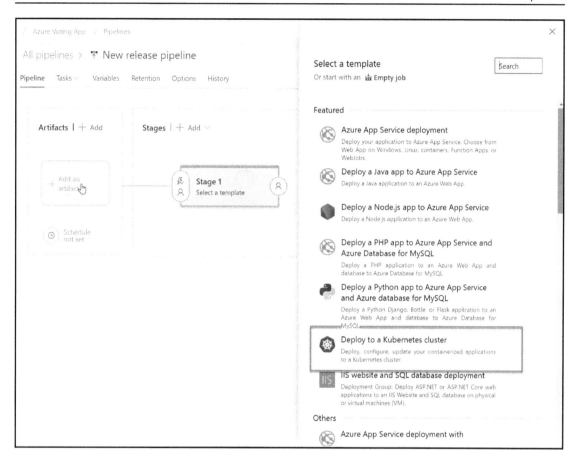

4. On the next page, define a stage name. We can choose to have multiple stages, such as deploy to pre-pod, deploy to test, and deploy to prod. Give it a name and click the **X** sign.

5. Now, let's add our artifacts source. In our case, we'll be initiating deployments based on the Azure repo, so we'll choose **Azure Repos...** as the source and choose our project. Click on **Add an Artifact** and provide some details, as follows:

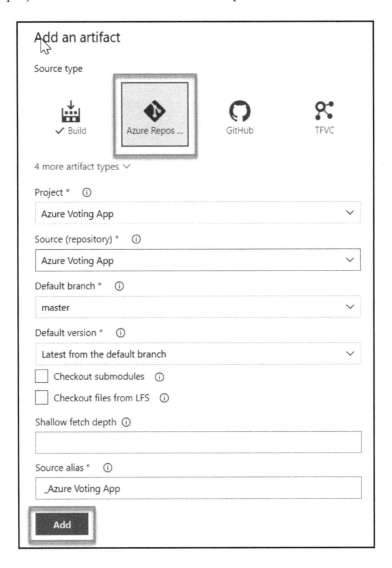

6. Let's enable **CD** for the **Artifacts** step. Click on the **Trigger** button and enable **CD**. This ensures that a release is started as soon as there's a new build available. You can also choose to have a release started on PRs:

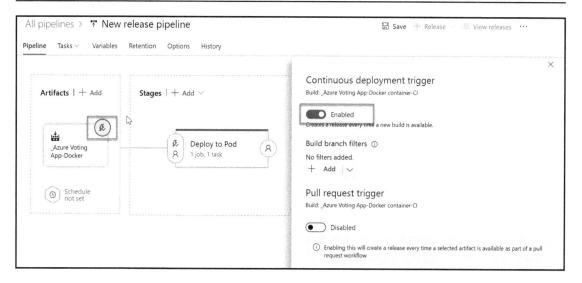

7. Now, let's configure a deployment task under the **Deploy to Pod** stage. Click on **Tasks** and select the **kubectl apply** job:

8. Now, we need to configure the deployment configuration. Click on **New** in the Kubernetes service connection:

- **Choose authentication**: Kubeconfig
- **Connection name**: Any name of your choice to identify the cluster
- **Server URL**: Copy from the `kubeconfig` file you copied earlier
- **KubeConfig**: Paste the entire `kubeconfig` file you copied earlier
- Click **Accept untrusted certificates**

9. Click **Verify connection**. Review your settings if you see an error.
10. You can select the Kubernetes Cluster using kubeconfig, service principal, or Azure integrated authentication:

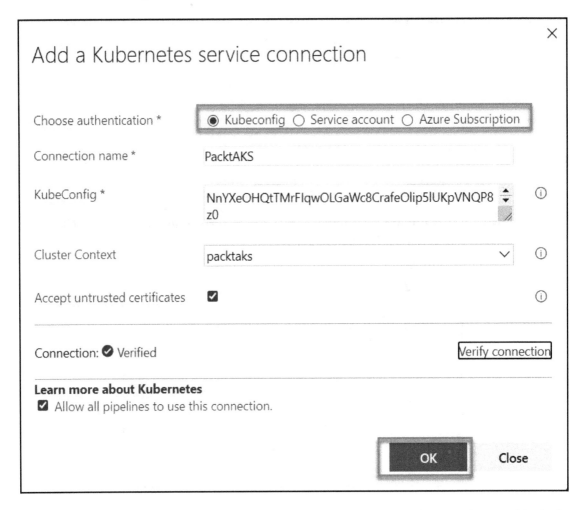

11. You can choose to deploy in a specific Kubernetes namespace or leave it blank if you want to deploy in the default namespace.
12. Under command, enter `apply`.

13. Click on **Choose configuration file** to provide a path to your deployment YAML file. Browse to your default directory and select the deployment YAML file. We can define additional options such as Kubernetes secrets and config maps if required. Click **Save** after verifying that all the configurations are valid:

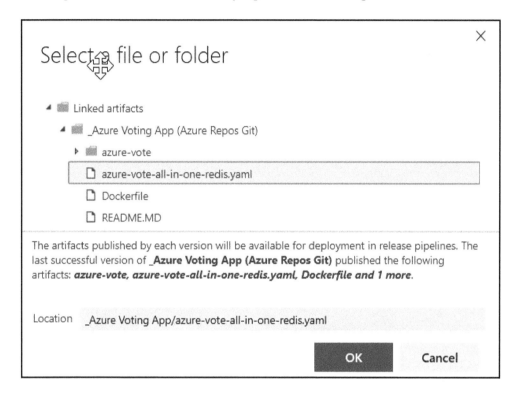

14. Now, we'll add another step in the pipeline so that we can update the images in AKS after deployment. This will ensure that, at every release, Kubernetes is pulling the latest images. Click on the **+** sign to add another task to the pipeline.
15. Select **Deploy to a Kubernetes cluster** when selecting a template.

16. Configure the task so that it uses the same Kubernetes connection. Under **Command**, keep `set` as the command and use `image deployments/azure-vote-front azure-vote-front=youracrname.azurecr.io/azurevotingapp:latest` as the argument:

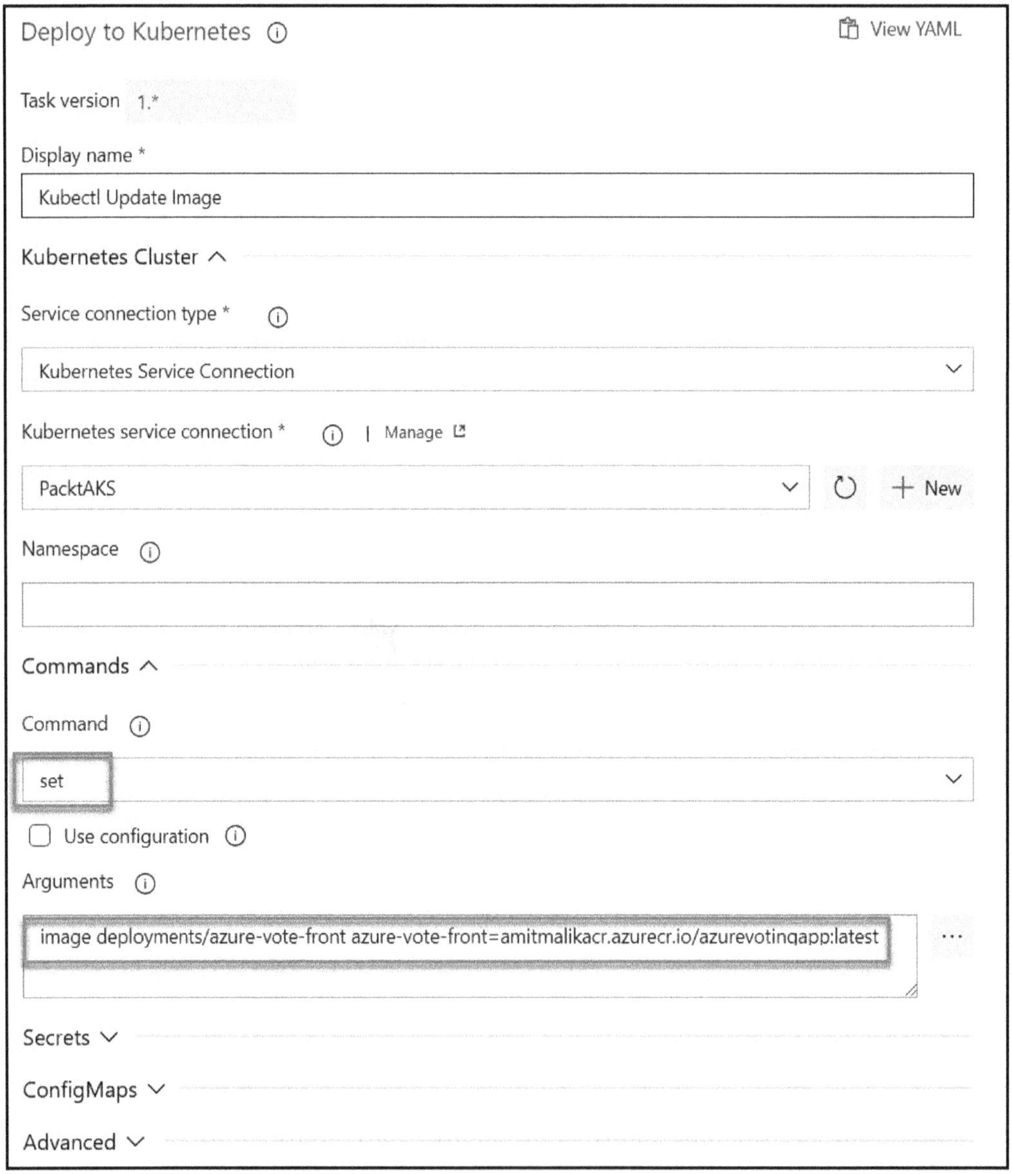

Deploy to Kubernetes ⓘ   📋 View YAML

Task version 1.*

Display name *

> Kubectl Update Image

Kubernetes Cluster ∧

Service connection type *   ⓘ

> Kubernetes Service Connection   ⌄

Kubernetes service connection *   ⓘ | Manage ⧉

> PacktAKS   ⌄   ↻   + New

Namespace ⓘ

>

Commands ∧

Command ⓘ

> set   ⌄

☐ Use configuration ⓘ

Arguments ⓘ

> image deployments/azure-vote-front azure-vote-front=amitmalikacr.azurecr.io/azurevotingapp:latest   ...

Secrets ⌄

ConfigMaps ⌄

Advanced ⌄

17. Click **Save** to save your changes.

Now, our release configuration is ready. We have already enabled CD by specifying triggers. Let's go ahead and initiate a release:

1. Click on **Release** and then **Create a release**:

2. Select the default values and click **Create**.
3. Now, the release should start. You can view release logs by going to **Releases**, selecting the release we created, and clicking on **Releases**. In our case, the release will be successful:

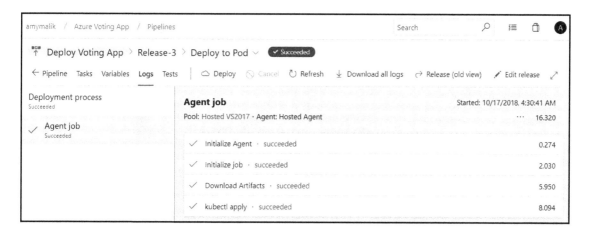

With that, our build and release configuration with full CI/CD automation is ready. Let's look at the AKS cluster to ensure that our application has been deployed properly and is accessible (with the release that we just did):

1. Connect to your AKS cluster using the CLI.
2. Run `kubectl get pods` and `kubectl get services`:

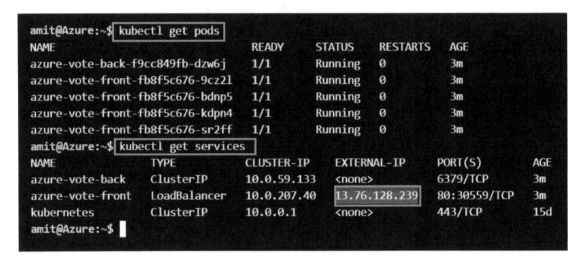

3. You can try launching the public IP to check that the application is working as expected:

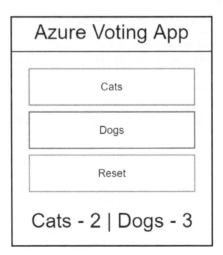

Next, we will be simulating an end-to-end CI/CD experience.

Simulating an end-to-end CI/CD experience

In the previous sections, we set up a CI/CD pipeline. Let's try to play around with it and experience the overall flow. Let's assume that there's a requirement for our voting app to start new voting for red or blue, instead of the cats or dogs voting system we had earlier. Let's go through this now:

1. Let's start by creating a work item for this change request. Log in to Azure Boards and click on **Create New Work Item**. We'll use **Feature** since we are making a change to the application:

2. Enter the task's details, including the task name, description, and other particulars, such as the reason for the task. Then, assign it an engineer and click **Save**:

3. Once the task has been assigned, the developer will go ahead and make the code change and raise a PR. We can do this using the portal. Browse to Azure **Repos** | **Files** | azure-vote | config_file.cfg and click **Edit**.

4. Change the values from Cats and Dogs to Red and Blue and click **Commit...**:

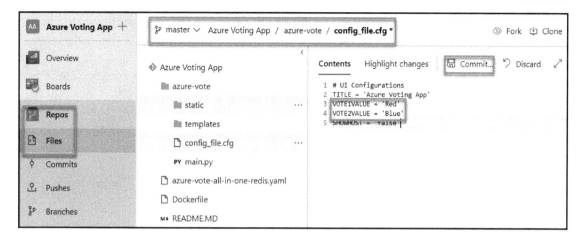

5. On commit, we can change the branch name to a new branch if want to go through a review and pull request process.

6. We will also link this commit to our work item:

7. Now, we can sit back, relax, and let Azure DevOps do its job. Commit will initiate a build operation that you can review in **Pipelines** | **Build**.

8. Once the build is successful, it will initiate a release operation and update the application. You can review the build and release logs to ensure that both have completed successfully.

9. Once the DevOps cycle has completed, you can try launching your application instance again (don't forget to clear the cache or refresh with *Ctrl + F5*). You should see that the voting options have now changed to Red and Blue.

10. Once the changes have been validated, the work item will be marked as completed.

Using Azure pipelines with GitHub

Azure pipelines are also available in the GitHub marketplace and can be integrated with GitHub projects directly. You can choose GitHub as your project source and perform a build and release operation using an Azure pipeline. This also enables CI with GitHub; that is, as soon as there's a PR/commit based on your configuration, Azure pipelines will run build/release operations and report the status on the GitHub PR page so that the approver can review the CI/CD logs and approve the PR if it's appropriate.

Azure pipelines is available on the GitHub marketplace to purchase and use: `https://github.com/marketplace/azure-pipelines`. Alternatively, you can specify GitHub as a source in Azure DevOps and pipelines will be available for your GitHub repository.

> The following is a good reference video showing the integration of GitHub with Azure pipelines: `https://channel9.msdn.com/Events/Microsoft-Azure/Azure-DevOps-Launch-2018/A102?ocid=player`.

Summary

In this chapter, we learned about Microsoft's latest set of services related to the DevOps process. We learned about various tools, including Azure Boards, Azure Repos, Azure pipelines, Azure test plans, and Azure Artifacts. We also set up a DevOps organization and configured the CI/CD pipeline for our sample application.

In the next chapter, we will learn about designing web apps for containers.

Questions

Answer the following questions to test your knowledge of this chapter. You can find the answers in the *Assessments* section at the end of this book:

1. Are Azure DevOps services available both on-cloud and on-premises?
    1. Yes
    2. No

2. How can we automate the deployment of the application to Azure Web Apps?
    1. Using an Azure pipelines build
    2. Using an Azure pipelines release
    3. Using Azure artifacts

3. Can a project manager use Azure DevOps for resource and delivery planning?
    1. Yes, with Azure boards.
    2. Yes, with Azure artifacts.
    3. No. Azure DevOps is only for developers.

Further reading

- **Introducing Azure DevOps blogs and demonstrations**: https://azure.microsoft.com/en-us/blog/introducing-azure-devops/
- **Azure DevOps services documentation**: https://docs.microsoft.com/en-in/azure/devops/user-guide/index?view=vsts
- **Microsoft DevOps blog**: https://blogs.msdn.microsoft.com/devops/
- **Azure Artifacts documentation**: https://docs.microsoft.com/en-us/azure/devops/test/index-tp?view=vsts

3
Building a Web and Microservices Architecture on Azure

By building robust microservices with tools such as Visual Studio, Service Fabric, and SQL databases, you will be able to modernize your existing architecture. Your application will then be more agile and scalable. The application will be able to adopt various technologies and development stacks, giving the team the possibility to use the tools of their choice.

This section contains the following chapters:

- Chapter 6, *Designing Web Applications*
- Chapter 7, *Scalability and Performance*
- Chapter 8, *Building Microservices with Service Fabric*

6
Designing Web Applications

In the previous chapter, we covered modernizing apps and infrastructure with DevOps. This chapter will cover Azure Web Apps, the different App Service Plans that are available, and the characteristics of the different App Service Plans. You will learn more about designing web apps for containers using Azure Container Services and Docker; how to design web apps for high availability, scalability, and performance using the Redis cache; autoscaling; app service environments; and more. You will also learn about how to design a custom web API and what Azure offers in terms of securing custom APIs.

The following topics will be covered in this chapter:

- Azure Web Apps
- App Service Plans
- Designing web apps for containers
- Designing web apps for high availability, scalability, and performance
- Designing and securing custom web APIs

Technical requirements

This chapter uses the following tool for the examples:

- Visual Studio 2019: https://visualstudio.microsoft.com/vs/

The source code for this chapter can be downloaded here: https://github.com/ PacktPublishing/Migrating-Apps-to-the-Cloud-with-Azure/tree/master/Chapter6/ PacktPubToDoAPI.

Azure Web Apps

Azure Web Apps is a part of Azure App Service and is where you can host your websites and applications in Azure. Using Web Apps, you only pay for the compute resources you use, not for the actual hosting of your site or application. Besides websites and applications, you can also host your web APIs and your mobile backends inside Azure Web Apps.

You can use a programming language of your choice for developing applications. At the time of writing, Azure Web Apps supports .NET, .NET Core, Java, Ruby, Node.js, PHP, and Python. These applications are hosted on Windows or Linux VMs that are fully managed by Microsoft and can easily be scaled using out-of-the-box features. Besides scaling, you can leverage other Azure features, such as security, load balancing, and insights and analytics. You can also use the DevOps capabilities, such as continuous integration and deployment from Azure DevOps, GitHub, Docker Hub, and other resources; SSL certificates; package management; staging environments; and custom domains.

Now let's take a look at the various App Service Plans.

App Service Plans

Azure web apps are hosted inside App Service Plans. Inside the app service plan, you can configure all of the required settings, such as the costs, the compute resources, and in what region you want to deploy your apps. There are different types of App Service Plans available in Azure—from free plans, where you share all of the resources with other customers and that are most suitable for development applications, to paid plans, where you can choose to host your apps on Windows VMs or Linux VMs and can set the available resources.

Azure offers the following service plan pricing tiers:

- **Dev/test**: Free and shared, your app runs on the same VM as other apps in a shared environment. This environment can also include apps from other Azure customers and users. Each app has a CPU quota and there is no ability to scale up or out. These App Service Plans are most suited for development and test apps or apps with less traffic. There is no SLA support for these two plans. The shared service plan offers the ability to add custom domains. The service plan is shown here:

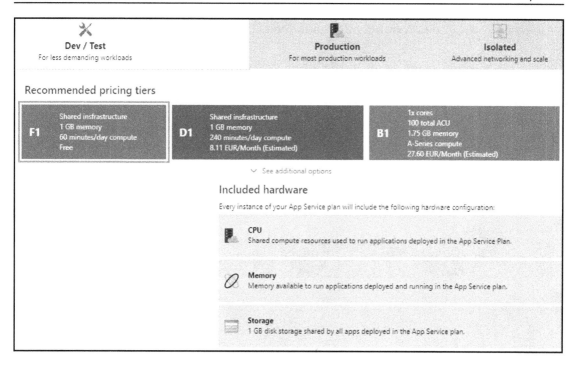

Free and shared app service plan in the Azure portal

- **Production**: This option includes the following tiers:
    - **Basic**: The basic tier is the first tier, where you can choose between different pricing ranges. It offers three tiers, and the available cores and RAM double for every tier. Apps run on dedicated Linux or Windows VMs and the compute resources are only shared between apps that are deployed inside the same app service plan. All apps inside the same app service plan reside in an isolated environment that supports SSL and custom domains. The basic tier offers scaling to three instances, but you need to do this manually. This tier is most suitable for development and test environments and applications with less traffic.
    - **Standard:** The standard tier also has three tiers to choose from. It offers custom domains and SSL support, autoscaling for up to 10 instances, and 5 deployment slots, which can be used for testing, staging, and production apps. It also provides daily backups and Azure Traffic Manager.

- **Premium:** Premium offers two types of tiers: premium and premium V2. They both offer all of the features of the standard tier, but the premium tier offers extra scale instances and deployment slots. The premium V2 tier runs on Dv2-series VMs, which offer faster processors and SSD drives and drastically increase the performance of your application. The various dedicated compute plans in the Azure portal are shown here:

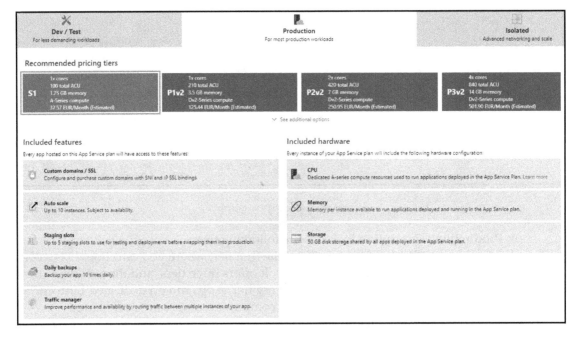

Dedicated compute plans in the Azure portal

- **Isolated**: The isolated tier offers full isolation for your applications by providing a private environment with dedicated VMs and virtual networks. You can also scale up to 100 instances. To create a private environment, App Services uses an **App Service Environment** (ASE), which will be covered in the next section. All apps run on Dv2-series virtual machines, so this tier offers high-performance capabilities. The isolated app service plan is most suitable for apps that need complete isolation because of high-security demands, for instance, but want to leverage all of the capabilities that Azure Web Apps offers, such as autoscale and deployment slots. The isolated service plan is shown here:

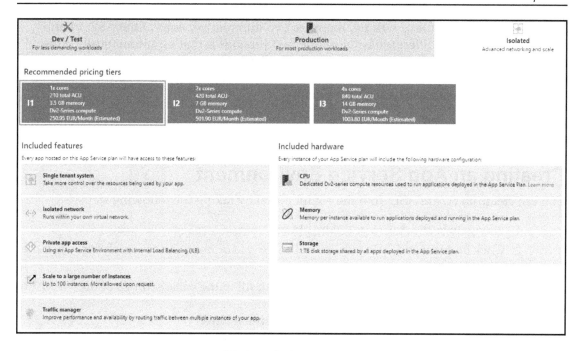

Isolated app service plan in the Azure portal

In the next section, we will look at the **App Service Environment**.

App Service Environment

The **App Service Environment** (ASE) is a feature of Azure App Service that provides a fully isolated environment for your web apps, mobile apps, API apps, and Azure functions. The ASE is deployed inside a subnet of the VNet, which provides full isolation and secure network access. ASEs are most suitable for apps that require high-scale workloads because they can be spread across a single or multiple Azure regions. Because of network isolation, ASEs are also very suitable for apps with high security requirements.

Only one ASE can be created per Azure subscription, and it can host up to 100 instances—from 100 app instances in a single app service plan to 100 App Service Plans with one app instance.

ASEs use frontends and workers; the former is suitable for automatic load balancing of the requests inside the ASE and the latter hosts the actual web apps inside the ASE. They are added automatically by Azure.

At the time of writing, there are two different versions of the ASE: v1 and v2. The difference between the two versions is that v2 automatically adds frontends and workers to the ASE, depending on the scale of the App Service Plans. In v1, you have to add these roles manually before you can scale out your app service plan.

Now, let's create an ASE!

Creating an App Service Environment

You can create an Azure ASE from the Azure portal by taking the following steps:

1. Navigate to the Azure portal by opening `https://portal.azure.com/`.
2. Click on **New** and type `App Service Environment` in the search bar. Click the **Create** button.
3. A new blade will open up where you can fill in the basic settings of the VM. Add the following:
   - **Subscription**: Select a subscription here.
   - **Resource group**: Create a new resource group and call it `PacktPubASE`.
   - **Name**: Type `PacktASE1`.
   - **Virtual IP Type**: Pick **External**. This creates an ASE that is accessible from the internet.

Then, click **Next: Networking**:

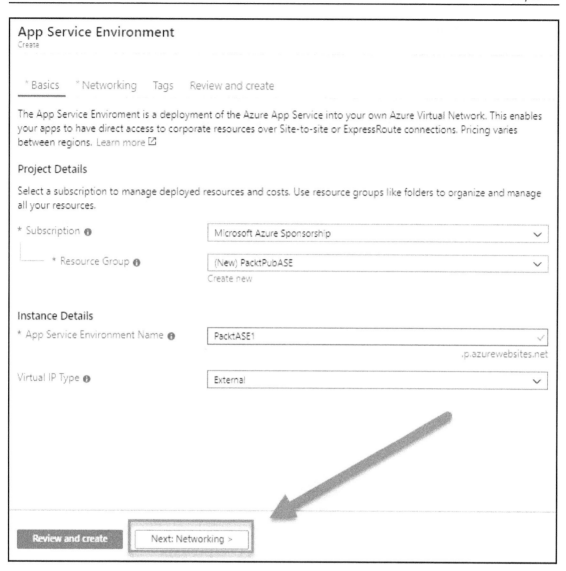

Basic ASE settings

4. In the networking blade, add the following values:
   - **Virtual Network**: Create a new VNet and call it `PacktPubASEVNet` and pick a region. Click **OK**.
   - **Subnet**: Create a new subnet and call it `PacktPubASESubnet`. Add the following values:

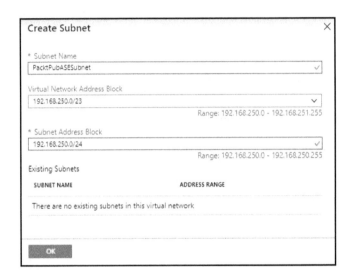

Subnet settings

- Click **OK**.

The networking blade will now look as follows:

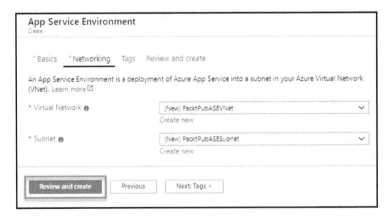

Network settings

- Click **Review and create** and then **Create**.

5. Click on **Create**. Azure will create an ASE, a virtual network, a route table, and an NSG for you.

6. You can now choose this ASE when you create a **New Azure App Service Plan**:

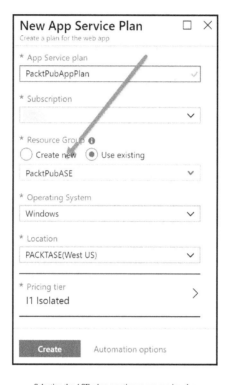

Selecting the ASE when creating an app service plan

Please note that the creation of an ASE can be quite expensive, so I strongly advise you to remove this when you are finished with your test.

For more information about Azure ASE, you can refer to the following Microsoft documentation: `https://docs.microsoft.com/en-us/azure/app-service/environment/intro`.

Now that we understand Azure Web Apps and App Service Environments, let's take a look at Web Apps for containers in the following sections.

Web Apps for containers

Web Apps for containers is part of the Azure App Service on Linux. You can also run Windows containers on it, but at the time of writing this book, this feature is still in preview. It lets you easily deploy and scale your own Docker-formatted images based on Linux distributions on Azure. Docker is based on open standards, which means it can run on all major Linux distributions and Windows Server 2016.

Docker containers are lightweight sandboxes on top of your OS. When your application is deployed inside a Docker container, the app cannot see or access all the other applications or processes that are running on the same OS. You can compare this to creating different VMs to host different types of workloads or applications, but without the overhead of the virtualization itself. Docker containers also share the same OS and infrastructure, whereas VMs need to have their own OS installed inside their own infrastructure.

With containers, you share the underlying resources of the Docker host and you build a Docker image that includes everything you need to run the application. You can start with a basic image and then add everything you need.

Docker containers are also extremely portable. You can deploy a Docker container, including all of the settings, such as configuration settings, a specific runtime, framework, and tooling, on a VM with Docker installed. You can then easily move that same container to the Azure App Service on Linux, and the application will still run as expected. This solves the "*it works on my machine*" problem that (almost) all developers face. This makes Docker not a virtualization technology, but an application delivery technology.

Docker containers are very suitable for building applications that leverage the microservices architecture, where parts of an application are loosely coupled and divided into separate services that all collaborate with each other. Each service can then be deployed into a separate container and written in their own programming language using their own configuration settings. A service can consist of a database, a web API, or a mobile backend, for instance. You can easily deploy multiple copies of a single application or database. The only thing to be aware of is that they all share the same OS. If your application needs to run on a different OS, you still have to use a VM.

For more information on the Azure App Service on Linux, you can refer to the following website: `https://docs.microsoft.com/en-us/azure/app-service/containers/app-service-linux-intro`.

Microsoft released a sample project called Developer Finder, which is available on GitHub. This will give you a great overview of the possibilities of Docker containers and is a good starting point for developing your own applications using Docker. You can refer to the following site: `https://github.com/azure-app-service/demoapp`.

Creating a web app for containers

A web app for containers can be created from the Azure portal.

In this example, I'm using the Docker Hub as a repository for Docker images. You can create an account using the following link: `https://hub.docker.com/`.

Follow these steps to create a project:

1. Navigate to the Azure portal by opening `https://portal.azure.com/`.
2. Click on **New** and, in the search bar, type `Web App for Containers`. Click on the **Create** button.
3. A new blade will open up where you can fill in the basic settings. Add the following values:
   - **Subscription**: Select a subscription here.
   - **Resource group**: Create a new resource group and call it `PacktPubContainers`.
   - **Name**: Type `PacktContainers`.
   - **Publish**: Select **Docker Image**.
   - **Operating System**: Select **Linux**.
   - **Region**: Choose **East US**.
   - **Linux Plan (East US)**: Keep the default value.
   - **Sku and size:** Here, you can also keep the default value. The premium plan gives us the ability to adjust the scaling properties later in this chapter.

Then, click **Next: Docker**:

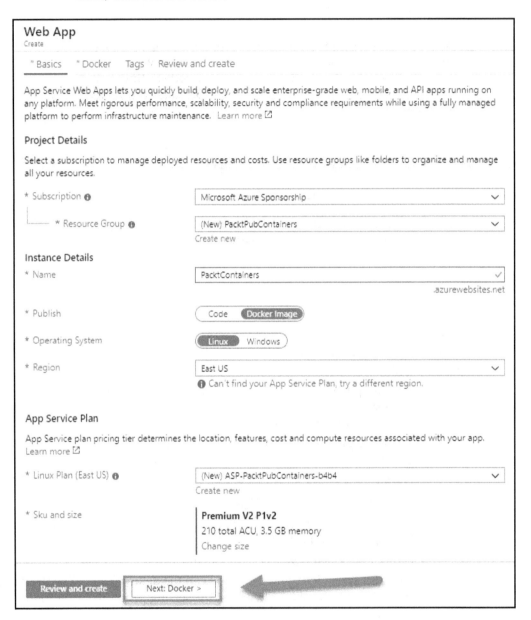

Basic settings

4. In the Docker settings blade, add the following values:
   - **Options: Single Container**
   - **Image Source: Quickstart**
   - **Sample: Static site**

   You can see them in the following screenshot:

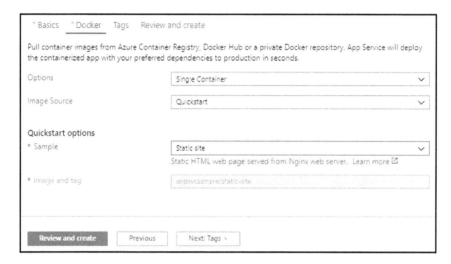

Docker settings

5. Click **Review and create** and then **Create.**
6. When the resource is created, go to **Resource**, select the **PacktContainers** Web App, and copy the URL to the clipboard:

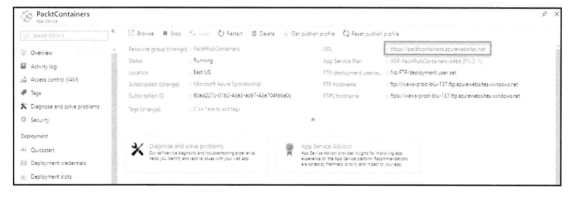

PacktContainers overview blade

7. Then, paste the URL into a browser. You will see that the static website is displayed. This website now runs in a container:

PacktContainers overview blade

We have now created a web app for containers instance with a static website in it. In the next section, we will take a look at how to design web apps to achieve optimum performance.

Designing web apps for high availability, scalability, and performance

Performance is an important issue to keep in mind when designing web apps. Web apps that are unresponsive or that perform badly will eventually lose all their visitors. They will simply hop onto another site. Azure provides multiple options so that you can make your web app highly available and scalable, which will result in better performance to keep your visitors on board.

> Besides the features that Azure offers to design for high availability, scaling, and performance, you can keep certain architecture patterns in mind when architecting your web app. You can refer to the following article from the Azure architecture center for these patterns: `https://docs.microsoft.com/en-us/azure/architecture/patterns/category/performance-scalability`.

High availability and performance

Azure provides several ways to make your web app perform better and to become highly available. You can use a **Content Delivery Network** (**CDN**) or a cache or you can copy your web app over to multiple regions, as explained in the upcoming sections.

Using a CDN

You can use a CDN to scale your websites globally. By using a CDN, your static content, such as HTML pages, style sheets, client-side scripts, images, documents, and files, are cached in different regions. This way, it takes less time to download the content because the static content is physically closer to the user, which increases the performance of your web app.

Azure CDN allows you to use custom domain names to access your content. This can be configured inside the Azure portal. You can refer to the following article to add a custom domain: `https://docs.microsoft.com/en-us/azure/cdn/cdn-map-content-to-custom-domain`. You can also enable HTTPS for your CDN: `https://docs.microsoft.com/en-us/azure/cdn/cdn-custom-ssl`.

Using Azure Cache for Redis

Azure Cache for Redis is based on the popular open source implementation, that is, Redis cache. It provides a secure cache with a memory key-value datastore that runs in an Azure data center and from which you can access your data. It can be used by different types of applications, including web apps, applications inside a virtual machine, or other cloud services. Caches can be shared by all applications that have the appropriate access key.

 Azure Cache for Redis will be discussed in more detail in `Chapter 10`, *Connecting to the Database*.

Azure Cache for Redis comes in the following tiers:

- **Basic**: This is a single-node cache, which is ideal for development, test environments, and non-critical workloads. This tier has no SLA.
- **Standard**: Provides a replicated cache. The data is automatically replicated between the two nodes. This tier offers an SLA.

- **Premium:** The premium tier has all of the standard features, and it provides bigger workloads, better performance, disaster recovery, and enhanced security. It also offers Redis persistence, which persists data that is stored inside the cache. Snapshots and backups can be created and restored in the case of failures. It also offers Redis Cluster, which automatically shares data across multiple Redis nodes, so that you can create workloads of bigger memory sizes (greater than 53 GB) and get better performance. It also offers support for Azure virtual networks, which gives you the ability to isolate your cache using subnets, access control policies, and more. You can provision Azure Cache for Redis from the Azure portal using an ARM template.

You can refer to the following article to download some sample ARM templates for deploying Azure Redis caches with different types of configuration settings: `https://docs.microsoft.com/en-us/azure/redis-cache/cache-redis-cache-arm-provision`.

Using Azure Traffic Manager

Another way of designing for availability and scalability is copying your web app over to multiple regions or data centers. Azure uses Azure Traffic Manager to spread the workload. Your web app can be reached by using a single URL, where Azure Traffic Manager will handle the load and locate the closest geographical region or the most suitable region for you at the DNS level. The following screenshot shows the Azure Traffic Manager profile page:

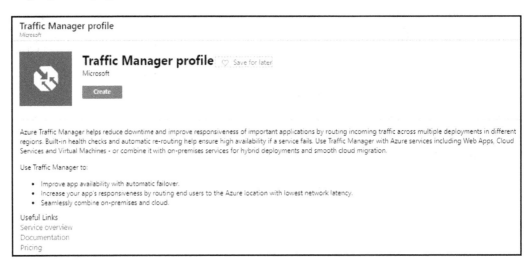

Azure Traffic Manager

When creating an Azure Traffic Manager profile from the Azure portal, you can choose between four different routing methods:

- **Performance**: Select this method when you have endpoints in different geographical locations and you want end users to use the closest endpoint in terms of the lowest network latency.
- **Weighted**: This method is most suitable when you want your application to be distributed evenly or according to certain weights that you define.
- **Priority**: Use this method when you want one endpoint to be the primary endpoint for all the traffic and provide backups in case the primary or the backup endpoints are unavailable.
- **Geographic**: This method is most suitable for scenarios where knowing a user's geographical region and routing them based on that is important. Localization of content can be a reason for choosing this method, for instance. Users are then directed to specific endpoints based on the geographical location where their DNS query comes from.

Scalability

Azure provides the ability to scale your web apps. One of the possibilities is to scale out, where you can scale your web apps globally. Scaling out means adding nodes to, or removing nodes from, a web app. This way, the load time is decreased when the web app is accessed from different locations. The other option is to scale up. Scaling up means adding resources to, or removing resources from, a web app, such as CPU or memory. When scaling up, you switch to another pricing tier inside your app service plan or pick a different app service plan.

 For more information about Azure App Service Plans, you can refer to the *App Service Plans* section of this chapter.

Let's take a look at the steps for scaling out and scaling up your web apps.

Scaling out

There are multiple ways to scale out your web app. You can scale out manually or automatically by using Azure autoscale. To use autoscale, use the following steps:

1. Under **Settings**, click on **Scale Out (App Service plan)**.

2. On the right-hand side of the screen, you can choose between manual scale and a custom autoscale. You can also increase or decrease the **Instance count**. The maximum instance count depends on the app service plan:

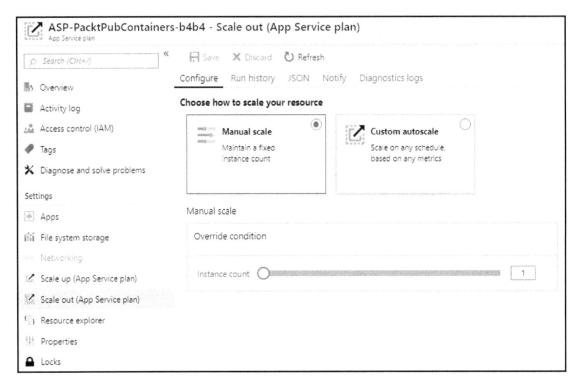

Azure app service plan scaling

3. Here, you can also turn on autoscale (only for the standard, premium, and isolated App Service Plans). You have to name the autoscale set and add at least one scaling condition. You can choose between scaling based on a metric or a specific instance count. When using a scale based on a metric, you need to add a scale rule:

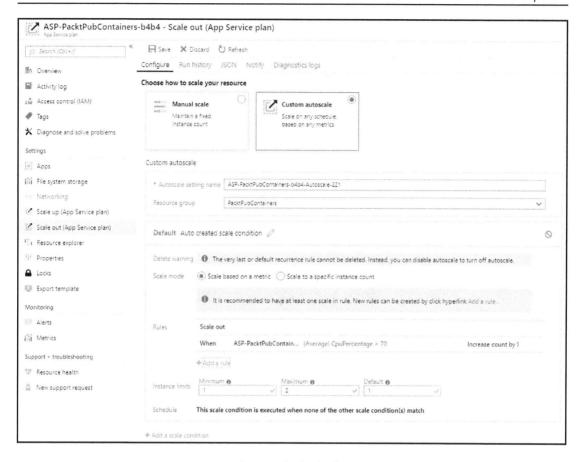

Azure app service plan autoscaling

Azure autoscale lets you configure a lot of settings that are beyond the scope of this book. You can refer to the following URL for more information on Azure autoscale and the available settings: `https://docs.microsoft.com/en-us/azure/monitoring-and-diagnostics/monitoring-understanding-autoscale-settings`.

Scaling up

You can choose a different pricing tier or app service plan to scale up your website. This can be done from the app service plan settings inside the Azure portal as well, such as when scaling out your web app:

1. Navigate to the Azure App Service settings in the Azure portal and, under **Settings**, click on **Scale Up (App Service plan)**.

2. You can then select a different app service plan, as shown in the following screenshot:

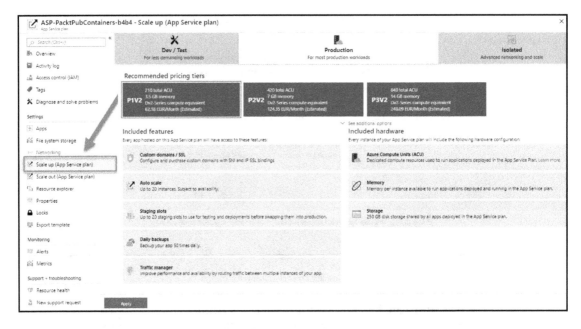

Azure app service plan scaling up

Next, we will be looking at designing and securing custom web APIs.

Designing and securing custom web APIs

Custom web APIs can be created using Visual Studio Code or Visual Studio 2019. For creating web APIs, the following programming languages are available:

- ASP.NET
- ASP.NET Core

- Angular
- React.js

Designing your web API

This demo will be created using .NET Core Framework 2.0 and Visual Studio 2019. Begin by opening up Visual Studio 2019 and following these steps:

1. Click on **File** | **New** | **Project** and, in the new **Project** window, select **ASP.NET Core Web Application**. Click **Create**. Call the project `PacktPubToDoAPI` and click **Create**.
2. A pop-up window will open up where you can select the **API** template. Select **ASP.NET Core 2.2** and click on **Create**:

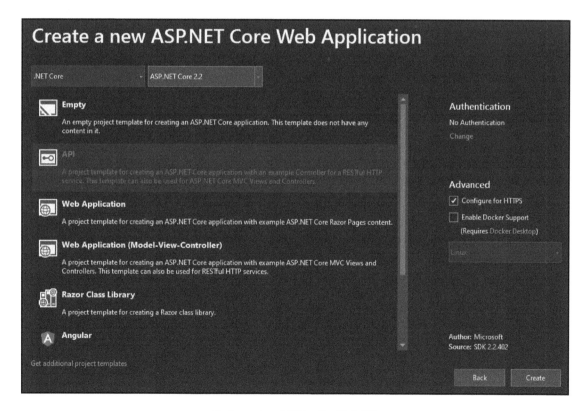

Creating a custom web API from Visual Studio 2019

3. Add a `Models` folder in the **Solution Explorer**. Right-click your project name and select **Add | New Folder**. Add a `TodoItem` class by right-clicking the `Models` folder and clicking **Add | Class**.

4. Update the `TodoItem` class with the following code:

```
namespace PacktPubToDoAPI.Models
{
    public class TodoItem
    {
        public long Id { get; set; }
        public string Name { get; set; }
        public bool IsComplete { get; set; }
    }
}
```

5. The next step is to add the database context class, which coordinates entity framework functionality. Add a `TodoContext` class inside the `Models` folder and replace it with the following code:

```
using Microsoft.EntityFrameworkCore;
using PacktPubToDoAPI.Models;

namespace PacktPubToDoAPI.Models
{
    public class TodoContext : DbContext
    {
        public TodoContext(DbContextOptions<TodoContext> options)
            : base(options)
        {
        }

        public DbSet<TodoItem> TodoItems { get; set; }

    }
}
```

6. The next step is to register the database context with the dependency injection container. You can do this by replacing the code in `StartUp.cs` with the following:

```
using Microsoft.AspNetCore.Builder;
using Microsoft.EntityFrameworkCore;
using Microsoft.Extensions.DependencyInjection;
using PacktPubToDoAPI.Models;

namespace PacktPubToDoAPI
{
```

```
public class Startup
{
    public void ConfigureServices(IServiceCollection services)
    {
        services.AddDbContext<TodoContext>(opt =>
opt.UseInMemoryDatabase("TodoList"));
        services.AddMvc();
    }

    public void Configure(IApplicationBuilder app)
    {
        app.UseMvc();
    }
}
}
```

7. In the **Solution Explorer**, right-click the `Controllers` folder and add a controller named `TodoController`. Replace the controller with the following code:

```
using System.Collections.Generic;
using Microsoft.AspNetCore.Mvc;
using PacktPubToDoAPI.Models;
using System.Linq;

namespace PacktPubToDoAPI.Controllers
{
    [Route("api/[controller]")]
    public class TodoController : Controller
    {
        private readonly TodoContext _context;

        public TodoController(TodoContext context)
        {
            _context = context;

            if (_context.TodoItems.Count() == 0)
            {
                _context.TodoItems.Add(new TodoItem { Name =
"Item1" });
                _context.SaveChanges();
            }
        }
    }
}
```

8. This code uses dependency injection in the constructor to inject `TodoContext` inside the controller. This context is used for the **Create**, **Read**, **Update**, and **Delete** (**CRUD**) methods on the data. The constructor adds an item to the in-memory database if it is empty.

9. The next step is to implement the CRUD methods. Add the following code to the constructor for the `Get` requests:

```
[HttpGet]
public IEnumerable<TodoItem> GetAll()
{
    return _context.TodoItems.ToList();
}

[HttpGet("{id}", Name = "GetTodo")]
public IActionResult GetById(long id)
{
    var item = _context.TodoItems.FirstOrDefault(t => t.Id == id);
    if (item == null)
    {
        return NotFound();
    }
    return new ObjectResult(item);
}
```

10. Add the following underneath for `Post` requests:

```
[HttpPost]
public IActionResult Create([FromBody] TodoItem item)
{
    if (item == null)
    {
        return BadRequest();
    }

    _context.TodoItems.Add(item);
    _context.SaveChanges();

    return CreatedAtRoute("GetTodo", new { id = item.Id }, item);
}
[HttpPut("{id}")]
public IActionResult Update(long id, [FromBody] TodoItem item)
{
    if (item == null || item.Id != id)
    {
        return BadRequest();
    }
```

```
        var todo = _context.TodoItems.FirstOrDefault(t => t.Id ==
id);
        if (todo == null)
        {
            return NotFound();
        }
        todo.IsComplete = item.IsComplete;
        todo.Name = item.Name;

        _context.TodoItems.Update(todo);
        _context.SaveChanges();
        return new NoContentResult();
    }
```

11. Finally, add the `Delete` request underneath the `Post` requests:

```
[HttpDelete("{id}")]
    public IActionResult Delete(long id)
    {
        var todo = _context.TodoItems.FirstOrDefault(t => t.Id ==
id);
        if (todo == null)
        {
            return NotFound();
        }

        _context.TodoItems.Remove(todo);
        _context.SaveChanges();
        return new NoContentResult();
    }
```

12. You can now deploy this web API to Azure using the **Publish** function in Visual Studio 2019. Right-click **Solution Explorer** and click on **Publish**. The publishing wizard will open. There, under **Publish**, click the **Start** button:

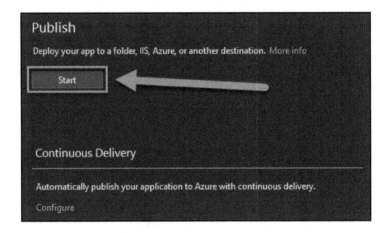

Publishing the app

13. On the next screen, select **App Service**, choose **Create new**, and click on **Publish**:

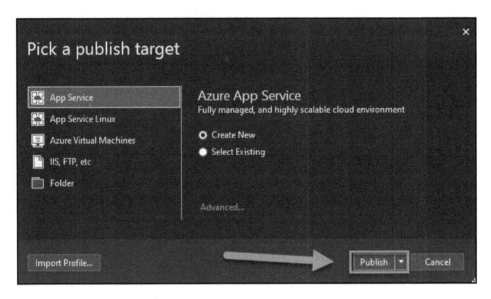

Publishing the web API to Azure from Visual Studio 2019

14. On the next screen, keep the default settings, but this time create a new resource group, call it `PacktAPIGroup`, and click **Create**:

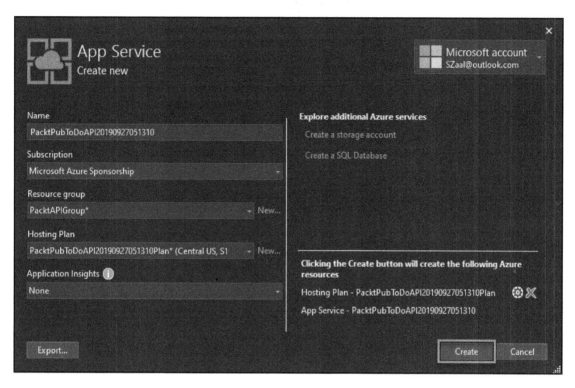

Selecting the Azure subscription from Visual Studio 2019

15. The web API is now deployed to Azure. After deployment, a browser will automatically be started and the API will be displayed.

This sample application is based on a sample from the Microsoft site. When you need any further instructions or information about the sample app, please refer to the following site: `https://docs.microsoft.com/en-us/aspnet/core/tutorials/first-web-api`.

Securing your web API

To secure your web API, you can use several options. You can use options provided by Azure or you can use your own authentication providers. A best practice, however, is to use the standard authentication options that are available for Azure app services.

You can use the following services in Azure to secure your web API:

- **Azure Active Directory (Azure AD)**: Azure AD offers traditional username and password identity management, roles management, and permissions management from the cloud. Also, it offers more enterprise solutions, such as multi-factor authentication, application monitoring, solution monitoring, and alerting.
- **Azure Active Directory Business to Consumer**: Azure Active Directory **Business to Consumer (B2C)** is a cloud identity-management solution for mobile and web applications. It offers out-of-the-box authentication providers that can be leveraged from your apps and custom APIs. Examples of out-of-the-box authentication providers are Facebook and Google.
- **Active Directory Federation Services**: You can use **Active Directory Federation Services (ADFS)** to secure your web API using the on-premises identities that are present in your organization. ADFS can be configured in conjunction with Azure AD in hybrid mode. You can then use the same APIs, such as the Microsoft Graph, to connect to your on-premises identities when you are using only Azure AD.
- **API Management**: You can use API Management to secure your web API as well. You can use advanced security policies, API keys, throttling for preventing DDOS attacks, and more, to add another layer of security on top of your web API.

Summary

In this chapter, we have covered designing web applications. We've covered Azure Web Apps and App Service Plans; how to design web apps for containers; how to design web apps for high availability, scalability, and performance; and how to design and secure custom web APIs.

In the next chapter, we will talk about scalability and performance.

Questions

Answer the following questions to test your knowledge of the information in this chapter. You can find the answers in the *Assessments* section at the end of this book:

1. Is Azure Cache for Redis a memory key-value datastore?
    1. Yes
    2. No

2. Which Azure service can you use to spread the workload over different regions?
    1. Azure Cache for Redis
    2. Azure Traffic Manager
    3. A CDN
    4. A web app

3. Can you use Azure B2C as an authentication provider for your applications?
    1. Yes
    2. No

Further reading

You can check out the following links for more information on the topics that were covered in this chapter:

- **Web apps documentation**: https://docs.microsoft.com/en-us/azure/app-service/
- **Azure App Service Plan overview**: https://docs.microsoft.com/en-us/azure/app-service/azure-web-sites-web-hosting-plans-in-depth-overview
- **Announcement of isolated app services**: https://azure.microsoft.com/nl-nl/blog/announcing-app-service-isolated-more-power-scale-and-ease-of-use/
- **App Service on Linux documentation**: https://docs.microsoft.com/en-us/azure/app-service/containers/
- **CDN documentation**: https://docs.microsoft.com/en-us/azure/cdn/
- **Redis cache documentation**: https://docs.microsoft.com/en-us/azure/redis-cache/
- **Integrating applications with Azure Active Directory**: https://docs.microsoft.com/en-us/azure/active-directory/develop/active-directory-integrating-applications
- **Active Directory B2C documentation**: https://docs.microsoft.com/en-us/azure/active-directory-b2c/

Scalability and Performance

In the previous chapters, we had a brief overview of Azure Web Apps, the different App Service plans that are available to us, and the characteristics of each of them.

This chapter introduces the objective of compute-intensive applications. We will cover how to design **High-Performance Computing** (**HPC**) and other compute-intensive applications using Azure services, how to determine when to use Azure Batch, and how to design stateless components to accommodate scale and containers within Azure Batch.

The following topics will be covered in this chapter:

- Working with HPC VMs
- Understanding Microsoft HPC pack
- Understanding Azure Batch

Technical requirements

To follow this chapter's samples, you need to have a valid Azure subscription (free 30-day trial or paid version).

The complete code files for this chapter can be found here: `https://github.com/` `PacktPublishing/Migrating-Apps-to-the-Cloud-with-Azure`.

Working with HPC virtual machines

Azure offers several VM series and sizes that are designed and optimized for compute-intensive tasks. They are also known as compute-intensive instances. At the time of writing this book, Azure offers the A8-A11, the N-series, and the H-series, which all support HPC workloads.

These series and sizes consist of hardware that is designed and optimized for compute-intensive, graphics-intensive, and network-intensive applications. They are best suited for modeling, simulations, and HPC cluster applications:

- The A-series offers RDMA networking, which provides ultra-low latency and high-bandwidth networking.
- The N-series is aimed at graphics-intensive and compute-intensive applications. They consist of different NVIDIA Tesla GPUs that are well-suited for deep learning applications, gaming applications, or virtualization.
- The H-series offers VMs that are specifically aimed at high performance. They offer fast Intel Xeon processors, SSD-based local storage, and DDR4 memory. These VMs are best suited for HPC workloads, such as batching, modeling, and simulations.

For more information on the hardware specifications of the N-series virtual machines, you can refer to the following article: `https://docs.microsoft.com/en-us/azure/virtual-machines/windows/sizes-gpu`.

For more information about high-performance VMs, you can refer to the following article: `https://docs.microsoft.com/en-us/azure/virtual-machines/windows/sizes-hpc?toc=%2Fazure%2Fvirtual-machines%2Fwindows%2Ftoc.json`.

Azure Marketplace offers several virtual machine images that are specifically designed for HPC, such as Azure data science VMs for Windows and Linux, D3View, and more. You can visit the marketplace by going to `https://azuremarketplace.microsoft.com/en-us/marketplace`.

Handling HPC workloads on-premises is often very difficult because you need to manage a large set of machines and scale them according to the calculation's needs. An on-premise infrastructure is often not ready for that.

With these types of VMs, you can use Azure to run compute-intensive Linux and Windows workloads, from parallel batch jobs to traditional HPC simulations. Here, you instantiate the resources and the scaling policy, and the Azure infrastructure will handle the rest.

Virtual machine scale sets

For high-performance computing with VMs, Azure offers a feature called **scale sets**. A scale set permits you to create a set of Azure VMs with the same characteristics and under load balancement. All of the VMs associated with a scale set have the same operating system and the same configuration. You can associate up to 1,000 VMs to a scale set (300 VMs if you upload your own images).

By using scale sets, you can automatically increase or decrease the number of instances accordingly to your workloads. If you need high performance to complete a particular task, you can scale up your VM set, perform the task, and then scale down the set, all of which is automatically managed by the platform. Obviously, for high performance, it's recommended that you use Azure VMs that support premium storage.

Regarding costs, scale sets have no extra costs. You pay for the computing resources you use, not for the management features offered by the scale set itself (load balancing, autoscaling, and so on).

A scale set can be created directly from the Azure portal by clicking on **Create a resource** and then searching for `scale set`. When found, select **Virtual machine scale set**:

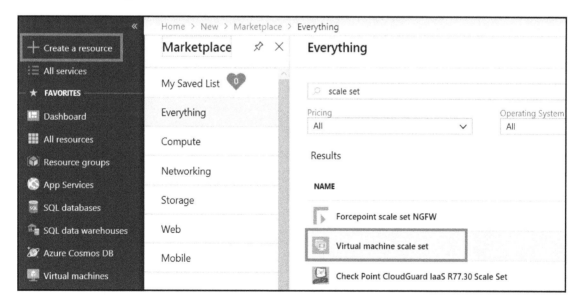

In the **Create virtual machine scale set** window, you need to do the following:

1. Provide a name for your scale set.
2. Select your **Subscription**, **Location**, and **Resource group.**
3. Select a **Username** and **Password** for the administrator account of the VMs in your scale set.
4. Select the number of instances (VMs) to create in your scale set and the instance size:

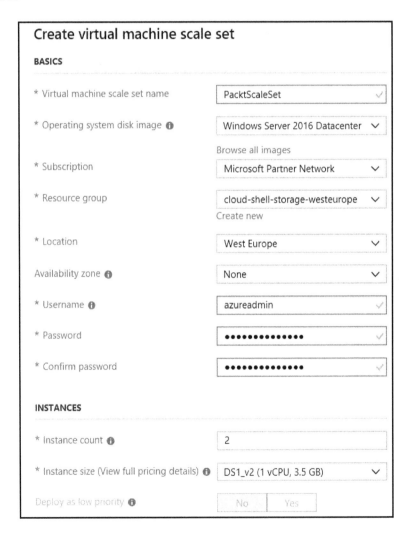

5. Choose a load balancing option. Select **Load balancer**.
6. Create a public IP address.
7. Select a domain label (this DNS label forms the base of the FQDN for the load balancer in front of the scale set).
8. Choose a virtual network.
9. Click **Create,** as shown in the following screenshot:

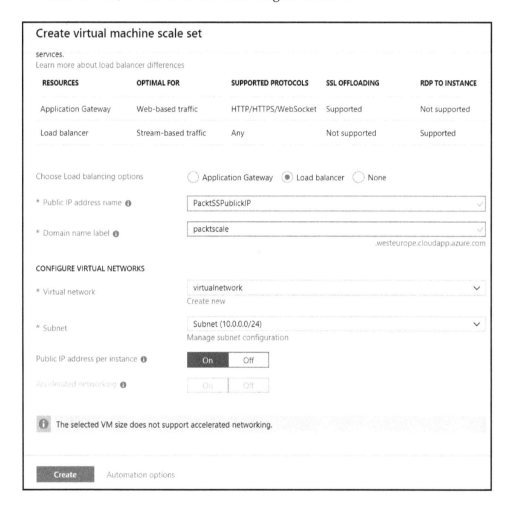

When the scale set has been created, in your Azure resources, you will have a load balancer, and this load balancer has NAT rules for traffic distribution (inbound NAT rules). You can connect to the VMs of this scale set by using these NAT rules (IP and port).

You can also create a scale set by using the Azure CLI and PowerShell with the following script:

```
$cred = Get-Credential

New-AzureRmVmss -ResourceGroupName "PacktResourceGroup" `
   -VMScaleSetName "PacktScaleSet" -Location "WestEurope" `
   -VirtualNetworkName "PacktVnet" -SubnetName "PacktSubnet" -
PublicIpAddressName "PacktPublicIPAddress" `
   -LoadBalancerName "PacktLoadBalancer" `
   -Credential $cred
```

Note that the `New-AzureRmVmss` command creates a scale set and uses a load balancer to distribute traffic between the VMs in the scale set.

You can list the VMs associated with a scale set by using the following command:

```
Get-AzureRmVmssVM -ResourceGroupName "PacktResourceGroup" -VMScaleSetName
"PacktScaleSet"
```

Every VM in the scale set has its own instance ID. You can retrieve specific information for a particular VM in the scale set by using its instance ID as a parameter in the following command:

```
Get-AzureRmVmssVM -ResourceGroupName "PacktResourceGroup" -VMScaleSetName
"PacktScaleSet" -InstanceId "1"
```

To increase or decrease the capacity of the scale set (number of VM instances running), you can use the following script:

```
# Retrieves the current scale set
$vmss = Get-AzureRmVmss -ResourceGroupName "PacktResourceGroup" -
VMScaleSetName "PacktScaleSet"

# Increase the capacity of the scale set to 5 VM instances
$vmss.sku.capacity = 5
Update-AzureRmVmss -ResourceGroupName "PacktResourceGroup" -Name
"PacktScaleSet" -VirtualMachineScaleSet $vmss
```

For other commands to automate tasks on your scale set, I recommend that you check out the following link: https://docs.microsoft.com/en-us/azure/virtual-machine-scale-sets/tutorial-create-and-manage-powershell.

You can monitor your scale sets by using **Azure Monitor for VMs**. It will permit you to monitor different performance counters about your Azure VMs in your scale set and it provides a set of predefined metrics that can be useful for handling performance and scalability.

More information about Azure Monitor for VMs can be found at the following link: `https://docs.microsoft.com/en-us/azure/azure-monitor/insights/vminsights-overview`.

Understanding Microsoft HPC Pack

Microsoft provides an HPC Pack for Windows Server 2012 and 2016 and Linux machines. This is a free offering and you can use this to create HPC clusters on your on-premises servers and Azure VMs.

You can install HPC Pack on a Windows or Linux server. These machines will automatically become the head nodes of the cluster. You can then add additional nodes to the cluster and run a job on it. This job will be distributed across all of the available nodes automatically.

It offers the following additional features:

- **Hybrid cluster**: You can set up hybrid clusters using on-premises servers and Azure VMs.
- **HPC Cluster Manager**: This is a tool for managing, deploying, and configuring HPC clusters.
- **PowerShell**: You can use HPC PowerShell to manage, configure, deploy, add, and execute jobs on the cluster.

You can use HPC Pack for designing effective cloud-native HPC solutions and hybrid HPC solutions. Both of these will be explained in the following sections.

Cloud-native HPC solutions

A cloud-native HPC solution uses HPC VMs and can scale up to thousands of instances and compute cores. It uses a head node, several compute nodes, and storage. The following Azure resources can be used to create a cloud-native HPC architecture:

- **HPC head node**: The head node runs in Azure on a Windows or Linux server VM. When you install the Azure HPC pack on this machine, it will become the head node automatically.
- **HPC compute nodes**: The HPC compute nodes are created using A8 and A9 instances. These instances provide RDMA networking, which can be used to achieve high bandwidth and microsecond latencies between the nodes.

- **Virtual Machine Scale Set** (**VMSS**): You can place the compute nodes in a **Virtual Machine Scale Set** (**VMSS**) for redundancy and availability. VMs that use RDMA for communicating with each other are placed in the same availability set.
- **Virtual network**: All of the Azure resources, such as the head node, compute nodes, and storage layer, are added to an Azure virtual network.
- **Storage**: The disks that are used for all of the different nodes are stored inside Azure Blob Storage.
- **ARM templates**: You can use ARM templates to deploy the applications to the nodes:

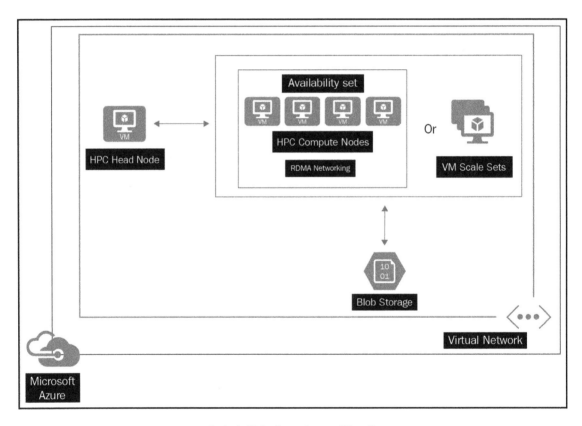

Cloud-native HPC architecture (courtesy of Microsoft)

In the next section, we'll look at an overview of the hybrid HPC architecture.

Hybrid HPC architecture

The hybrid HPC architecture uses some of the building blocks that are used for a cloud-native HPC architecture, which are complemented by the on-premises part. The following Azure resources will be used in this scenario:

- **HPC head node**: The head node runs on your on-premises environment. It can be installed on a VM in Azure as well or on a Windows or Linux server VM, and just like the cloud-native architecture, you can install Azure HPC Pack on it and it will become the head node automatically.
- **HPC compute nodes**: The HPC compute nodes in your on-premises environment can be Linux or Windows servers with sufficient compute power. The VMs in Azure are created using A8 and A9 instances and provide RDMA networking.
- **Virtual machine scale sets**: You can place the compute nodes in Azure inside a VMSS for redundancy and availability. VMs that use RDMA for communicating with each other are placed in the same availability set.
- **Virtual network**: The Azure resources, such as the compute nodes and storage layer, are added to an Azure virtual network.
- **ExpressRoute**: ExpressRoute offers a secure and reliable connection between your on-premises environment and Azure. These connections don't go over the public internet but use a private connection, which is usually set up between an ExpressRoute broker and Azure.
- **VPN Gateway**: A VPN gateway offers an endpoint between Azure and your on-premises network and enables secure connectivity and communication between the different nodes in the HPC cluster. This connection uses the public internet.

- **Storage**: The disks that are used for the nodes that are hosted in Azure are stored inside Azure **Blob Storage**:

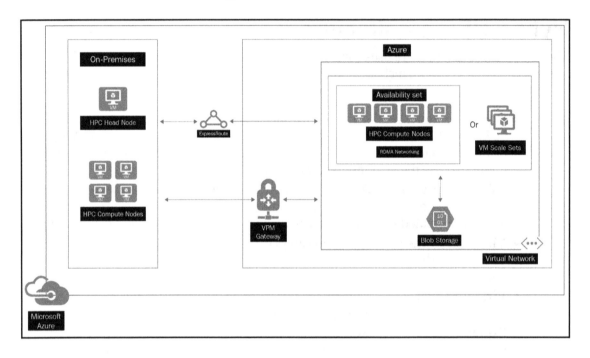

Hybrid HPC architecture (courtesy of Microsoft)

In the next section, we'll learn how to design and deploy an HPC cluster on-premises.

Deploying an HPC cluster on-premises

To design and deploy an HPC cluster on-premises, follow these steps:

1. Choose your cluster topology for the cluster. The HPC pack supports five different topologies:
   - **Topology 1**: Compute nodes isolated on a private network
   - **Topology 2**: All nodes on enterprise and private networks
   - **Topology 3**: Compute nodes isolated on private and application networks
   - **Topology 4**: All nodes on enterprise, private, and application networks
   - **Topology 5**: All nodes on an enterprise network

2. Deploy one or more head nodes (you need more than one if you want high availability) for your cluster. You need to install Windows Server 2016 (or 2012R2) on your head node and then HPC Pack. This head node computer has to be under an Active Directory domain and, for HPC Pack's installation, you need an administrator account.

3. Configure the cluster. The deployment to-do list of HPC Cluster Manager will guide you on how to set up the cluster. You need to configure the HPC cluster network by following the **Network Configuration Wizard** in HPC Cluster Manager, define the naming convention for the new nodes that are added to the cluster, and (optionally) add users to your cluster.

4. After the cluster configuration, you can add nodes to the cluster (by using the manual option or the bare metal option). For the manual option, you need to install HPC Pack on your computer and then select **Join an existing HPC cluster by creating a new compute node.**

Understanding Azure Batch

Azure Batch is a service that helps developers scale their workloads over VMs (Windows or Linux) or containers, without the need to manage the infrastructure. With Azure Batch, you can run large-scale, parallel, and HPC applications efficiently in the cloud. Batch computing is most commonly used for applications that regularly process, transform, or analyze large volumes of data. Typically, HPC applications that run on Azure Batch include deep learning applications, image rendering applications, media encoding applications, and Monte Carlo simulations. Azure Media Services uses Azure Batch internally for media encoding as well.

The Azure Batch service uses Azure compute as its infrastructure, which means that you can use both Windows or Linux VMs to host your applications or workloads. Azure uses the A8/A9 series VMs with RDMA networking internally for the nodes and is fully responsible for creating and managing those VMs. Azure adds these nodes to a pool inside the Azure Batch account.

Inside the Azure Batch account, a job can be created that will run the workload on the pool. Your workload is then added to the Batch queue and split up into several tasks so that they can run in parallel. Azure Batch scales those tasks automatically, and they can be scheduled as well. Your workloads, which are called tasks, are added to the Batch queue and spread over the managed pool of VMs and can be scaled automatically. Most of these tasks can run completely independently, but for some HPC workloads, it might be necessary for the tasks to communicate with each other. In that case, Azure Batch uses persistent storage to store output data for retrieval by other tasks. By default, Azure Blob Storage is used for this, but you can use other storage types as well. The tasks communicate with each other using a runtime called **Message Passing Interface** (**MPI**), and the outcome of all of these different tasks can be consolidated into a single result:

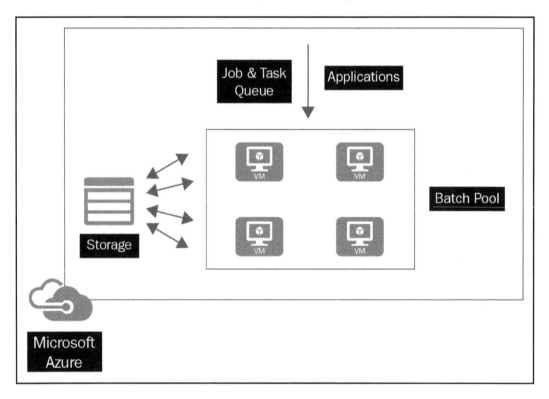

Azure Batch architecture

To automate the creation of Azure Batch processes, Azure Batch uses a JSON template (not to be confused with an ARM template; this one is different). In this template, you can automate the creation of the Batch pool, including the VM sizes, the operating system, and the number of nodes (the number of VMs). You can use the Azure CLI for automation as well.

A Batch pool consists of VMs that can be created using images from the Azure Marketplace, cloud services (a standard guest image from Azure), custom images (a custom VHD from a storage account), and specific graphic and rendering images.

 You can use low priority VMs for Azure Batch. This reduces the cost of VMs significantly. This discount is only available for Azure Batch, that is, for all of the VM sizes Azure Batch supports, and in all regions. For more information on these prices, you can refer to the following web page: https://azure.microsoft.com/en-us/pricing/details/batch/.

Creating an Azure Batch service

In this example, we are going to create a Batch pool by using the Azure portal. This will give you some extra information about the different settings for Azure Batch, such as how to start your applications on a pool of VMs.

To create an Azure Batch pool, you can refer to the following steps:

1. The first step is to create an Azure Batch account in the Azure portal. You can refer to the following article to create one: `https://docs.microsoft.com/en-us/azure/batch/batch-account-create-portal`. I've created an Azure Batch account called `packtpub` in a **Resource group** called `PacktBatchGroup`:

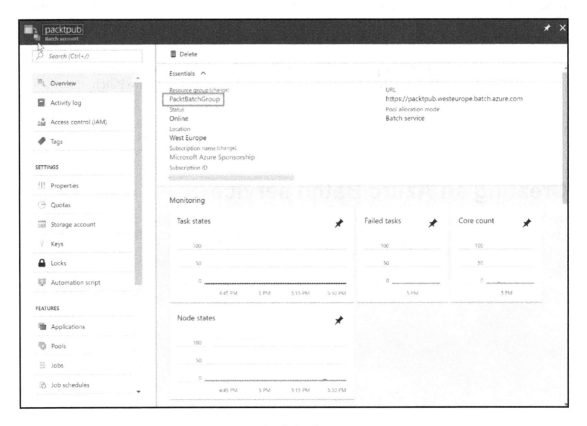

Azure Batch service

2. Next, click on **Pools** in the left-hand side menu and click on **Add**. Add the following values:
   - **Pool ID**: `packtpool1`
   - **Display name**: `PactPool`
   - **Image Type**: **Cloud Services (Windows Only)**
   - **NODE SIZE**: **Standard A1**
   - **SCALE MODE**: **Auto Scale**

- **Formula**: $TargetDedicated=0 (you can refer to the following article about **Automatic Scaling Formulas** for more information: https://docs.microsoft.com/en-us/azure/batch/batch-automatic-scaling)

- **Start Task**: **Disabled** (here, you can provide a command for the startup of executables or other workloads)

3. Leave the other default values for the rest of the settings and click on **OK**:

Azure Batch pool settings

For the virtual network settings, you can run your Batch pool inside a VNet. This way, the VMs can communicate with other VMs that are not part of the Batch pool, such as file servers or license servers.

4. After creating the Batch pool, you can select **Application packages** from the left-hand side menu to upload your executables, libraries, or other metadata that is associated with your application. To upload packages, you have to create or link an Azure storage account. Application packages are uploaded as ZIP files that consist of all of the necessary files. These files are installed on the VMs automatically by Azure:

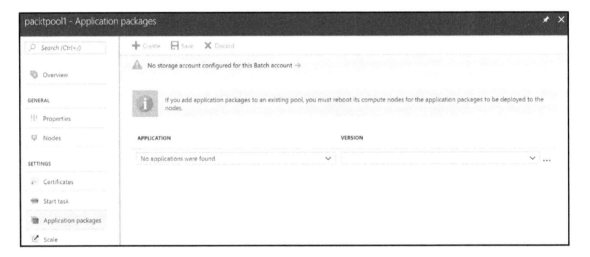

Azure Batch application packages

5. You can also provide the **Start task** properties from the left-hand side menu.

 This is just one way of creating a Batch service. There are more methods that you can use, such as using Visual Studio, calling the Batch API directly, or using the CLI or PowerShell.

Stateless components

Azure Batch uses parallel actions to process workloads. To fully leverage this capability, applications need to be split up into single and stateless tasks, called multi-instance tasks. By default, a Batch task is executed on a single compute node. By enabling multi-instance tasks, the task is executed on multiple compute nodes.

These multi-instance tasks are submitted to the Batch job and then distributed over the available nodes inside the Batch pool. Azure Batch automatically creates one primary task and several subtasks based on these multi-instance settings. The tasks that run in parallel use Azure Storage to save and retrieve the data that's used by the different tasks:

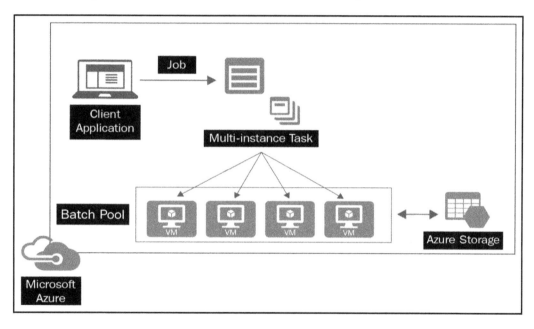

Azure Batch jobs and tasks

These multi-instance tasks can be created in code using the Batch .NET SDK or the Python SDK.

For more information on creating an Azure Batch solution using the Batch .NET SDK, you can refer to the following tutorial: `https://docs.microsoft.com/en-us/azure/batch/tutorial-parallel-dotnet`.

Containers on Azure Batch

Azure Batch also supports the deployment of containers. You can use Docker containers or Singularity. Singularity is similar to Docker, but it is primarily designed to run on shared HPC clusters in on-premises environments and for super-computing installations.

Singularity does not require root privileges to execute containers. It allows applications to leverage GPUs and specialized networking within the privileged scope of the executing user. This makes Singularity compatible with permissions-constrained HPC environments. Where Docker was originally designed to run Linux containers, Singularity can import Docker images and run Windows containers as well (it works completely independently of Docker).

Singularity can be run from Azure Cloud Shell without any installation and can be installed from the Azure Batch Shipyard release. This is an open system for enabling simple, configuration-based container execution on Azure Batch. No knowledge of the Azure Batch .NET SDK is needed; only configuration files are used here.

For more information about containers on Batch Shipyard, you can refer to the following GitHub page: `https://github.com/Azure/batch-shipyard`.

Executing a Batch job from code

Azure Batch jobs can be executed via code by using the Azure CLI (PowerShell scripts) or by using the Azure Batch .NET API.

In the following example, we'll learn how to use the Azure Batch .NET API to run an Azure Batch job that executes a custom application (.NET console application) in several cores simultaneously. We are assuming that you have previously done (as described in this book) the following:

- Created a Batch service account
- Created a storage account
- Copied a custom console application called MyApp (via the .exe and .config files) in to your Azure storage container (*step 4* of the *Creating an Azure Batch Service* section)

To execute a Batch job, follow these steps:

1. Open Visual Studio and create a console application project (this is called BatchServiceApp here):

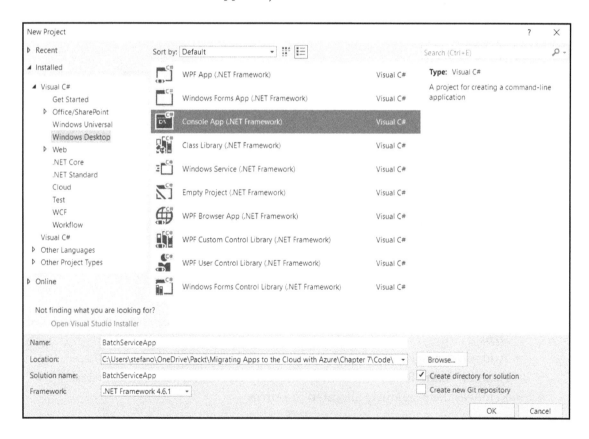

2. Then, we need to add the references to the `Azure.Batch` NuGet package:

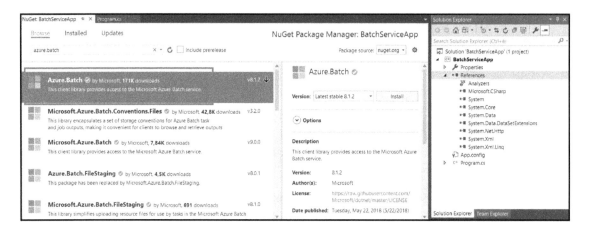

3. Then, we need to add a reference to the `WindowsAzure.Storage` NuGet package:

In our console application, we need to create a series of long-running tasks in the Azure Batch service to execute our MyApp application. For every instance, the code does the following:

- Starts an instance of an Azure Batch client
- Adds a pool to the Azure Batch service (with dedicated resources, cores, and VM size)
- Adds an Azure Batch job in the pool
- Adds an Azure Batch task to the previously created job and starts the task
- Removes the previously allocated resources

The complete code (for reference) is as follows. In `Main` of the program, we create the batch instances:

```
using Microsoft.Azure.Batch;
using Microsoft.Azure.Batch.Auth;
using Microsoft.Azure.Batch.Common;
using System;
using System.Collections.Generic;
using System.Linq;
using System.Text;
using System.Threading.Tasks;

namespace BatchServiceApp
{
 class Program
 {
   static void Main(string[] args)
   {
     //Creating Batch service to process data on 3 codes in parallel
     for (int i = 0; i < 3; i++)
     {
       var processTask = new Task(() => RunProcess("Code"
+i),TaskCreationOptions.LongRunning);
       processTask.Start();
     }
   Console.ReadLine();
   }

static void RunProcess(string code)
 {
   BatchSharedKeyCredentials cred = new
BatchSharedKeyCredentials("https://<Account Name>.
<Region>.batch.azure.com", "<AccountName", "<Account Key>");
   BatchClient client = BatchClient.Open(cred);

   AddApplicationPool(client, code);
   AddCloudJob(client, code)
   //Remove if any tasks already exists
   DeleteCloudTask(client, code);
   AddCloudTask(client, code);
   DeleteCloudJob(client, code);
   DeleteApplicationPool(client, code);
 }
```

In the `RunProcess` function, we retrieve the Azure Batch credentials and instantiate the Batch client. Then, we create the application pool and the cloud job:

```
static void AddApplicationPool(BatchClient client, string code)
  {
    var poolId = "applicationpool" + code;
    IPagedEnumerable<CloudPool> pools = client.PoolOperations.ListPools();
    foreach (CloudPool pool in pools)
    {
      if (pool.Id.Equals(poolId))
      {
        Console.WriteLine("Pool already available for id : " + pool.Id);
        return;
      }
    }

    CloudPool newPool = client.PoolOperations.CreatePool(
      poolId: poolId,
      targetDedicatedComputeNodes: 3, // 3 compute nodes
      virtualMachineSize: "small", // single-core, 1.75 GB memory, 225 GB
disk
      cloudServiceConfiguration: new CloudServiceConfiguration(osFamily:
"3"));
    newPool.Commit();
    Console.WriteLine("Created the pool for Code : " + code);
  }

static CloudJob AddCloudJob(BatchClient client, string code)
{
 var poolId = "applicationpool" + code;
 var jobId = "cloudjob" + code;
 IPagedEnumerable<CloudJob> jobs = client.JobOperations.ListJobs();
 foreach (CloudJob job in jobs)
 {
   if (job.Id.Equals(jobId))
   {
     Console.WriteLine("Job already available for id : " + job.Id);
     return job;
   }
 }

 CloudJob newJob = client.JobOperations.CreateJob();
 newJob.Id = jobId;
 newJob.PoolInformation = new PoolInformation() { PoolId = poolId };
 newJob.Commit();
 Console.WriteLine("Created the Cloud job for Code : " + code);
 return newJob;
}
```

Then, we create the cloud task to start our application:

```
static void AddCloudTask(BatchClient client, string code)
{
  var poolId = "applicationpool" + code;
  var jobId = "cloudjob" + code;
  CloudJob job = client.JobOperations.GetJob(jobId);
  ResourceFile programFile = new
ResourceFile("http:////MyApp.exe","MyApp.exe");
  ResourceFile appConfigurationData = new
ResourceFile("http:////MyApp.exe.config",
    "MyApp.exe.config");
  string taskName = "applicationtask" + code;

 CloudTask task = new CloudTask(taskName, "MyApp.exe " + code);
 List<ResourceFile> taskFiles = new List<ResourceFile>();
 taskFiles.Add(appConfigurationData);
 taskFiles.Add(programFile);
 task.ResourceFiles = taskFiles;
 job.AddTask(task);
 job.Commit();
 job.Refresh();

 client.Utilities.CreateTaskStateMonitor().WaitAll(job.ListTasks(),TaskState
 .Completed, new TimeSpan(0, 30, 0));
 Console.WriteLine("Process completed successfully for code :" + code);
 foreach (CloudTask taskInProgress in job.ListTasks())
 {
   Console.WriteLine("Process " + taskInProgress.Id + " Output:\n" +
 taskInProgress.GetNodeFile(Constants.StandardOutFileName).ReadAsString());
 }
}
```

At the end of the execution of the cloud task, all of these resources are deleted:

```
static void DeleteCloudTask(BatchClient client, string code)
 {
 var jobId = "cloudjob" + code;
 IPagedEnumerable<CloudJob> jobs = client.JobOperations.ListJobs();
 foreach (CloudJob checkjob in jobs)
 {
   if (checkjob.Id.Equals(jobId))
   {
     CloudJob job = client.JobOperations.GetJob(jobId);
     foreach (CloudTask task in job.ListTasks())
     {
       task.Delete();
     }
```

```
    }
  }
  Console.WriteLine("Cloud tasks deleted for code : " + code);
}

static void DeleteCloudJob(BatchClient client, string code)
{
var jobId = "cloudjob" + code;
client.JobOperations.DeleteJob(jobId);
Console.WriteLine("Cloud Job deleted for code : " + code);
}

static void DeleteApplicationPool(BatchClient client, string code)
{
  var poolId = "applicationpool" + code;
  client.PoolOperations.DeletePool(poolId);
  Console.WriteLine("Application pool was deleted for code : " + code);
}
}
}
```

You have successfully executed your Batch job.

Summary

In this chapter, we covered compute-intensive applications. We covered how to design HPC and other compute-intensive applications using Azure services, how to determine when to use Azure Batch, and how to design stateless components to accommodate scale and containers on Azure Batch.

In the next chapter, we will cover the web application objective.

Questions

Answer the following questions to test your knowledge of the information in this chapter. You can find the answers in the *Assessments* section at the end of this book:

1. You want to create HPC clusters in your on-premises environment. Should you use Azure Batch?
    1. Yes
    2. No

2. When creating HPC VMs, should we use the H-series?
   1. Yes
   2. No

3. To automate the creation of Azure Batch processes, should we use ARM templates?
   1. Yes
   2. No

Further reading

Check out the following links for more information on the topics that were covered in this chapter:

- **HPC VM sizes**: https://docs.microsoft.com/en-us/azure/virtual-machines/windows/sizes-hpc?toc=%2Fazure%2Fvirtual-machines%2Fwindows%2Ftoc.json
- **Options with HPC Pack to create and manage a cluster for Windows HPC workloads in Azure**: https://docs.microsoft.com/en-us/azure/virtual-machines/windows/hpcpack-cluster-options
- **Batch documentation**: https://docs.microsoft.com/en-us/azure/batch/
- **HPC, Batch, and Big Compute solutions using Azure VMs**: https://docs.microsoft.com/en-us/azure/virtual-machines/linux/high-performance-computing
- **Deploying applications to compute nodes with Batch application packages**: https://docs.microsoft.com/en-us/azure/batch/batch-application-packages
- **Solution architecture: On-premises HPC implementation bursting to Azure**: https://azure.microsoft.com/en-us/solutions/architecture/hpc-on-prem-burst/
- **Solution architecture: HPC clusters deployed in the cloud**: https://azure.microsoft.com/en-us/solutions/architecture/hpc-cluster/
- **Solution architecture: Big compute solutions as a service**: https://azure.microsoft.com/en-us/solutions/architecture/hpc-big-compute-saas/

8
Building Microservices with Service Fabric

In this chapter, we will be covering Azure Service Fabric. We will start by giving an overview of all of the capabilities of Azure Service Fabric. Then, we will dive into creating a microservice application from scratch using Azure Service Fabric. We will create an application in both .NET and Java.

The following topics will be covered in this chapter:

- Overview of Azure Service Fabric
- Creating an Azure Service Fabric cluster
- Creating a Service Fabric .NET application
- Creating a Service Fabric Java application

Technical requirements

The code files for this chapter can be found here:

`https://github.com/PacktPublishing/Migrating-Apps-to-the-Cloud-with-Azure/tree/master/Chapter8`

This chapter uses the following tools for its examples:

- Service Fabric runtime, SDK, and various tools: `https://docs.microsoft.com/en-us/azure/service-fabric/service-fabric-get-started`
- Visual Studio 2019: `https://visualstudio.microsoft.com/vs/`
- Eclipse 2019: `https://www.eclipse.org/downloads/download.php?file=/technology/epp/downloads/release/2019-09/R/eclipse-java-2019-09-R-linux-gtk-x86_64.tar.gz`

Understanding Azure Service Fabric

Azure Service Fabric is an orchestration platform from Microsoft that can be used to deploy, manage, and package microservices and containers. It is similar to Docker Cloud and Kubernetes, but Service Fabric is a service that was created by Microsoft.

Another difference between these three is that Service Fabric is the only one that is fully integrated with other services of the Azure platform. Examples of this tight integration with the Azure platform include the fact that Azure Service Fabric can use API Management, Event Hub, and IoT Hub out of the box as stateless gateways. When using other providers, stateless gateways are mostly built manually. You can import Docker images into Azure Fabric as well, but the orchestration of the Docker containers is then fully handled by Azure Service Fabric.

Azure Service Fabric offers a lightweight runtime for building distributed, scalable, stateless, and stateful microservices that can run inside containers. Using Service Fabric, you can deploy the microservices and containers across a cluster of machines. On top of that, it offers comprehensive application management capabilities to deploy, provision, upgrade, patch, delete, and monitor applications and services on containers. Service Fabric is tailored to create full, cloud-native applications that can start small and eventually scale up to thousands of machines over time.

Besides the tight integration in Azure, Service Fabric can be deployed on Windows Server machines inside your own data center as well on Azure. Service Fabric can also be deployed on Windows, Linux, and Azure Stack. Microsoft also released Service Fabric Mesh, a full PaaS solution that allows you to run applications on top of Service Fabric without having to maintain the cluster beneath it.

There are a number of Azure PaaS solutions or resources that run on Service Fabric, such as Azure SQL Database, Cosmos DB, Intune, IoT Hub, Event Hubs, Skype, Cortana, Power BI, and Microsoft Dynamics. The following diagram gives an overview of Azure Service Fabric:

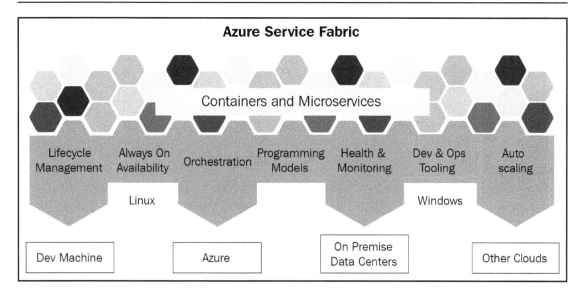

Azure Service Fabric overview

Applications use the Service Fabric programming models to create and manage services. There are Service Fabric APIs that can be used in custom applications to take full advantage of the platform's features and application frameworks. You can deploy guest executables, which don't use the Service Fabric APIs, but can use the capabilities of the underlying platform. Guest executables are treated as stateless services and are deployed across different nodes inside a cluster. They can benefit from affinity, anti-affinity, failover, application life cycle management, and discovery capabilities, for instance.

Stateless and stateful microservices

Azure Service Fabric offers the ability to build applications that consist of microservices or containers. In Azure Service Fabric, you can create stateless and stateful services, which are explained in more detail in the following sections.

Stateless services

Stateless services are currently the norm in cloud applications. A service is considered stateless when it doesn't contain data that needs to be stored reliably or has to be made highly available. When an instance of a stateless services shuts down, the state and all internal data are released and lost. So, any state that is present is entirely disposable and doesn't require synchronization, replication, persistence, or high availability.

A common example of how stateless services are used in Azure Service Fabric is a frontend that exposes a public-facing API for a web application. The stateless frontend service will then pass on the request to the stateful services, which will then complete the request. In this example, the client call is redirected to a known port (for example, 80), on which the stateless service is listening. The stateless service then determines whether the call is from a trusted party and to which service it needs to be redirected. Then, the stateless service forwards the call to the correct partition of the stateful service and waits for a response. When a response is received, it replies to the original client. So, in this example, the stateless service acts as a gateway and only redirects the request without persisting any state.

Stateful services

Unlike Stateless services, stateful services *do* have to store some portion of the state, which must be kept consistent and present for the service to function correctly.

An example of a stateful service is a service that constantly needs to calculate a rolling average based on certain values it receives. To achieve this, it must have the current set of incoming requests that it needs to process, as well as the current average. This average needs to be stored in an external store by each service, which retrieves and processes the incoming request. This data can be stored inside Azure Tables Storage or another type of database, such as Azure SQL Database, Azure Cosmos DB, or Azure Database for MySQL.

When using Azure Service Fabric, services aren't required to store their state externally. Service Fabric takes care of storage for both the service code and the service state.

This makes Service Fabric an extremely fast solution for certain application scenarios. These application scenarios are explained in more detail in the following section.

Azure Service Fabric application scenarios

There are a couple of application scenarios where Azure Service Fabric applications are very useful:

- **Scalable services**: To allow the state of the services to be scaled out across a cluster, you can partition the services. The individual services are then created and removed on the fly. This allows services to be scaled from a few instances on a couple of nodes up to thousands of instances on many nodes easily. Then, they can be scaled in easily as well.

- **High available services:** Service Fabric offers fast failover by creating multiple secondary service replicas. If a node or a service goes down due to hardware or other failures, one of the secondary replicas is promoted as the primary replica with minimal loss of service.

- **Session-based interactive applications**: Service Fabric is a great solution for applications requiring low latency reads and writes, such as online gaming or instant messaging applications. With Service Fabric, you don't have to create a separate store or cache, which increases network latency.

- **Data analytics and workflows**: The fast reads and writes are very suitable for applications that process events or streams of data. Service Fabric also enables applications that use processing pipelines, where results must be reliable and passed on to the next stage without any loss. Examples of these types of applications are transactional and financial applications.

- **Data gathering, processing, and IoT**: Service Fabric has low latency while using stateful services, which makes it an ideal solution for processing data on millions of devices where the data for the devices and the computation are co-located.

Programming models

Service Fabric supports two different programming models that can be used to build scalable and stateful services in Visual Studio 2017. They are called Reliable Services and Reliable Actor programming models. By leveraging these models inside your code, Azure can guarantee that the services are consistent, scalable, reliable, and available inside Azure Service Fabric. Service Fabric integrates with ASP.NET Core as well, so you can write both stateless and stateful ASP.NET Core applications that take advantage of these reliable collections and the orchestration capabilities of Service Fabric.

The basic concepts regarding Reliable Services and Reliable Actor programming models are explained in the following sections.

The Reliable Services programming model

An Azure Service Fabric application contains one or more services that run your code. By using the Reliable Service model, you can create both stateless and stateful services. The Reliable Services programming model offers the following capabilities for your services:

- It gives you access to all of the Service Fabric programming APIs directly. Your services can do the following:
    - Query the system
    - Report the health of all of the entities inside a cluster
    - Receive notifications about configuration and code changes
    - Find and communicate with other services
    - Use Reliable Collections
    - Give access to many other capabilities, in several programming languages
- There's a pluggable communication model, by means of which you can use HTTP with Web API, WebSockets, custom TCP protocols, and more. You can use out-of-the-box communication options or provide your own.
- For stateful services, you can store your state consistently and reliably by using **Reliable Collections**. These collections are similar to C# collections. Reliable Collections store your state next to your compute, with the same high availability and reliability that is offered by other highly available external stores. This model improves latency since compute and state are co-located.

Reliable Services in Service Fabric are different from services you may have written before. Service Fabric provides the following for Reliable Services:

- **Reliability**: In the case of machine failures or network issues, or in cases where the service itself encounters errors or crashes and fails, your service still stays up. For stateful services, the state is preserved, even in the case of network or other failures.
- **Availability**: The service is reachable and responsive. Service Fabric handles this part and maintains the desired number of running copies.
- **Scalability**: The services are decoupled from the hardware and they can scale out or scale in when necessary, adding or removing hardware or other resources. Services are partitioned to ensure that they can scale and handle partial failures and that they can be created and deleted dynamically via code.
- **Consistency**: Any information stored in the service is consistent—even across multiple reliable collections within a service. Changes across collections within a service can be made in a transactionally atomic manner.

For more information regarding the available programming models for Azure Service Fabric, you can refer to the following Microsoft documentation: `https://docs.microsoft.com/en-us/azure/service-fabric/service-fabric-reliable-services-introduction`.

The Reliable Actor programming model

Reliable Actors is a Service Fabric application framework based on the **Virtual Actor** pattern. This actor-pattern-based application framework is built on top of Service Fabric Reliable Services. It provides an API with a single-threaded programming model that uses the scalability and reliability capabilities of Service Fabric.

The actor pattern is a model that is used for distributed systems. An actor is an isolated and independent unit of compute and state with a single-threaded execution. The actor pattern is used for distributed systems where a large number of actors can execute simultaneously and independently of each other. Actors can communicate with each other and they can create more actors.

The actor design pattern can be a good fit for several distributed system problems and scenarios, but, as with any software design pattern, careful consideration of the constraints of the pattern and the framework implementing it must be made. This pattern is most suitable in the following scenarios:

- Your application needs a large number (thousands or more) of small, independent, and isolated units of state and logic.
- You need to work with single-threaded objects that do not require significant interaction from external components.
- Your actor instances won't block callers with unpredictable delays by issuing I/O operations.

For more information on the Reliable Actor programming model, you can refer to the following Microsoft documentation: `https://docs.microsoft.com/en-us/azure/service-fabric/service-fabric-reliable-actors-introduction`.
For more information on the Virtual Actor pattern, you can refer to the following website: `https://www.microsoft.com/en-us/research/project/orleans-virtual-actors/?from=http%3A%2F%2Fresearch.microsoft.com%2Fen-us%2Fprojects%2Forleans%2F`.

Life cycle management

With Azure Service Fabric, you can manage entire life cycles of your microservice applications. It supports several different tasks, from developing microservices to deployment, management, and maintenance. To accomplish this, Azure Service Fabric provides different roles that can operate independently. These different roles are as follows:

- **Service developer**: The service developer develops generic microservices that can be leveraged in different applications. The developer uses the Reliable Services and Reliable Actor programming models to create these microservices.
- **Application developer**: The application developer creates applications by using the various services that have been developed by the service developer. The application developer creates the application manifest.
- **Application administrator**: This application administrator creates the application configuration files and creates the deployment packages. The administrator uses PowerShell to create the application packages.
- **Operator**: The operator deploys the application, monitors the application's health and performance after deployment, and maintains the physical infrastructure. The operator uses PowerShell, the CLI, or the RESTful API to deploy the application.

 For more information on the Service Fabric application's life cycle features, you can refer to the following article: `https://docs.microsoft.com/en-us/azure/service-fabric/service-fabric-application-lifecycle`.

Azure Service Fabric Mesh

Azure Service Fabric Mesh is a PaaS service that can be used to deploy a microservices application without the need for you to create your own Service Fabric cluster. You don't have to manage the virtual machines, storage, or networking.

Applications that are hosted on Service Fabric Mesh will run and scale automatically without the need to worry about the underlying infrastructure. It consists of clusters of thousands of machines, and all of the cluster operations are hidden from the developers. You can only deploy the code and specify the resources, availability requirements, and resource limits. Service Fabric Mesh will then automatically allocate the infrastructure and make sure that the deployed applications are highly available automatically. Using Service Fabric Mesh, developers are only responsible for building applications using the available programming models for Azure Service Fabric.

 At the time of writing this book, Azure Service Fabric Mesh is still in preview.

In the upcoming section, we are going to set up a Service Fabric cluster inside the Azure portal.

Creating an Azure Service Fabric cluster

To set up a Service Fabric cluster inside the Azure portal, follow these steps:

1. Navigate to `https://portal.azure.com/` and log in with your administrator credentials.
2. Create a new resource and, in the search box, type in `Service Fabric Cluster`.
3. Create a new cluster.
4. A new blade will open, where you can provide the configuration values for your new Service Fabric cluster. Select **Basics** and add the following values:
   - **Cluster name**: `packtsfcluster`
   - **Operating system**: Select **WindowsServer 2016-Datacenter-with-Containers** (the default option).
   - **User name**: Type `packtuser`.
   - **Password**: Type `packtpassword1!`.
   - **Subscription**: Select a subscription here.

- **Resource group**: Create a new resource group and name it `packtsfcluster`.
- **Location**: Select a location:

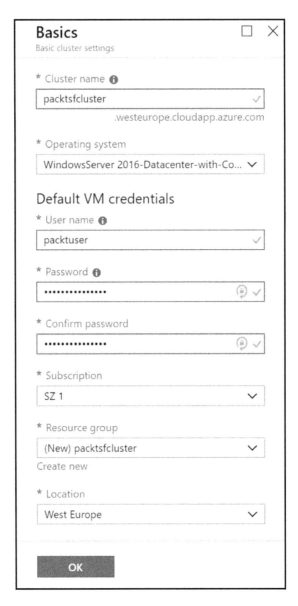

Basic settings

5. Next is the **Cluster configuration**. Add the following values:
    *   **Node type count**: **1**. The number of VMs, VM sizes, and their properties are defined by node types. Your cluster can consist of more than one node type, but the primary node type (the first one that you define on the portal) must have at least five VMs. This is the node type where Service Fabric system services are placed.
    *   **Node Type 1**: Click on this to configure the primary node type:
        *   **Node type name**: Type `nodetype1`.
        *   **Durability tier**: Select **Silver**. This will create five VMs. You can select **Bronze**, which has a minimum of one VM associated with it, **Silver** (five VMs), and **Gold** (five VMs with full node SKUs). For more information about durability tiers, you can refer to the following article: `https://docs.microsoft.com/en-us/azure/ service-fabric/service-fabric-cluster- capacity#the-durability-characteristics-of-the- cluster`.
        *   **Virtual machine size**: **Standard_D2_v2** series VMs have SSD drives that are highly recommended for stateful applications.
        *   **Custom endpoints**: Type `80, 8081`. Here, you can enter a list with ports that you want to expose through the Azure Load Balancer to the public internet for your applications.
        *   **Enable reverse proxy**: Check the box. This setting facilitates the ability of microservices running in a Service Fabric cluster to discover and communicate with other services that have HTTP endpoints.

- **Reverse proxy port**: Type `19081` (the default value):

Cluster configuration settings

- Click **Create** and **OK**.

6. Next is the **Security** configuration. Add the following values:
   - **Configuration type**: Choose **Basic**.
   - **Key vault**: Click on this option to create a new key vault. Service Fabric uses certificates to provide authentication and encryption for securing a cluster and its applications. Service Fabric uses X.509 certificates to secure a cluster and to provide application security features. To do this, you must use Azure Key Vault, which we will discuss in `Chapter 12`, *Securing Your Azure Services*, to manage certificates for Service Fabric clusters in Azure. Select **Create a new vault** in the next blade:
     - **Name**: Type `packtsfkeyvault`.
     - **Resource group**: Create a new one, and name it `packtsfkeyvault`.
     - **Pricing tier**: Choose **Standard**.
     - **Access policies**: Leave this as the default value.
     - **Virtual Network access**: Leave this as **All networks can access** (the default setting).
     - Click the **Create** button, and you will have successfully created the key vault. Now, click **OK**:

Security settings

7. Now that the key vault has been created, you can set the access policies. Select **Edit access policies for packtsfkeyvault**. A new blade will open. Here, select **Click to show advanced access policies**. Enable the following fields:
   - **Azure Virtual Machines for deployment**
   - **Azure Resource Manager for template deployment**

8. Click the **Save** button and close the **Access policies** blade:

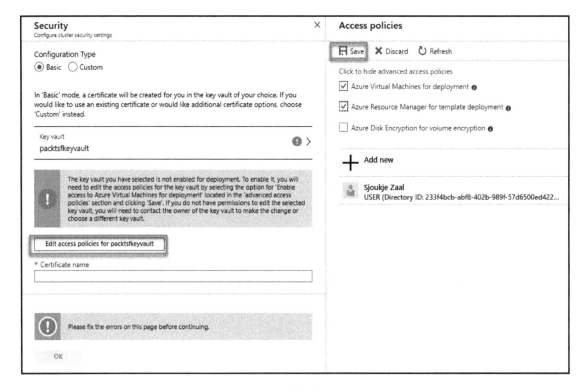

Access policies settings

9. Set the certificate name as `sfcluster-<region name>`.
10. Click **OK**. The certificate will be created.

The **Summary** page will open automatically. Azure will perform a final validation of the configuration values and present you with an overview of the outcome:

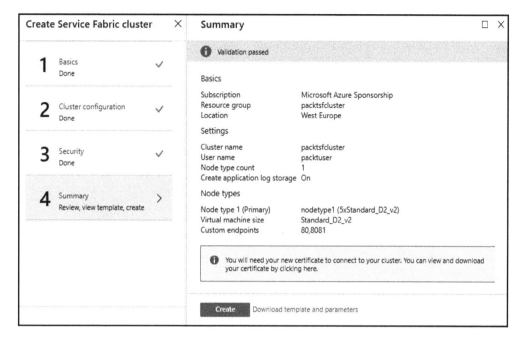

Service Fabric cluster settings summary

Download the certificate by clicking the link in the information box. You will need this to connect to your cluster. After downloading the certificate, click **Create**.

The Service Fabric cluster has been created. After creation, you can navigate to the Service Fabric cluster overview page:

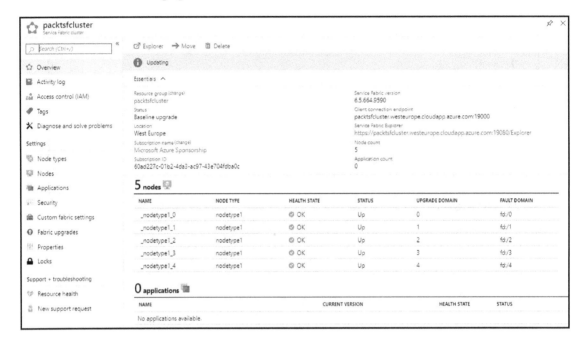

Service Fabric cluster overview page

 TIP
Creating a Service Fabric Production cluster in production involves some planning. For more information on planning your production cluster, you can refer to the following website: https://docs.microsoft.com/en-us/azure/service-fabric/service-fabric-cluster-capacity.

Now that we have created an Azure Service Fabric cluster, we can start creating an application that can be deployed inside the cluster.

Creating a Service Fabric .NET application

In this demo, we are going to create a .NET Azure Service Fabric application in Visual Studio 2019. This sample project contains a single application with multiple services, demonstrating the basic concepts needed to get you started with building highly available, scalable, distributed applications.

However, before we can create the application, we need to set up our development environment, which we will do in the upcoming section.

Setting up your development environment

To set up your development environment for building and running Azure Service Fabric applications, you need to install the Service Fabric runtime, SDK, and tools to start creating Service Fabric applications. The download link can be obtained from the *Technical requirements* section at the beginning of this chapter.

After downloading the required tools, run the executable, which will execute the web platform installer. Here, you can install the Microsoft Azure Service Fabric SDK. Make sure that the SDK that you are installing is targeted at Visual Studio 2017.

Creating the application

After installing the SDK and the tools, you can start creating the application:

1. Open Visual Studio 2019 in administrator mode and create a new project.
2. Type `Service Fabric` in the top menu, and select the **Service Fabric Application** project:

Creating a new Service Fabric application

3. Click **Next.**

4. Name the application `PackSFApplication`, select a location, and click **Create**:

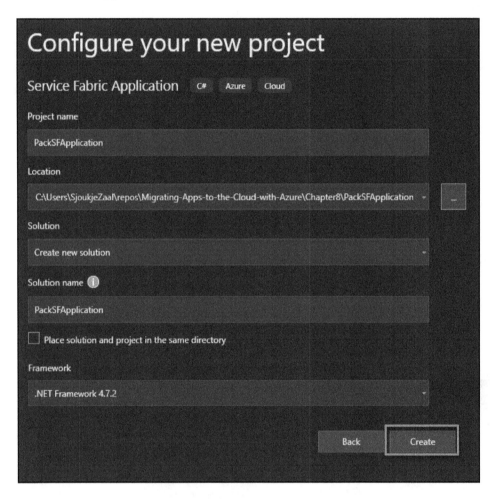

Creating a new Service Fabric application

5. In the following screen, select **Stateful Service**, name the service `PacktStatefulService`, and click **Create**:

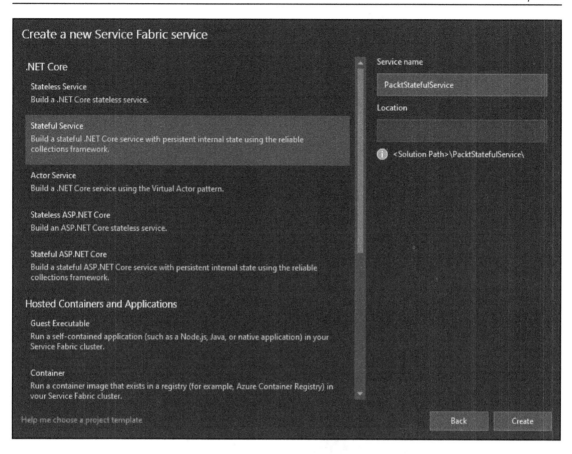

Service Fabric templates

The application and the Stateful Service will have been created, and the projects will be displayed in the solution explorer. A couple of artifacts will have been created automatically by Visual Studio:

- **Publishing profiles**: These are profiles for deploying to different Service Fabric cluster environments.
- **Scripts**: These are PowerShell scripts for deploying or upgrading your Service Fabric application to a Service Fabric cluster.

- **Application definition packages**: This includes the `ApplicationManifest.xml` file under `ApplicationPackageRoot`, which describes your application's structure and composition. Associated application parameter files can be found under `ApplicationParameters`, which can be used to specify environment-specific parameters. Visual Studio will select an application parameter file that's specified in the associated publish profile:

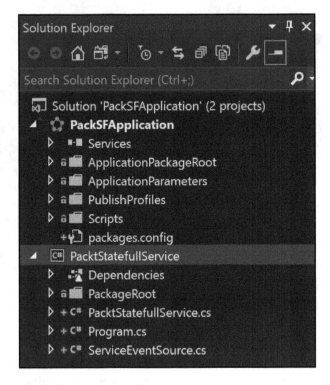

Visual Studio Solution Explorer

Visual Studio generates sample code for the stateful service that can be used for this demo as well. It will give you a basic understanding of the different artifacts that are needed to create an application for Azure Service Fabric. It uses Reliable Collections for storing values.

6. Open `PacktStatefulService.cs` and scroll down to the `RunAsync` method. This consists of a counter that increments each time the service is called. The code appears as follows:

```
protected override async Task
RunAsync(CancellationToken cancellationToken)
{
    // TODO: Replace the following sample code with
your own logic
    // or remove this RunAsync override if it's not
needed in your service.

    var myDictionary = await
this.StateManager.GetOrAddAsync<IReliableDictionary<string,
long>>("myDictionary");

    while (true)
    {
cancellationToken.ThrowIfCancellationRequested();

        using (var tx =
this.StateManager.CreateTransaction())
        {
            var result = await
myDictionary.TryGetValueAsync(tx, "Counter");

ServiceEventSource.Current.ServiceMessage(this.Context,
"Current Counter Value: {0}",
                result.HasValue ?
result.Value.ToString() : "Value does not exist.");

            await myDictionary.AddOrUpdateAsync(tx,
"Counter", 0, (key, value) => ++value);

            // If an exception is thrown before calling
CommitAsync, the transaction aborts, all changes are
            // discarded, and nothing is saved to the
secondary replicas.
            await tx.CommitAsync();
        }

        await Task.Delay(TimeSpan.FromSeconds(1),
cancellationToken);
    }
}
```

7. Before you run the application, change the number of nodes in the **Service Fabric Local Cluster Manager**. You can access this in the system tray (when it is not displayed in the system tray, you need to start it by opening the Service Fabric Local Cluster Manager from the available applications). Then, click **Switch Cluster Mode** and select **5 Node**. In a production environment, this will mean that the service runs on five different machines. The local cluster that is used by Visual Studio will host the five nodes on one machine:

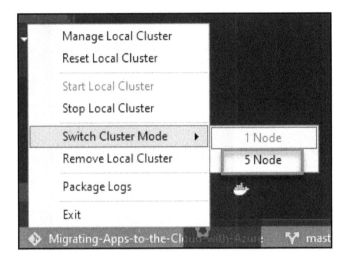

Service Fabric Local Cluster Manager

8. Now, click *F5* to run the application. Click **yes** when a message box pops up asking you to grant the `ServiceFabricAllowedUsers` group read and execute permissions to your Visual Studio project directory.

9. A local cluster for debugging will be created by Visual Studio. The **Diagnostic Events** screen will open and this is where you will be able to see the counter incrementing:

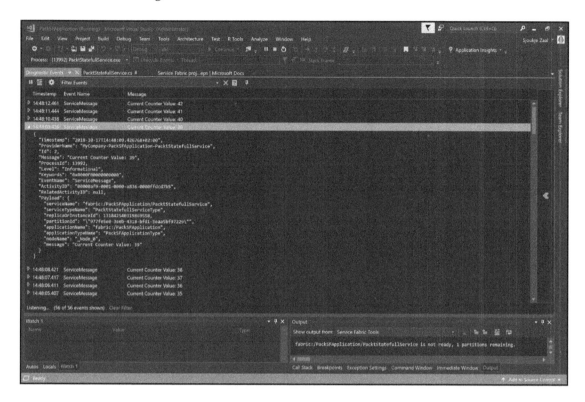

Debugging the application

10. The Service Fabric Explorer tool can display a visual representation of the cluster as well. Again, open the **Service Fabric Local Cluster Manager** in the system tray. Right-click the icon and select **Manage Local Cluster**. This will open a web page with a visual representation of a cluster. Here, you can view the health of the nodes and the application, restart machines, view errors, and more:

Visual representation of a local Service Fabric cluster

For this book, we are creating a simple demo to show you the basics of an Azure Service Fabric application. For an actual deep dive into Azure Service Fabric, you will need more than one chapter.

 To create a more advanced application that uses all of the concepts that were explained in the previous sections, you can refer to the following sample application on GitHub: `https://github.com/Azure-Samples/service-fabric-dotnet-getting-started`. Alternatively, you can refer to the following tutorial: `https://docs.microsoft.com/en-us/azure/service-fabric/service-fabric-tutorial-create-dotnet-app`.

Deploying the application

Deploying the application into the Service Fabric Cluster that we created earlier can easily be done directly via Visual Studio. To deploy the application, follow these steps:

1. First, the certificate that we downloaded when we created the Service Fabric cluster in the Azure portal needs to be installed on your local machine.

2. Then, right-click `PackSFApplication` and select **Publish**:

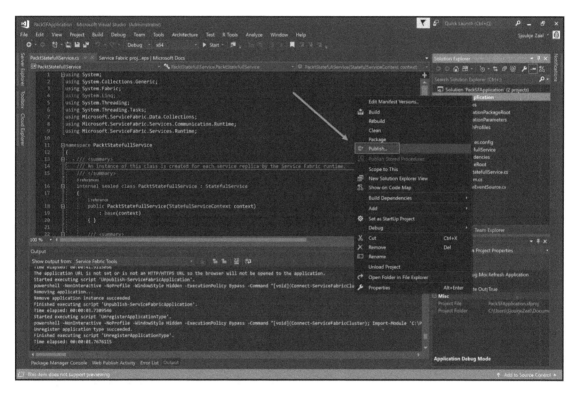

Publish setting in Visual Studio 2017

3. Select the **Service Fabric Cluster Connection Endpoint** from the drop-down menu and click **Publish**:

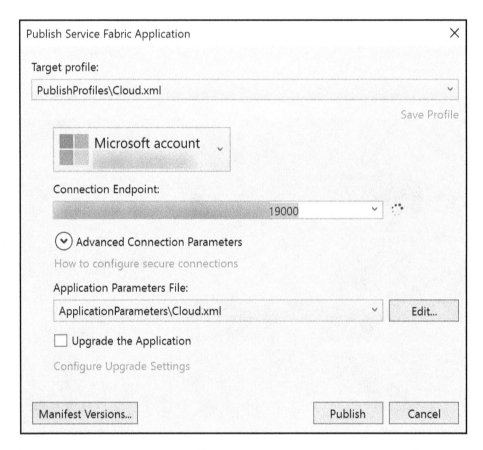

Publishing the Service Fabric application

4. The application will be published to the cluster in Azure. After deployment, navigate to the Service Fabric cluster overview page in the Azure portal and you will see that the application has been deployed:

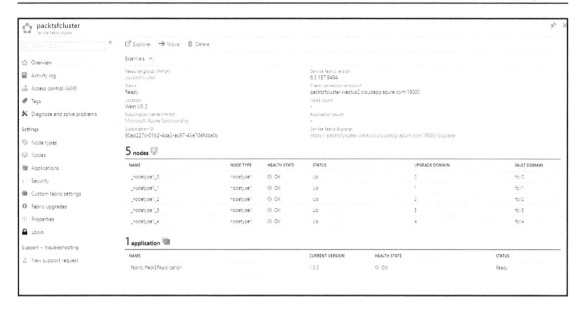

Service Fabric application deployed to Azure

In this section, we have covered how to create a Service Fabric application in .NET. In the next section, we are going to create an application for Service Fabric in Java.

Creating a Service Fabric Java application

In this demo, we are going to create a Java Azure Service Fabric application in Eclipse 2019. The sample project contains a single application with multiple services, demonstrating the basic concepts needed to get you started building highly available, scalable, and distributed applications.

But before we can create the application, we first need to set up our development environment, which we will do in the next section.

Setting up your development environment

To set up your development environment for building and running Azure Service Fabric applications, you will need a Linux or Mac developer machine with an installation of Eclipse. In this chapter, we will be using Linux (Ubuntu 16.04) and Eclipse 2019 with Gradle as the build system, but Eclipse Neon or later will suffice. You will also need to ensure that the `apt-transport-https` and `curl` packages are installed by executing the following command:

```
sudo apt-get install apt-transport-https curl
```

You need to install the Service Fabric runtime, SDK, and `sfctl` CLI to start creating Service Fabric applications. The simplest way to do this is to use the script installation by executing the following command:

```
sudo curl -s
https://raw.githubusercontent.com/Azure/service-fabric-scripts-and-template
s/master/scripts/SetupServiceFabric/SetupServiceFabric.sh | sudo bash
```

Setting up a local Service Fabric cluster

To run your application locally, set up a local Service Fabric cluster. To do this, execute the following command:

```
sudo
/opt/microsoft/sdk/servicefabric/common/clustersetup/devclustersetup.sh
```

Once the script has completed, open your favorite web browser and go to the Service Fabric Explorer at `http://localhost:19080/Explorer`. Establishing the cluster is a long-running process, so it may take several minutes for you to successfully get the following page:

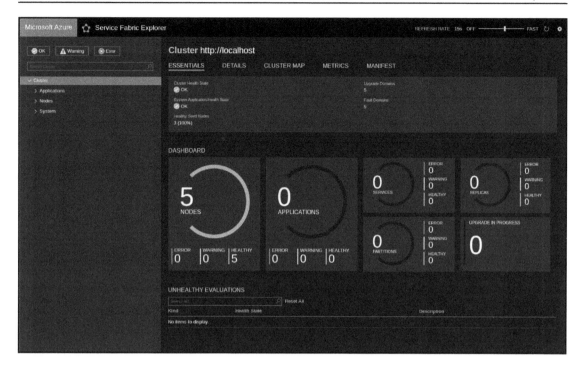

Visual representation of a local Service Fabric cluster

Installing the Eclipse plugin for service fabric

To install the Eclipse plugin for Service Fabric, start Eclipse and go to **Help | Install New Software...**:

1. Click **Add**.
2. In the **Add Repository** window, enter `http://dl.microsoft.com/eclipse` in the **Name** and **Location** input fields, and then click **Add**:

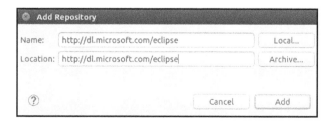

Add Repository dialog

3. Select **Azure ServiceFabric Plugin for Eclipse** and click **Next**:

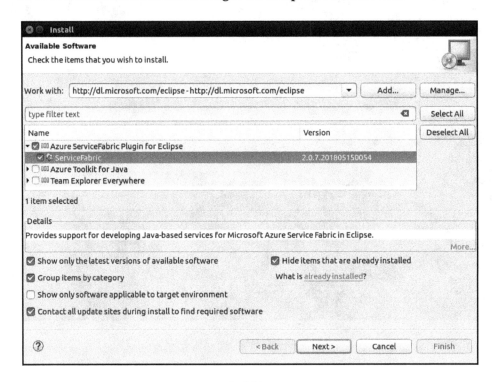

Install dialog

4. Review the installation details and click **Next**:

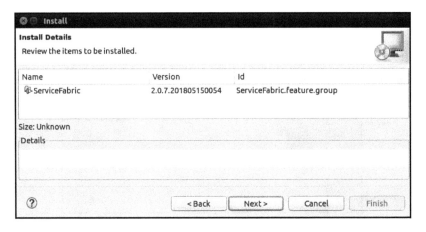

Install Details dialog

5. Accept the license agreement and click **Finish:**

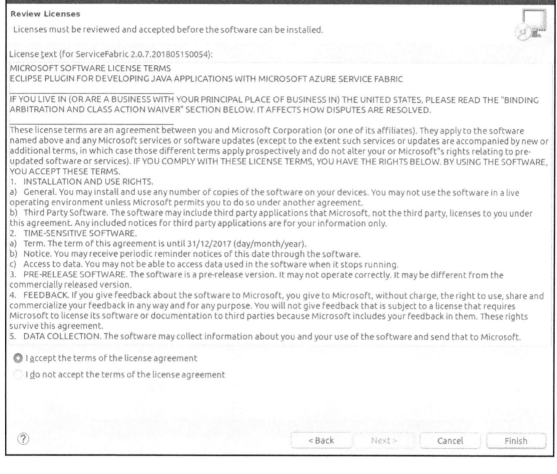

Review Licenses dialog

6. Once the installation has completed, restart Eclipse.

Creating the application

After installing the SDK and tools, you can start creating the application:

1. Open Eclipse and got to **File** | **New** | **Other**..., select **Service Fabric Project**, and click **Next**:

Select a wizard dialog

2. Enter the project name, `PackSFApplication`, and click **Next**:

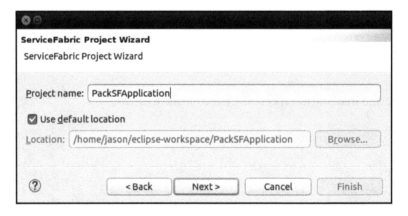

ServiceFabric Project Wizard dialog

3. Select **Stateful Service**, name the service `PacktStatefulService`, and click **Finish**:

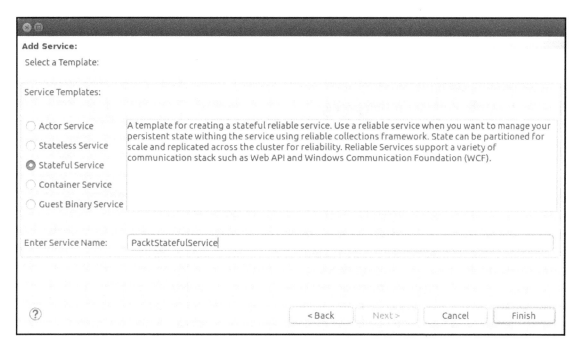

Add Service dialog

4. When the **Open Associated Perspective** window opens, click **Open Perspective**:

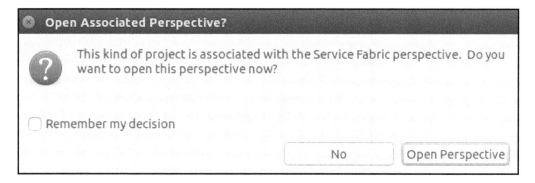

Open Associated Perspective dialog

The Service Fabric application and the stateful service have now been created and the projects displayed in the package explorer. Key artifacts that were created by Eclipse are the following:

- **Publishing profiles**: These are profiles for deploying to different Service Fabric cluster environments.
- **Scripts**: These are Shell scripts for deploying or upgrading your Service Fabric application to a Service Fabric cluster.
- **Application definition packages**: This includes the `ApplicationManifest.xml` file under `PackSFApplicationApplication`:

Package Explorer

Eclipse generates sample code for the stateful service, which can be used for this demo as well. It will provide a basic understanding of the different artifacts that are needed to create an application for Azure Service Fabric. It uses Reliable Collections for storing values:

1. Open `PacktStatefulService.java` and scroll down to the `runAsync` method. This consists of a counter that increments each time the service is called. The code looks like the following:

```
@Override
protected CompletableFuture<?> runAsync(CancellationToken
cancellationToken) {
    Transaction tx = stateManager.createTransaction();
    CompletableFuture<ReliableHashMap<String, Long>> mapFuture =
stateManager.<String,
Long>getOrAddReliableHashMapAsync("myHashMap");
    return mapFuture.thenCompose((map) -> {
        return computeValueAsync(map, tx, cancellationToken);
    }).thenCompose((v) -> {
        return commitTransaction(tx);
    }).whenComplete((res, e) -> {
        closeTransaction(tx);
    });
}
```

2. Right-click your Service Fabric application and, from the context menu, select **Service Fabric | Publish Application...**.
3. In the **Publish Application** window, select `PublishProfiles/Local.json` and click **Publish**:

Publish Application dialog

4. The demo application is now deployed to your local Service Fabric cluster. Open your favorite web browser and go to `http://localhost:19080/Explorer`, where you will see a visual representation of your cluster and can view the health of the nodes and application, restart machines, view errors, and more:

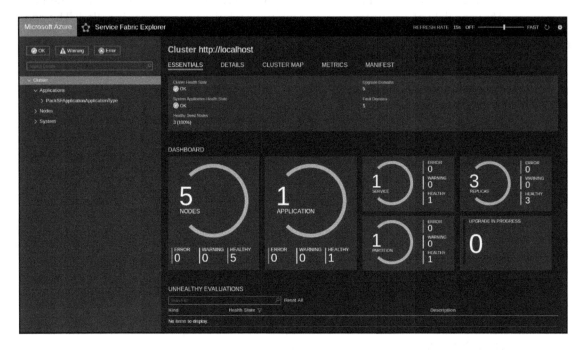

Service Fabric Explorer

 For this book, we are creating a simple demo to show the basics of an Azure Service Fabric application. For an actual deep dive into Azure Service Fabric, you will need more than one chapter. To create a more advanced application that uses all of the concepts explained in the previous sections, you can refer to the sample application on GitHub at `https://github.com/Azure-Samples/service-fabric-java-getting-started`, or the following tutorial: `https://docs.microsoft.com/en-us/azure/service-fabric/service-fabric-tutorial-create-java-app`.

Deploying the application

Deploying the application into the Service Fabric cluster that we created earlier can easily be done from Eclipse directly. To deploy the application, observe the following steps:

1. First, the certificate that we downloaded when we created the Service Fabric cluster in the Azure portal needs to be installed on your local machine.

2. Now, convert the certificate into PEM format by executing the following command:

```
openssl pkcs12 -in your-cert.pfx -out your-cert.pem -nodes -passin
pass:your-password
```

3. Open the `Cloud.json` file in Eclipse under the `PublishProfiles` directory and configure the endpoint and credentials as follows:
   - **ConnectionIPOrURL**: "`[your hostname]`"
   - **ConnectionPort**: "`19080`"
   - **ClientKey**: "`[path to your PEM file]`"
   - **ClientCert**: "`[path to your PEM file]`"

4. Right-click your Service Fabric application and, from the context menu, select **Service Fabric | Publish Application...**.

5. In the **Publish Application** window, select `PublishProfiles/Cloud.json` and click **Publish**:

Publish Application dialog

The demo application is now deployed to your Service Fabric cluster. After deployment, navigate to the Service Fabric cluster overview page in the Azure portal, and you will see that the application has been deployed:

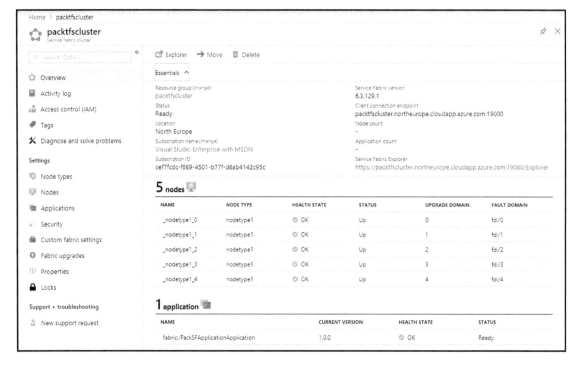

Service Fabric application deployed to Azure

Summary

In this chapter, we learned about the Azure Service Fabric ecosystem and covered the different application scenarios where Service Fabric applications are the most suitable. We also covered building a basic cloud-native microservice application using Azure Service Fabric in both .NET and Java.

In the next chapter, we are going to create scalable systems with Azure functions.

Questions

Answer the following questions to test your knowledge of the information that you covered in this chapter. You can find the answers in the *Assessments* section at the end of this book:

1. What is the Azure Service Fabric PaaS offering called?
    1. Azure Service Fabric Clusters
    2. Azure Service Fabric Mesh
    3. Azure Service Fabric Manager
    4. Azure Service Fabric Nodes

2. Is Azure Service Fabric suitable for DevOps environments?
    1. Yes
    2. No

3. What are the programming models for Azure Service Fabric called?
    1. Unreliable Actor programming model
    2. Unreliable Services programming model
    3. Reliable Actor programming model
    4. Reliable Services programming model

Further reading

You can check out the following links for more information regarding the topics that were covered in this chapter:

- **Overview of Azure Service Fabric**: https://docs.microsoft.com/en-us/azure/service-fabric/service-fabric-overview
- **What is Service Fabric Mesh?**: https://docs.microsoft.com/en-us/azure/service-fabric-mesh/service-fabric-mesh-overview
- **Service Fabric application life cycle**: https://docs.microsoft.com/en-us/azure/service-fabric/service-fabric-application-lifecycle
- **Service Fabric cluster capacity planning considerations**: https://docs.microsoft.com/en-us/azure/service-fabric/service-fabric-cluster-capacity#the-durability-characteristics-of-the-cluster
- **Reliable services overview**: https://docs.microsoft.com/en-us/azure/service-fabric/service-fabric-reliable-services-introduction
- **Configuring a Service Fabric cluster**: https://docs.microsoft.com/en-us/azure/service-fabric/service-fabric-cluster-creation-via-portal

4
Going Serverless and Deploying to the Cloud

Tools such as Azure Functions and Azure App Service enable you to make your application serverless. This gives your organization a unique advantage by reducing the time it takes to develop an application, bringing cost savings, and promoting innovation.

This section contains the following chapters:

- Chapter 9, *Building Scalable Systems with Azure Functions*
- Chapter 10, *Connecting to the Database*
- Chapter 11, *Managing and Deploying Your Code*
- Chapter 12, *Securing Your Azure Services*

Building Scalable Systems with Azure Functions

9

Azure Functions is a great way to write small pieces of code that are highly scalable, reusable, and cheap. They're a so-called serverless solution, meaning you only need to worry about the code and not the server running your code.

The following topics will be covered in this chapter:

- Understanding serverless computing
- Creating an Azure function
- Working with triggered functions
- Creating Azure Functions in Visual Studio
- Deploying Azure Functions
- Timer triggered functions
- Input and output bindings
- Azure Functions proxies
- Best practices

Technical requirements

You will need to use the following tools for the examples in this chapter:

- **Visual Studio 2019**: https://www.visualstudio.com/downloads/

The source code for this chapter can be downloaded here: https://github.com/PacktPublishing/Migrating-Apps-to-the-Cloud-with-Azure/tree/master/Chapter9.

Understanding serverless computing

Before we talk about Azure Functions, let's discuss so-called serverless computing, which is kind of a misnomer since your code will definitely run on servers. Anyway, serverless computing isn't completely wrong, either, since it allows you to run code without worrying about servers and infrastructure at all (or the dreaded system administrators, for that matter). Serverless computing allows you to run code without doing any server management. As we've already mentioned, your code will still run on servers, but the server management is done by your cloud vendor (Azure, in our case) and is completely hidden from developers. While Azure Functions is one implementation of serverless, it's not the only one. Another popular application of serverless is Azure Logic Apps, which allows you to create workflows with relative ease. In this chapter, however, we're only going to focus on Azure Functions.

In serverless computing, server allocation happens dynamically, which has two huge implications: scaling is easy and you're only paying when you're actually using resources. Let's expand on both.

Dynamic scaling

One very cool feature of serverless and Azure Functions is that Azure scales servers up and down dynamically. A **function** can be a piece of code that you can call using an HTTP request. So, when you're calling a function a hundred times in a loop, and each execution takes a couple of seconds, Azure can decide to scale up a couple of servers so that you're not waiting for ages to complete the execution processes.

However, there are some limitations to scaling. You never get more than 200 servers and Azure only scales up one server every 10 seconds at most. One server can still handle more than one execution at a time, though, so if you have 200 servers, you can probably handle some thousands of executions in parallel.

Dynamic pricing

In Azure, you only pay for resources you're using, and since servers are allocated dynamically, you're not paying for functions that you're not using. Even when your functions are executing, it's quite cheap. With an App Service plan, you allocate a server that is always up and running; depending on your tier (let's say, basic, normal, and enterprise) you're paying about €40 – €1,000 a month, even when your application does absolutely nothing. Your functions can run on an App Service plan (which is great when you already have one), but it's recommended to create a consumption plan.

With a consumption plan, you pay per use. The actual costs are a bit difficult to calculate since it's a mix of per-second resource consumption and the number of executions. That being said, your first million executions and 400,000 GB are free. If you have a small to medium-sized company with a few functions for fun or for some special use cases, you're probably running them for free. Once you get past the free executions, you're still only paying a few cents per million executions and a thousandth of a cent per GB per second. In conclusion, functions are pretty cheap.

Keep in mind that once your functions start to scale up servers, your costs may double.

Disadvantages of serverless computing

Serverless computing is very cool, but it comes with some limitations as well. There is, of course, the aforementioned scaling limitations. Also, you'll have no control over your server. On one hand, this is very easy and convenient, but on the other hand, it poses some limitations, such as not being able to install any third-party applications you may need.

One of these applications may also be your actual runtime. Azure Functions supports C# and F# in .NET and .NET Core, JavaScript (with Node.js), Java, Python, and PowerShell Core. Other than that, version 1.x of the Azure Functions runtime had experimental support for various languages, such as Python and PHP, but those were dropped in version 2.x. Microsoft will undoubtedly add support for other languages in the future, but for now, you're limited to C#, F#, JavaScript, and Java.

Creating an Azure function

Azure Functions are usually small pieces of code that can be executed on Azure without us having to deploy a server. This solution is often called **Function as a Service**, or **FaaS**. For this reason, functions can also be seen as microservices or even nanoservices. They're lightweight and enable a small piece of functionality. Functions are based on Web Apps, as discussed in `Chapter 6`, *Designing Web Applications*. They even show in your Web Apps overview. However, functions aren't exactly the same as Web Apps, so they come with some limitations. For example, while Web Apps support logging to files, functions can only use Application Insights for monitoring, which we will discuss in `Chapter 13`, *Diagnostics and Monitoring*. Having **ARR affinity** or **always on** functionality in functions also wouldn't make much sense, so they're not visible in the configuration settings. Likewise, functions don't have **default documents** or **path mappings**. Depending on your plan, you also can't scale up or out as this is handled for you automatically.

In terms of migrations, as we discussed in `Chapter 1`, *Strategies for Application Modernization Using Azure,* you can use functions for everything except rehosting. Because an Azure function is really just that – a function – it's so small that you can easily replace one (C#) function at a time and migrate it to Azure (given that it meets certain requirements; see the *Best practices* section at the end of this chapter for more information). You can easily move one or two functions to Azure and perform refactoring. You could even move some services to Azure Functions as a form of rearchitecture. Automatic import and export processes allow us to rewrite functions because triggers and bindings make this sort of work relatively easy. We will discuss this in more detail later in this chapter. Finally, when you completely rewrite an application, you can move some functions and processes to Azure Functions.

For our first example, we're going to create an Azure function in the Azure portal.

Creating a Function App

The first thing we need to do is create a Function App. This is the container where your functions live. Creating a Function App is pretty much the same as creating an App Service, with a few minor changes. Follow these steps to create the Function App:

1. Go to **Create a resource** and find **Function App.**
2. In the blade that opens, type in an app name that's unique across all of Azure.
3. Select a subscription.
4. Select or create a resource group.
5. Select your preferred OS (Windows or Linux).
6. Choose your hosting plan. As we mentioned previously, you can use a regular hosting plan, but a consumption plan (the default) is recommended.
7. Pick a location (pick whatever is close to you).
8. Select your runtime stack (.NET, Java, or JavaScript at the time of writing; we'll go for .NET).
9. Select or create a storage account. Azure uses a storage account to store your functions' code.
10. Finally, you can choose to create Application Insights for your Azure Function App.
11. When you've filled everything out, you can click **Create** and the Function App will be created. This might take a few minutes:

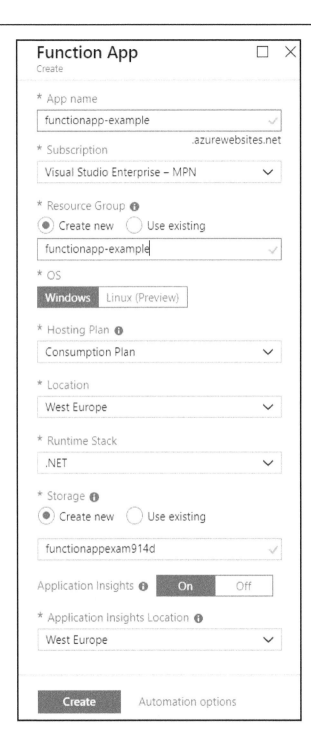

Creating a function

Once your Function App has been created, you can create an actual function:

1. Browse to **App Services** or to **Function Apps**. Once you've click on either of these options, you'll be taken to your **Function Apps**.

2. From the **Function Apps** screen, you can manage and create your functions:

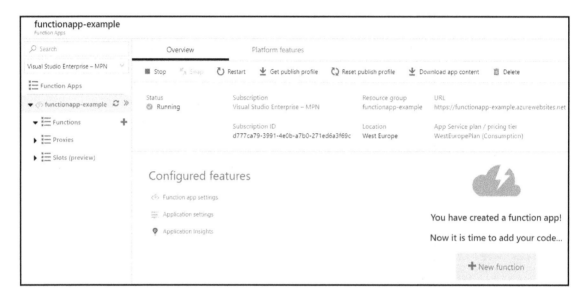

3. The easiest way to create a function is by just clicking the big **+ New function** button, so let's do that.

4. First, you'll be presented with a couple of development environments, that is, **Visual Studio**, **VS Code**, **Any editor + Core tools**, and **In-portal**. From here, choose **In-portal** (we'll use Visual Studio later).

5. Next, you have to pick a trigger; either a **Webhook + API**, a **Timer**, or **More templates**.
   The Azure UI is a bit flaky and inconsistent here, so pick **More templates** and pick the **HTTP Trigger**. This is the same as picking **Webhook + API**, except you get to pick a name for your function.

6. Now, you'll need to provide a name and authorization level for your function. I already know the default function template, so I'm naming my function `SayHello` and I'm leaving the authorization level on the default function level.

7. On the next screen, you'll find a simple function that takes the value of a name parameter from either the body or the query string and returns `Hello, {name}`.

8. Hit the **Run** button and inspect the log and debug screens that pop up.

9. In the following screenshot, you will see a **</> Get function URL** button at the top, which gives you the URL, as well as the function key, which is necessary to call the function (since we chose the function authorization level). Copy the URL and append `&name=[your name]` to it (for me, it's `https://functionapp-example.azurewebsites.net/api/SayHello?code=[code]&name=[name]`).

10. Paste the URL into your browser's URL field. You should see `Hello,  [name]`:

In the next section, we're going to use our newly created HTTP function.

Consuming your HTTP function

While performing a `GET` request in your browser is nice, you're probably going to use this to call functions from your own code, and probably using the `POST` method. Luckily, this isn't very difficult to do. Open up Visual Studio, create a new .NET Core console app, and put the following code in the `Program.cs` file:

```
using System;
using System.Net.Http;
using System.Text;
```

```
namespace ConsoleApp1
{
    class Program
    {
        static void Main(string[] args)
        {
            using (var client = new HttpClient())
            {
                string url = "[your URL]";
                var content = new StringContent("{\"name\": \"[your
name]\"}", Encoding.UTF8, "application/json");
                client.PostAsync(url, content).ContinueWith(async t =>
                {
                    var result = await
t.Result.Content.ReadAsStringAsync();
                    Console.WriteLine("The Function result is:");
                    Console.WriteLine(result);
                    Console.WriteLine("Press any key to exit.");
                    Console.ReadKey();
                }).Wait();
            }
        }
    }
}
```

Of course, you'll need to change `[your URL]` to your URL and `[your name]` to your name. This code will simply call your function and display the result, that is, `Hello,` `[your name]`, in the console window.

Function management

Now, you can change the code of your function and play around with it. In the menu on the left, you'll see your function, along with the **Integrate**, **Manage**, and **Monitor** submenus. The **Integrate** menu lets you change your allowed HTTP methods (defaults to `GET` and `POST`); from here, you can change the route template, the request parameter name, and the authorization level. You can also add additional inputs or outputs, as shown in the following screenshot:

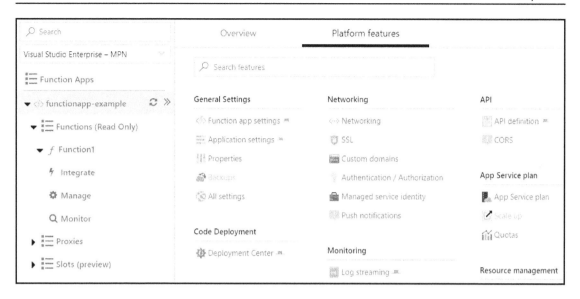

Under the **Manage** menu item, you can create, copy, renew, and revoke keys. You need these for functions with authorization levels of **Function** or **Admin**. For admin-level functions, you need the 7 key (which I don't recommend; you don't want to hand out master keys). For function-level functions, you can use either keys that are specific to that function or keys that give access to any function under the Function App. You can also disable or delete your function here.

Under **Monitor**, you can find your function executions, check whether they were successful, how long they took to complete, the result code, and so on. It can take up to 5 minutes for an execution to pop up here. If you chose to turn on Application Insights, you can also go to Application Insights from here.

For the management of your Function App, you can click the Function App and go to the **Platform** features tab. Since a consumption plan still runs on servers, you can edit some settings, such as application settings, IP restrictions, custom domains, and authentication and authorization. It's not as extensive as it is for a regular web app, but it gives you a bit more control over how your functions can be used.

Last but not least, when you browse to the storage account you selected or created, you'll also find the `azure-webjobs-hosts` and `azure-webjobs-secrets` blob containers. In your files, you'll find a file share. Both hold the files that are necessary for your functions to run.

Working with triggered functions

You can call HTTP functions yourself from a browser (if GET is enabled), from your code (using an HTTP client), or using another program that supports HTTP requests. Another really cool feature that's at the core of functions is that they can be triggered by various events, thereby enabling an event-driven programming architecture. For example, a function can be triggered when a message is put on a Service Bus queue, when a blob is changed or added to a storage account, or when a document changes in Cosmos DB. There are various other triggers that I personally haven't needed yet, but there are triggers for Event Grid, Azure Active Directory, Outlook, and more. You'll see them for yourself when you create a new function.

Creating a triggered function

Speaking of which, let's create a function that triggers on a Service Bus queue and writes the contents to a blob in a storage account (creating a blob file may trigger yet another function). First, we'll have to create a queue in a Service Bus:

1. Go to **Create a resource** and search for Service Bus.
2. Again, we have to pick a Service Bus name that is unique across Azure.
3. Choose the basic pricing tier, which is fine for our use case.
4. Choose your subscription.
5. Select or create a resource group.
6. Pick a location.
7. Hit **Create** and wait for the Service Bus to deploy.

Next, we can create our function:

1. Create a new function, which you can now do by clicking the big + behind **Functions**.
2. Choose the Azure Service Bus Queue trigger.
3. You may have to install an extension, which can take a few minutes.
4. Pick any name you like; I simply left it as the default.
5. You'll have to create a Service Bus connection, which is as easy as clicking **New** and choosing your Service Bus and Policy, both of which can be left as in the default states if you only have one Service Bus.
6. Pick a queue name; I'm leaving it as the default, that is, myqueue.
7. Hit **Create**.

Next, you'll be taken to the code screen. The default implementation for this type of trigger is just a log statement (which you can read under **Monitor**) that logs the queue message. While we don't have IntelliSense or a lot of help from the code editor, we can write some simple code that creates a blob file:

```
#r "Microsoft.WindowsAzure.Storage"

using Microsoft.WindowsAzure.Storage;
using System;
using System.Threading.Tasks;

public static async Task Run(string myQueueItem, ILogger log)
{
    log.LogInformation($"C# ServiceBus queue trigger Function processed
message: {myQueueItem}");
    var storAccount = CloudStorageAccount.Parse("[connectionstring]");
    var client = storAccount.CreateCloudBlobClient();
    var container = client.GetContainerReference("queue-messages");
    await container.CreateIfNotExistsAsync();
    var blob = container.GetBlockBlobReference(Guid.NewGuid().ToString());
    blob.Properties.ContentType = "text/plain";
    await blob.UploadTextAsync(myQueueItem);
}
```

Let's explain the preceding code. First of all, the first line, `#r` `"Microsoft.WindowsAzure.Storage"`, imports the Azure Storage package, which gives us access to the `Microsoft.WindowsAzure.Storage` namespace, which contains all the classes for working with storage accounts and blobs in Azure.

`var storAccount = CloudStorageAccount.Parse("[connectionstring]");` needs to be edited because you need to replace `[connectionstring]` with your own connection string. You can find this in the Azure portal. Go to your storage account and find your access keys. Copy the connection string of either `key 1` or `key 2`.

Other than that, this is some pretty self-explanatory code that you can use to create a container named `queue-messages` (if the container doesn't already exist) and upload a text file with the text from the queue item.

You can run the code and actually change the text for `myQueueItem` in the portal. Once you've run the code, go to your storage account and find the `queue-messages` blob container. You'll see that there's a file inside it. Once you open the file, you should see the text that you inserted in the debug window.

If all works as it should, we're going to see this work with the actual queue:

1. Go to your Service Bus instance.
2. Go to **Queues.**
3. Hit **+ Queue** to create a queue.
4. Name the queue `myqueue` and leave all the defaults as they are.
5. Hit **Create** and wait for the queue to be created.

Unfortunately, tooling for Service Bus queues and topics is a bit limited. The only way we can add messages to the queue is by writing code. It isn't hard, but it would be nice if we could do this from the portal.

Now, open up Visual Studio and create a .NET Core console app. Install the `Microsoft.Azure.ServiceBus` package using NuGet and place the following code in the `Program.cs` file:

```
using Microsoft.Azure.ServiceBus;
using System.Text;

namespace ConsoleApp1
{
    internal class Program
    {
        private static void Main(string[] args)
        {
            string text = "This is a text";
            byte[] bytes = Encoding.UTF8.GetBytes(text);
            QueueClient client = new QueueClient("[connectionstring]",
"myqueue");
            client.SendAsync(new Message(bytes)).Wait();
            client.CloseAsync().Wait();
        }
    }
}
```

You need to replace `[connectionstring]` again. You can find it in your Service Bus account under shared access policies. Then, go to the `RootManageSharedAccessKey` policy. Copy either the primary or secondary connection string.

Now, run the console app. You should see the message appear in your queue (either through a spike on the overview page or in your queue's active messages). It shouldn't take long before your function picks it up and creates a new blob file.

Creating Azure Functions in Visual Studio

So far, we have only created functions in the Azure portal, but this isn't ideal. First, the portal doesn't provide proper tools for writing complex code. Second, your code isn't included in source control. Third, your code isn't covered in unit tests and automated builds. Finally, you can never deploy your functions to other environments through continuous deployment. So, while it's nice for simple use cases, try to avoid creating functions in the portal and use Visual Studio instead.

Now, we are going to create our functions using Visual Studio 2017. To follow along with these examples, you need to have the Visual Studio Azure development workload installed, which you can select when you install or modify Visual Studio. To check whether you have it or not, open Visual Studio, create a new project, and look for the **Azure Functions** project template (under **Cloud**):

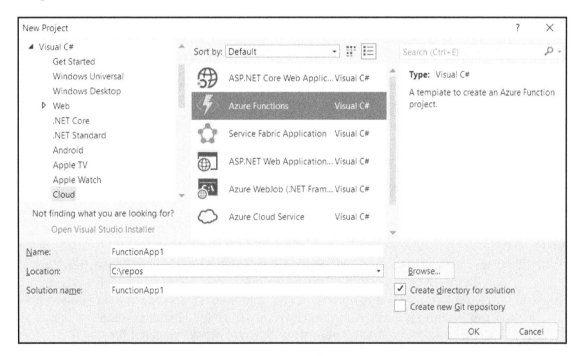

Follow these steps to create an Azure function:

1. Create a new Azure Functions project. You can keep the default `FunctionApp1` name.

2. On the next screen, we'll need to select a **Blob trigger**, which triggers when a blob is uploaded.

3. Make sure you select the Azure Functions v2 (.NET Standard) runtime. If this isn't available, you may have to update your function tools.

4. You'll need a storage account, so select this option from in the **Storage Account** settings. The default storage account is an emulator, but it has limited capabilities and we'll need the storage account eventually anyway.

5. The **Connection string setting** is just a name for your connection string; I've named it `StorageAccount`.

6. The **Path** is the name of your blob container; you can leave as the default, that is, `samples-workitems`:

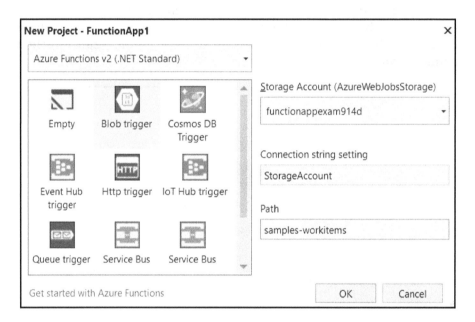

7. Once the project has been created, you need to set your connection string. You can do this in two ways: first, we can go into `local.settings.json`, add a `StorageAccount` value under `Values`, and give it the value of your connection string (recommended). Alternatively, you can change the connection in your code to `AzureWebJobsStorage` since this was already created for you. I recommend doing the former. Since we're using the same storage account, we can copy the connection string from the `AzureWebJobsStorage` setting.

8. Go into the Azure portal, find your storage account, and create the `samples-workitems` blob container.

9. Hit *F5* in Visual Studio to run your function and upload a file to your blob container. You should see the file being logged in your console window:

Let's do something with the file. We can send an email whenever a file is uploaded and add the file as an attachment:

```
using Microsoft.Azure.WebJobs;
// [...]

namespace FunctionApp1
{
    public static class Function1
    {
        [FunctionName("Function1")]
        public static async Task Run([BlobTrigger("samples-
workitems/{name}", Connection = "StorageAccount")]Stream myBlob, string
name, ILogger log)
        {
            log.LogInformation($"C# Blob trigger Function Processed blob\n
Name:{name} \n Size: {myBlob.Length} Bytes");
            // [...]
            await client.SendMailAsync(mail);
        }
    }
}
```

The preceding code is pretty straightforward. Don't forget to replace `[your account]` with your Outlook username and `[your password]` with your Outlook password. In a production environment, you'd put this somewhere in your configuration file, but for this example, that's not really important.

If you run the code again and upload a file to your blob container, you should get an email after a few seconds. You can open the attachment to see it's the same as the file you uploaded. Of course, you can do all kinds of stuff with a file upload, such as make a log to a database, put a message on a queue, read the file and process its contents, and so on.

One warning, though – your Azure Functions uses the file storage to store certain data, which also includes which triggers are and aren't handled. So, when you create a new function and make it trigger on existing blob storage, it will trigger for all the files that are already in the container because it hasn't triggered on them yet. Due to this, you may want to move or delete a file once you've processed it.

Deploying Azure Functions

So far, we've created our functions directly in the Azure portal, but now we've created one using Visual Studio. This means we need to deploy this function to Azure ourselves. We have two obvious choices here: deploy using Visual Studio, which is a manual task, or deploy using Azure DevOps, which enables continuous integration and deployment.

Deploying using Visual Studio

First, let's deploy using Visual Studio 2017 since it's quick and easy. A little warning up-front, though: this will overwrite the functions that are already in your Function App, so you'll lose them. Follow these steps to deploy using Visual Studio:

1. Right-click your project and select **Publish....** You'll be presented with a popup that lets you create a new Function App or select an existing one.
2. Since we already have a Function App, we can select an existing one.
3. Select **Run from ZIP (recommended)**. This puts your function in a read-only state, but it will closely match your release when you use Azure DevOps in the next section. Besides, you don't even want to be able to change functions in the portal since we want our changes to be in source control.
4. When you click the **Publish** button, you can select your Function App.
5. Click **OK**. Your function will be published to the portal:

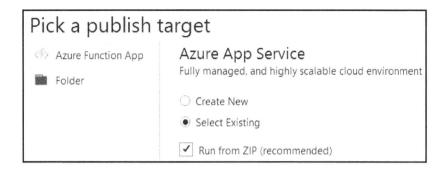

6. Browse to the Azure portal and check that your function was successfully deployed.
7. Upload a file to your blob storage and check that the file has been mailed to you.

As you can see, your functions are read-only since it explicitly says so in the portal: your app is currently in read-only mode because you are running from a package file. When running from a package, the filesystem is read-only and no changes can be made to the files. To make any changes, update the content in your ZIP file and in the WEBSITE_RUN_FROM_PACKAGE app settings.

Publishing from Visual Studio seems a little buggy. You may want to overwrite this release without a package file to check what this looks like when you edit your Function, but Visual Studio will raise an error and will report that there was *"invalid access to memory location"*. It's still easier than going through your build and release pipelines and I sometimes use it on development environments to quickly test something on Azure (after which I push my changes and release through Azure DevOps).

Deploying using Azure DevOps

The next step is to release your Azure Function through Azure DevOps. The first thing we need to do is get our Visual Studio solution in Git source control. After that, we need to create a build and release pipeline. Let's get started:

1. Browse to your Azure DevOps instance.
2. Create a new repository in your project.
3. Use Visual Studio to connect to your new repository. Your local.settings.json file will be ignored by default, so make sure that you manually add it to source control.
4. Push your solution to the repository.
5. Go to **Pipelines** and select **Builds**.

6. Create a new **Build**.
7. Change the name of your build to **Function App Build**.
8. Select the repository you've just made as a source.
9. Select the .NET Core template.
10. Go to the **Publish** task and turn off **Publish Web Projects**.
11. Go to the **Triggers** tab and select **Enable continuous integration**.
12. **Save & queue** your build, as shown in the following screenshot:

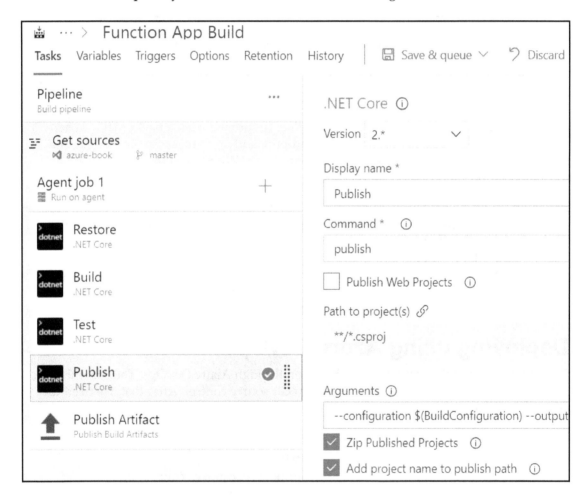

Your build should now start, so wait for it to finish. If everything goes well, your build should pass in a minute or two.

The next step is to create the release pipeline:

1. Go to your release pipelines in Azure DevOps.
2. Create a new release pipeline.
3. Change the name of your release to **Function App Release**.
4. Select the Azure App Service deployment template.
5. Select your build as the artifact source.
6. Change the default version of your artifact to **Latest**.
7. Enable continuous integration on the little lightning icon on **Artifacts**.
8. Go to the **Tasks** tab.
9. Change the **Stage name** to `Development`.
10. Select your **Azure subscription**.
11. Authorize your subscription if you haven't done so already.
12. Change the **App type** to **Function App**.
13. Select your Function App under **App service name**, as shown in the following screenshot:

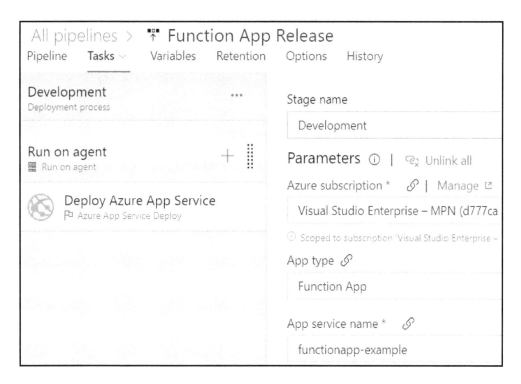

14. Under the Azure App Service Deploy task, under the **Additional Deployment** options, uncheck **Take app offline**. Leaving this option checked can result in deployment failures for Function Apps.

15. Under **Application and Configuration Settings**, add a new app setting with the name **StorageAccount** and your storage account connection string. This is the same setting that's in your `local.settings.json` file; you can make this a secret variable that's different for each environment.

16. Save your release pipeline.

17. Create a new release.

Note that your function is still in read-only mode, but the message as to why has changed: *"Your app is currently in read-only mode because you have source control integration enabled. To change edit mode visit Function app settings."*

Now, upload a blob and see your function in action! If you're not getting an email within a few minutes, check your function's monitor and Application Insights to figure out what's wrong. Before doing anything else, try restarting the Function App.

 You may receive an email from Microsoft saying that there's been some unusual activity on your account. That's true – you're suddenly sending emails from Azure. You can confirm this was you. If you don't want to confirm this, just go to the function monitor and check whether your function was triggered but failed because of an SMTP exception.

Timer triggered functions

So far, we've seen functions triggered by HTTP requests and functions triggered by events, such as a message being queued and a blob being created, but there's another very useful trigger type, which is simply a timer trigger. With a timer, you can execute your function every minute or hour, once a day, on set hours, and on basically any schedule you can think of (with a minimum interval of a minute). Think of nightly cleanup jobs or weekly reporting.

Using the cron syntax

The syntax that's used for timer triggers is called **cron**; it's widely used in Unix-like operating systems and it comes from the Greek word for time, chronos. The syntax is often short, convenient, and very difficult to get right, kind of like regular expressions. There's an easy online tool that can help you figure out your cron expressions: `https://crontab.guru/`.

There are five components in cron – minute, hour, day of the month, month, and day of the week. The asterisk (*) means any value, so the cron expression * * * * * means trigger on any minute, of any hour, on any day, of any month, or, simply put, trigger every minute. 0 0 * * * triggers at minute 0 of hour 0 (so 00:00, or 12 AM) of any day, so that's every day at midnight. 0 8 * * 1-5 triggers every weekday at 8 AM (weekdays go from 0 to 6, or Sunday to Saturday, so 1 - 5 means Monday to Friday).

Expressions can be much more complicated, but let's hope you don't need them.

Now, for the bad news (or good, depending on if you need it): Microsoft decided to add a second component to their cron expressions, so they don't adhere to the standard. As a result, you'll probably add a 0 before all your cron expressions, such as 0 0 8 * * 1-5, which is still every weekday at 8 AM.

Writing a second function

Let's write a second function that triggers every 10 seconds. We can use the */10 syntax, which uses the interval operator. So, that's every 10th second of every minute, every hour, and so on. We're simply going to use a `log` statement and show the next occurrence of the function. The following code goes in the same file as the Blob trigger function:

```
[FunctionName("TimerTrigger")]
public static void DoStuff([TimerTrigger("*/10 * * * * *", RunOnStartup =
true)]TimerInfo myTimer, ILogger log)
{
    log.LogInformation($"I was triggered at
{DateTime.Now.ToLongTimeString()}.");
    log.LogInformation(myTimer.FormatNextOccurrences(1));
}
```

If you enabled continuous integration and deployment, you can simply commit and push the code and Azure DevOps will deploy this code to Azure. You should see two functions now: `Function1` and `TimerTrigger`. You can change those names by changing the value of the `FunctionName` attribute in your code. Wait a few minutes and check out your new function's **Monitor** page. You should see some logs there:

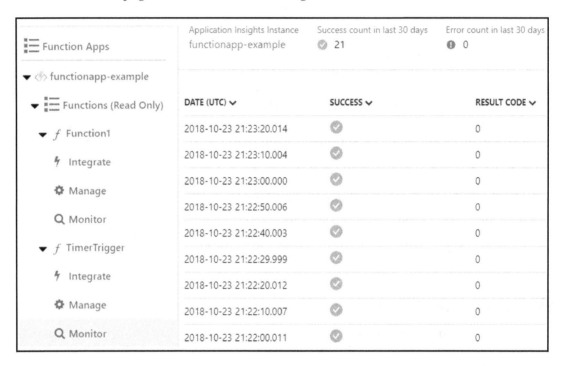

If you don't want your `TimerTrigger` to trigger every 10 seconds, you can disable this from your **Functions** overview, even in read-only mode:

In the next section, we're going to look at bindings, which enable near real-time processing for various events.

Input and output bindings

Another optional but cool feature of Azure Functions are bindings. With bindings, you can bind input and output values to Azure resources. For example, in our first example, we triggered a queue message, which we then wrote to a blob manually. What if I told you we could do this with just a single line of code? In the upcoming section, we'll learn how to add bindings in the portal.

Adding bindings in the portal

You can add bindings in the Azure portal. Create a new Function App (one that isn't in read-only mode) to get started. Now, follow these steps:

1. Create a new function.
2. Pick the Azure Service Bus Queue trigger.
3. Install the extension if you have to.
4. Pick a name for your function or leave it as the default.
5. Select a Service Bus connection or create a new one; you should still have the Service Bus from the previous example.
6. Pick a new queue name so that it doesn't interfere with our previous example (unless you don't have that anymore).
7. When your function has been created, add `return myQueueItem;` to the code:

```
using System;
using System.Threading.Tasks;

public static string Run(string myQueueItem, ILogger log)
{
    log.LogInformation($"C# ServiceBus queue trigger Function
processed message: {myQueueItem}");
    return myQueueItem;
}
```

8. Head over to the **Integrate** menu.
9. At the top right of the screen, click **+ New Output**.
10. Pick **Azure Blob Storage**.
11. On the next screen, install the blob extension if you have to.
12. Check the **Use Function return value** box.

13. Change the **Path** to `outcontainer/{rand-guid}.txt`.
14. Hit the **Save** button:

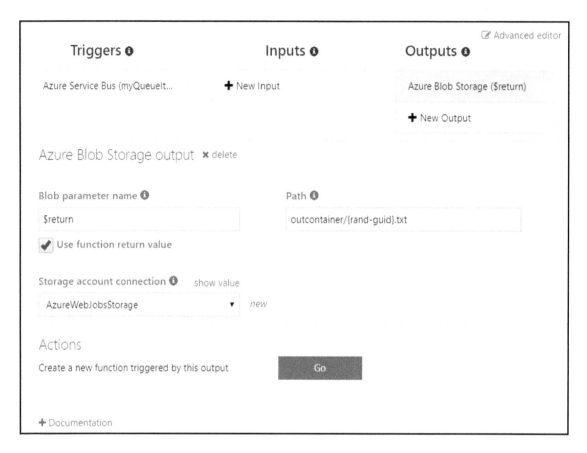

15. Test your function by adding something to the queue. You can use the console app we created earlier in this chapter to do so. If everything went right, you should see a file in the out container of your storage account.

It's also possible to use one or more output parameters using the C# `out` keyword:

1. Go into the **Integrate** menu of your function.
2. In your output, uncheck the **Use Function return value** box.
3. Change the **Blob parameter name** to `myblob`.

4. Add an output parameter to your function and assign it with `myQueueItem`:

```
using System;
using System.Threading.Tasks;

public static void Run(string myQueueItem, ILogger log, out
string myblob)
{
    log.LogInformation($"C# ServiceBus queue trigger Function
processed message: {myQueueItem}");
    myblob = myQueueItem;
}
```

5. Test your function.

Input bindings work pretty much the same way, except it's a bit difficult to add extra information to a triggered function, so here's a contrived example:

1. Go into the **Integrate** menu of your function.
2. At the top of the screen, click **+ New Input**.
3. Pick the Azure Blob Storage.
4. Now, go into your blob storage and pick any (small) text file that's already there.
5. Change the path value to `[your-storage]/[your-filename]`. The content of this file will be passed into your function.
6. Change the code of your function so that it gets the `inputBlob` parameter:

```
using System;
using System.Threading.Tasks;

public static void Run(string myQueueItem, ILogger log, string
inputBlob, out string myblob)
{
    log.LogInformation($"C# ServiceBus queue trigger Function
processed message: {myQueueItem}");
    myblob = $"{myQueueItem} - {inputBlob}";
}
```

7. Finally, test your function.

As you can see, input and output parameters can make life a lot easier.

Adding bindings in Visual Studio

We can do the same in Visual Studio. The following examples are the same as what we did in the portal, but in C# code.

To use a return output, add a return attribute. The following example triggers on a Service Bus queue and outputs a blob file:

```
[FunctionName("WriteFile")]
[return: Blob("outcontainer/{sys.randguid}.txt", FileAccess.Write,
Connection = "StorageAccount")]
public static string WriteFile([ServiceBusTrigger("myqueue", Connection =
"ServiceBus")]string myQueueItem, ILogger log)
{
    log.LogInformation($"C# ServiceBus queue trigger Function processed
message: {myQueueItem}");
    return myQueueItem;
}
```

We can also use the output blob as an output parameter. Notice the out keyword:

```
[FunctionName("WriteFile")]
public static void WriteFile([ServiceBusTrigger("myqueue", Connection =
"ServiceBus")]string myQueueItem, ILogger log,
    [Blob("queue-messages/{sys.randguid}.txt", FileAccess.Write, Connection
= "StorageAccount")]out string myblob)
{
    log.LogInformation($"C# ServiceBus queue trigger Function processed
message: {myQueueItem}");
    myblob = myQueueItem;
}
```

The input parameter is pretty much the same. Again, I'm missing a real value to use on the input parameter, so I'm just using a random text file that's already there:

```
[FunctionName("WriteFile")]
public static void WriteFile([ServiceBusTrigger("myqueue", Connection =
"ServiceBus")]string myQueueItem, ILogger log,
    [Blob("queue-messages/somefile.txt", FileAccess.Read, Connection =
"StorageAccount")]string inputBlob,
    [Blob("queue-messages/{sys.randguid}.txt", FileAccess.Write, Connection
= "StorageAccount")]out string myblob)
{
    log.LogInformation($"C# ServiceBus queue trigger Function processed
message: {myQueueItem}");
    myblob = $"{myQueueItem} - {inputBlob}";
}
```

In the next section, we're going to have a more in-depth look at bindings.

Understanding bindings

In the previous examples, we used a string to represent blob files and Service Bus queue items. The runtime somehow recognizes this and all is well. However, if you use an `int` or a class you've created, things will break. That being said, a string isn't the only thing you can bind to. For example, a blob can be represented by a stream, `TextReader`, `Byte[]`, `CloudBlockBlob`, and more. The same goes for the Service Bus queue item, which could also be a message. This means your function could look as follows:

```
public static void WriteFile2([ServiceBusTrigger("myqueue", Connection =
"ServiceBus")]Message myQueueItem, ILogger log,
    [Blob("queue-messages/somefile.txt", FileAccess.Read, Connection =
"StorageAccount")]Stream inputBlob,
    [Blob("queue-messages/{sys.randguid}.txt", FileAccess.Write, Connection
= "StorageAccount")]out byte[] myblob)
```

The implementation would be completely different, of course. One thing you can do, though, is use the properties of your trigger object in the paths of your input and output parameters. This means you can do something like the following:

```
[FunctionName("WriteFile")]
public static void WriteFile([ServiceBusTrigger("myqueue", Connection =
"ServiceBus")]Message myQueueItem, ILogger log,
    [Blob("queue-messages/{Label}.txt", FileAccess.Read, Connection =
"StorageAccount")]string inputBlob,
    [Blob("queue-messages/{sys.randguid}.txt", FileAccess.Write, Connection
= "StorageAccount")]out string myblob)
{
    log.LogInformation($"C# ServiceBus queue trigger Function processed
message: {myQueueItem}");
    myblob = inputBlob;
}
```

Instead of receiving a string, we're receiving a message object and we're using the label property of that object to find our input blob file.

In the preceding example, we used blobs and Service Bus queues, but there are plenty of other triggers and bindings, such as `CosmosDBTrigger` and the Cosmos DB binding known as `QueueTrigger`, table binding, and so on. Again, the official Microsoft documentation on these subjects is pretty extensive, so I suggest that you have a look at them. They can be found in this chapter's *Further reading* section.

Azure Functions proxies

Another cool but simple feature of Azure Functions is proxies. The **Proxies** menu item is directly under your functions in your Function App. With proxies, you can put a small, lightweight proxy in front of basically anything.

Creating a proxy

To show you that really anything goes, we're going to set up a proxy to `https://www.microsoft.com/en-in/`:

1. Create a new Function App.
2. Go to **Proxies.**
3. Click the **+ New proxy** button.
4. Give your proxy a name, such as `MyFirstProxy`:

5. Define a **Route template**. This is the path after the base URL. Put `myfirstproxy` here.

6. We can also specify which HTTP methods are allowed. Select **Selected methods** and click the **GET** method.

7. The backend URL is the URL that your proxy is actually going to call, so put `https://microsoft.com` here.

8. Hit the **Create** button.

9. Now that the proxy has been created, you'll get your proxy URL, so copy it and enter it in your browser. Check that you'll be taken to `microsoft.com`.

Next, create a new function with an HTTP trigger. You can leave all the defaults as they are. Make sure you copy the URL, including the access code. Now, go to your proxy and change the backend URL to that of your function. You can now access the function with your proxy's URL. The name query parameter is passed to your proxy and passed down to your actual function.

Proxies for testing

One of the cool things about proxies is that you don't need a backend URL. You can create a new proxy and leave the backend URL empty. Instead, look at the response override. For example, suppose you have to call a service to create a customer and the service returns the new customer ID. The problem is, no such service exists yet. With a proxy, you can easily create a mock service that simply returns HTTP code `201` (created) with an ID in the body. Let's take a look at how this works:

1. Create a new proxy.

2. Name it `CreateCustomer`.

3. Set `customers/create` as the root template.

4. For the selected methods, choose `GET` (we're doing this so that we can easily test this in the browser; normally, this would be a `POST`).

5. Open up the response override options.

6. Put `201` in the status code field.

7. Put `{ "id": "123" }` in the body.

8. Test this in the browser. If everything goes well, you should get a JSON with an ID of `123`.

Perhaps a hard-coded ID doesn't cut it and you need something that you can control. To do this, you can reference variables in your body (and in other fields):

1. Replace `123` with `{request.querystring.id}`.
2. Add `?id=321` to your URL in the browser.
3. Again, check that you now get a JSON with an ID of `321`:

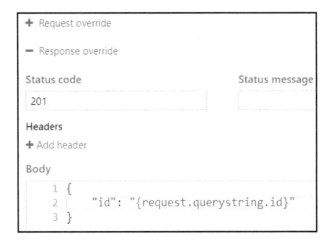

You can use variables in your route template, as well as elsewhere. For example, you can use the `customers/{id}` route template and then return `{ "id": "{id}" }`. Now, if you browse to `/customers/123`, you'll get a JSON with `id 123`.

You can override request query parameters and headers and response headers in the same way. For example, suppose you want to return the text `<p>This is NOT HTML</p>` which, obviously, should not be interpreted as HTML. When you return that value and try it out in your browser, you'll see that `<p>` and `</p>` are not shown and that your value is interpreted as HTML. By adding a `Content-Type` header and giving it the value `text/plain`, your browser will know to just show the body as plain text and not interpret it as HTML.

To reference application settings that have been configured at the Function App level, you can use the `%setting_name%` syntax.

There's also an advanced editor that has all your proxies in JSON format. Using this JSON, you can deploy your proxies just like you can deploy your functions. Simply add a `proxies.json` file to your Visual Studio solution and be sure to set its **Build Action** to **Content** and **Copy to Output Directory** to **Copy always** in the properties.

Best practices

Last but not least, let's consider some best practices when working with Azure Functions. There's plenty more to be said about working with functions, but these are some easy to follow best practices that will help you a great deal when it comes to writing maintainable functions:

- **Use Visual Studio and Azure DevOps**: First, and I cannot stress this enough – if you need more than trivial functions, write them using Visual Studio and source control and deploy them using Azure DevOps. It's quick and easy to set up, so you have no excuses!
- **Avoid long-running Functions**: Functions should be small and lightweight. Larger functions with many dependencies or with lots of code can cause unexpected timeouts. If you have one big function, try splitting it up into many small functions instead. Microsoft even recommends that some HTTP triggers queue the payload, have them handled by another trigger that triggers on the queue, and return a response immediately.
- **Functions should not depend on other Functions**: Functions should interact using triggers, such as blob or queue triggers, not by calling another function directly through HTTP. If you really need functions to communicate with each other, you can use Azure Logic Apps or Durable functions (which were not discussed in the chapter).
- **Your functions should be stateless**: Pass any information that a Function needs to do its job to the Function and make sure it returns the same outcome every time it's called with that same input, regardless of the time of day, the value in a database, or the continent it's running on. If you really need stateful functions, consider using durable functions.
- **Use different Function Apps in different environments**: Don't mix the production and test environments. Your Function Apps, functions, and proxies can be deployed automatically using Azure DevOps, so have a separate deployment for all your environments and make sure your functions are triggered by the right environments.

Summary

In this chapter, we learned about Azure Functions and the serverless architecture and how they can enable an event-driven architecture. We also looked at various types of functions and triggers. Besides writing our own functions, we also deployed functions using Visual Studio and Azure DevOps.

With Azure Functions proxies, we can create lightweight proxies that either route to other backend URLs or that return mock data for testing purposes.

In the next chapter, we're going to look at the various databases Azure has to offer.

Questions

Answer the following questions to test your knowledge on the information that was provided in this chapter. You can find the answers in the *Assessments* section at the end of this book:

1. Which language cannot be used to write Azure Functions in the v2 runtime?
    1. Python
    2. C#
    3. Java
    4. F#
    5. JavaScript

2. Which of the following cannot be used to trigger Azure Functions?
    1. Blob Storage
    2. Cosmos DB
    3. External files
    4. Timer
    5. Microsoft Graph Excel tables
    6. Service Bus
    7. Table storage

3. What isn't possible using proxies?
    1. Limiting allowed HTTP methods
    2. Leaving the backend URL blank
    3. Deploying using Azure DevOps
    4. Using JavaScript for conditional routing
    5. Entering a backend URL from outside your Azure environment
    6. Returning HTML
    7. Overriding headers

Further reading

Check out the following links to find out more about what was covered in this chapter:

- **An introduction to Azure Functions**: `https://docs.microsoft.com/en-us/azure/azure-Functions/Functions-overview`
- **Azure Functions Developers Guide**: `https://docs.microsoft.com/en-us/azure/azure-Functions/Functions-reference`
- **Functions pricing**: `https://azure.microsoft.com/en-us/pricing/details/Functions/`
- **Supported languages in Azure Functions**: `https://docs.microsoft.com/en-us/azure/azure-Functions/supported-languages`
- **Creating your first Function in the Azure portal**: `https://docs.microsoft.com/en-us/azure/azure-Functions/Functions-create-first-azure-Function`
- **Azure Functions' triggers and bindings concepts**: `https://docs.microsoft.com/en-us/azure/azure-Functions/Functions-triggers-bindings`
- **Develop Azure Functions using Visual Studio**: `https://docs.microsoft.com/en-us/azure/azure-Functions/Functions-develop-vs`
- **Timer triggers for Azure Functions**: `https://docs.microsoft.com/en-us/azure/azure-Functions/Functions-bindings-timer`
- **Working with Azure Functions proxies**: `https://docs.microsoft.com/en-us/azure/azure-Functions/Functions-proxies`
- **Optimizing the performance and reliability of Azure Functions**: `https://docs.microsoft.com/en-us/azure/azure-Functions/Functions-best-practices`
- **Durable Functions overview**: `https://docs.microsoft.com/en-us/azure/azure-Functions/durable-Functions-overview`

10
Connecting to the Database

Databases are very important in software. When moving your databases to Azure, you have a few databases to choose from, ranging from traditional SQL databases to NoSQL databases. In this chapter, we're going to look at the various database options that are available to us. When you opt for the Microsoft stack, you'll likely use Azure SQL or Cosmos DB, but databases from other vendors, such as MariaDB and Redis, are also offered as PaaS or IaaS solutions.

The following topics will be covered in this chapter:

- Working with Azure SQL
- Connecting to SQL Server Management Studio
- Connecting to Azure SQL from .NET Core
- Connecting to Azure SQL from Java
- Understanding Cosmos DB
- Working with the MongoDB API
- Working with the Redis cache database

Technical requirements

You will need the following tools to complete the examples in this chapter:

- **SQL Server Management Studio (SSMS):** https://docs.microsoft.com/en-us/sql/ssms/download-sql-server-management-studio-ssms
- **Visual Studio 2017:** https://www.visualstudio.com/downloads/
- **Eclipse 2019:** https://www.eclipse.org/downloads/download.php?file=/technology/epp/downloads/release/2019-09/R/eclipse-java-2019-09-R-linux-gtk-x86_64.tar.gz

The source code for this chapter can be downloaded here: https://github.com/PacktPublishing/Migrating-Apps-to-the-Cloud-with-Azure/tree/master/Chapter10.

Working with Azure SQL

SQL Server is Microsoft's flagship database. It was released almost 30 years ago and it's still going strong today. So, of course, Azure has its own options for running SQL Server databases. The costs for SQL Server databases range from about €4 (basic) to over €18,093 (business-critical 80 vCores and 4 TB), so there should be something between those price ranges that fits your needs.

Picking your version

You have two options when it comes to hosting a SQL Server database in Azure. You either go for Azure SQL Server, which gives you a nice database instance without much hassle, or you host a VM and install SQL Server on that. Azure SQL is a **Platform as a Service (PaaS)** solution, while a VM is an **Infrastructure as a Service (IaaS)** solution. Since the IaaS solution that's installing your database on a VM is basically the same as hosting your own on-premises version of SQL Server, except on a machine running in the cloud, we're not going to talk about that in this chapter. This chapter will focus on PaaS solutions.

If you're looking for IaaS solutions, Azure has plenty of VM images that come with preinstalled (SQL) databases, such as SQL Server 2008 all the way up to the newest release, in different versions such as Standard and Enterprise, and even with different service packs installed. You're not limited to SQL Server either; you can pick images with Oracle, Postgres, MySQL, MongoDB, Neo4j, and plenty of others. The IaaS solution is ideal for a rehost or lift-and-shift migration, as discussed in `Chapter 1`, *Strategies for App Modernization Using Azure*.

When you're looking for a SQL PaaS solution, your options are much more limited. There's Azure Database for MySQL, PostgreSQL, and MariaDB in preview, and then there's Azure SQL, which I'm going to discuss here. I'm not going to discuss all four SQL databases, but if you're interested in MySQL, PostgreSQL, or MariaDB, you can check out the links in the *Further reading* section at the end of this chapter. Azure SQL is not the same as the on-premises version of SQL Server. They share the same engine, but Azure SQL doesn't give you the same type of control that SQL Server gives you. This is inherent to PaaS because you're not controlling the infrastructure, so you don't have access to the underlying OS. That being said, for a lot of databases, the transition will be rather painless. All your SQL code is still supported, after all. As such, migrating to PaaS solutions can usually be done while refactoring, rearchitecting, or rebuilding. See the *Further reading* section at the end of this chapter for a side-by-side feature comparison.

You can also use the **Data Migration Assistant** (**DMA** – see the *Further reading* section), which helps you by looking for compatibility issues, such as unsupported or partially supported features, in your current database and Azure SQL (or any other SQL Server database).

Microsoft recommends hosting SQL Server in a VM for quick migrations to Azure as it closely resembles what you have on-premises. However, there is a third option: the Azure SQL Database Managed Instance. It provides nearly 100% compatibility with the latest Enterprise edition of your on-premises SQL Server. In this chapter, we're not going to use this, though, as it's not (yet) available in all locations or on all subscription types, it's quite expensive (starting at over €1,000), and it can take up to 6 hours to create.

Creating an Azure SQL Database

Creating an Azure SQL Database is surprisingly easy. Follow these steps to do so:

1. Either find your SQL databases or go to **Create a resource** and find **SQL Database**.
2. In the blade that opens, select a subscription.
3. Select or create a resource group.
4. Give the database a name. This is your database, so it doesn't have to be unique across Azure.
5. The next part is a little tricky; we need to create an actual server:
    1. Provide a name for your server; it has to be unique across all of Azure.
    2. Enter the name of your server's admin.
    3. Enter a password that meets the requirements (Azure will show you what those requirements are if you don't meet them).
    4. Confirm the password.
    5. Select a location.
    6. Keep **Allow Azure services to access server** checked. For non-development purposes, it's recommended to uncheck this option as it gives any Azure resource access to your server, even those not in your current subscription.
6. Now, we can go back to the SQL database settings. We don't want an elastic pool right now.

7. The pricing tier is interesting; you can go for the **Basic** tier here, which is already more than we need. I've picked standard with some extra **DTUs**:

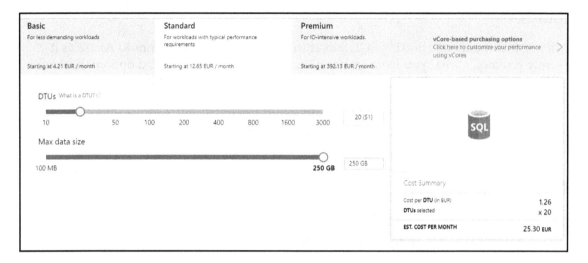

8. Leave the collation.
9. When you have filled everything out, you can click **Create** and the SQL database will be created; this may take a few minutes:

Let's look at the settings that may not be familiar to you. First, there's a server you have to create. Even though Azure SQL is a PaaS solution, you get some control over your server, mostly in terms of backups and security, which will be discussed in `Chapter 12`, *Securing Your Azure Services*, and `Chapter 14`, *Designing for High Availability and Disaster Recovery*.

With a server, you have a set number of resources that you pay for during the month. When you have multiple databases with varying and unpredictable periods of usage, a server may be sitting idle a lot of the time and peaking a few times a day or week. To overcome this problem, Azure introduced SQL elastic pools, which autoscale individual databases within set parameters as necessary. So, databases under light loads consume fewer resources while databases under heavy loads consume more resources. By placing these databases in a pool, you can save costs since they can share resources.

Pricing tiers

The cost of your SQL database depends on two things: the size of your data and the number of DTUs you have. There are three DTU-based tiers: Basic, Standard, and Premium. The Basic tier gives you five DTUs and a maximum of 2 GB of data. A DTU is a bundled measure of compute, storage, and IO resources. Simply put, the more DTUs you have, the more resources you have available and the better your database will perform.

For any serious database load, you should use either the Standard or the Premium database tiers. They cap out at 1 TB of data and 3,000 DTUs and 4 TB of data and 4,000 DTUs, respectively. The maximum amount of storage changes as you select more DTUs. The Premium tier also offers zone redundancy, meaning your database is replicated across availability zones in a single region. `Chapter 14`, *Designing for High Availability and Disaster Recovery*, discusses high availability in more detail.

The Basic, Standard, and Premium tiers offer simple and preconfigured resources at a predictable price. For more flexibility, control, and transparency, there are the vCore-based pricing options (which can be found under **vCore-based purchasing options**, next to **Premium**). Here, there are three new pricing tiers: **General Purpose**, **Hyperscale**, and **Business Critical**. With these tiers, you can choose vCores, which measure compute power, and data storage independently. Each tier has its own **IO operations per second** (**IOPS**) and latency, which are included in the DTUs on the other tiers. What's very interesting, however, is the serverless offering, which is priced based on usage. This tier offers you the option to auto-pause your database after a certain time of inactivity, during which you only pay for storage but not for computing power. The database (and billing) resumes automatically when activity occurs. Finally, these tiers also allow you to use Azure Hybrid Benefit, which allows you to save costs by **Bringing Your Own License** (**BYOL**).

Using your database in the portal

It's time to start using our Azure SQL instance. Find your SQL databases in the Azure portal and go to the Query editor (which is in preview at the time of writing). You'll need to log in using the admin user and password that you used when creating the server. Using **Active Directory Single Sign-On** (**AD SSO**) is supported, but is not in the scope of this chapter. Once you're logged in, you can create, save, open, and run queries, and you can edit data. The first thing we're going to do here is run a query to create a table. So, run the following query:

```
CREATE TABLE dbo.Person
(
    Id int NOT NULL IDENTITY (1, 1),
    FirstName nvarchar(255) NOT NULL,
    LastName nvarchar(255) NOT NULL,
    PRIMARY KEY (Id)
)
```

If you're used to SSMS, don't hit *F5* as this will only refresh your browser. Instead, click the **Run** button:

Now that we have created a table, we can put some data in it. Go to **Edit Data (Preview)**, acknowledge that this is a preview feature (if that's still applicable), and enter some data by clicking **Create New Row**, entering data, and clicking **Save**:

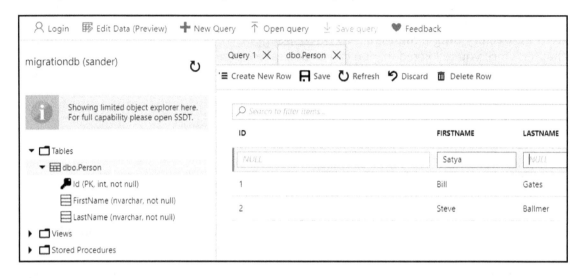

Besides **Tables**, you can also view **Views** and **Stored Procedures** in the portal. You can add a **View** and a **Stored Procedure** using the following code:

```
CREATE VIEW PersonView
AS
(
  SELECT Id
    ,FirstName
    ,LastName
  FROM Person
)

GO

CREATE PROCEDURE GetPerson
(
  @Id INT
)
AS
BEGIN
    SET NOCOUNT ON

  SELECT Id
    ,FirstName
    ,LastName
```

```
    FROM Person
    WHERE Id = @Id
END
```

While you can't do anything with **Views** or **Stored Procedures** from the portal, you can check that they actually work by simply executing a new query. Unlike SSMS, the portal can't show multiple result windows, so you'll have to execute the following SQL queries in separate query windows:

```
SELECT * FROM PersonView
EXEC [dbo].[GetPerson] @Id = 3
```

All in all, the portal provides you with a very basic experience and we need more sophisticated tools to do any real development in Azure SQL.

Connecting to SQL Server Management Studio

As it says right there in the portal, the query editor is pretty limited and we should use **SQL Server Data Tools** (**SSDT**) instead. We aren't going to do that, though; instead, we're going to use SSMS. So, download SSMS if you haven't done so already (this can be found in the *Technical requirements* section at the beginning of this chapter) and fire it up. In the **Connect to Server** dialog, enter your server name, which you can find in your SQL Server's (not your SQL database's) properties and should be `[name you choose].database.windows.net`, and the login and password that you used when you created your server.

Now, you should see a popup that asks you to sign in to Azure – do that now. Then, another popup will ask you whether you want to allow your IP address or your subnet range to connect to your server. Do that too. Make sure you're not adding a public IP address, by the way, such as the one from the free Wi-Fi at your local Starbucks:

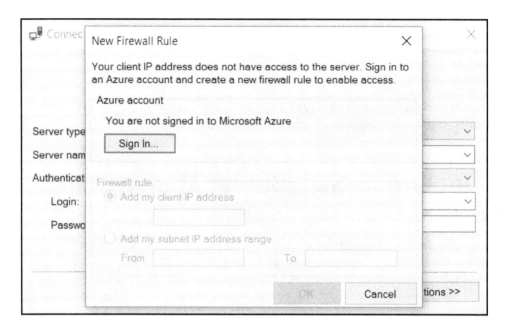

If you get an error, just like I did, you can also do this manually in the Azure portal. Copy the IP address from the SSMS popup, go to your SQL Server, and find **Firewalls and virtual networks** in the menu. Once there, create a new rule. Name it something like [your name] [your location] IP, fill in your IP address in the **START IP** and **END IP** boxes, and click the **Save** button:

If you try to connect using SSMS again, you should have no problems this time.

You should now see your **Object Explorer** as you're used to, but with some differences. Most notably, my development SQL Server environment shows me 10 folders, while Azure SQL Server only shows two: `Databases` and `Security`. We are missing the menu item management, the **SQL Server Agent**, **XEvent Profiler**, and other items. As I mentioned previously, these items can be made available to you using VMs or Managed Instances. For Azure SQL, you'll mostly be looking at other options in the Azure portal or for workarounds, such as sending emails with logic apps and SendGrid or lifting your **SQL Server Integration Services** (**SSIS**) packages to Azure with data factories:

Moving all your use cases is not in the scope of this book, but if you're using such services, make sure you have an acceptable alternative before moving to Azure. Other than that, you can now write queries; edit data; create tables, stored procedures, functions, and views; and do everything in your database that you could when using an on-premises SQL Server.

Connecting to Azure SQL from .NET Core

For developers, connecting to a SQL database in Azure works exactly the same as connecting to an on-premises SQL Server instance. We can use good old ADO.NET or Entity Framework for this. The following two examples assume you've created the `Person` table and inserted some data, as described in the previous section.

Connecting using ADO.NET

Let's make a connection and print our data using ADO.NET. Create a new .NET Core console application using Visual Studio 2017. In .NET Core, it's necessary to install the `System.Data.SqlClient` package using NuGet. This package contains the necessary classes, such as `SqlConnection` and `SqlCommand`, which have been around since the very first version of .NET:

```
using System;
using System.Data;
using System.Data.SqlClient;

namespace AzureSqlConnectionConsole
{
    internal class Program
    {
        private static void Main(string[] args)
        {
            using (SqlConnection connection = new
SqlConnection("Server=tcp:[your server].database.windows.net,1433;" +
                "Initial Catalog=migrationdb;Persist Security Info=False;"
+
                "User ID=[your username];Password=[your password];" +
"MultipleActiveResultSets=False;Encrypt=True;TrustServerCertificate=False;C
onnection Timeout=30;"))
                using (SqlCommand command = new SqlCommand("SELECT Id,
FirstName, LastName FROM Person", connection))
                {
                    connection.Open();
                    using (SqlDataReader reader =
command.ExecuteReader(CommandBehavior.CloseConnection))
                    {
                        while (reader.Read())
                        {
                            Console.WriteLine($"{reader["Id"]} -
{reader["FirstName"]} {reader["LastName"]}");
                        }
                    }
                }
            Console.WriteLine("Press any key to continue.");
            Console.ReadKey();
        }
    }
}
```

This code connects to the database, executes the SELECT command, and prints the results to the console window. You can find your connection string in the Azure portal. In your database, find the **Connection** strings menu item and copy the ADO.NET connection string. Next to ADO.NET, you'll find JDBC, ODBC, and PHP connections. Be sure to replace your server, username, and password in the previous example, or just your username and password in the connection string from the Azure portal.

Connecting using Entity Framework Core

Another option you can use to connect to your Azure SQL Database is using **Entity Framework (EF)**. Create another .NET Core console application and install the Microsoft.EntityFrameworkCore.SqlServer package using NuGet. EF Core only supports code-first, although you can scaffold existing databases. This basically means that you'll need all your tables, views, and stored procedures in code as well. The downside is obviously that this is a bit of work, although scaffolding does this for you. The upside to this is that you'll always be able to generate your database from code. This allows you to use migrations, which incrementally build your database from code. For the first example, let's simply recreate the previous example using EF:

```
using Microsoft.EntityFrameworkCore;
using System;
using System.Linq;

namespace AzureSqlEntityFrameworkConnection
{
    internal class Program
    {
        private static void Main(string[] args)
        {
            using (var context = new MigrationDbContext())
            {
                var persons = context.Person.ToList();
                foreach (Person p in persons)
                {
                    Console.WriteLine($"{p.Id} - {p.FirstName}
{p.LastName}");
                }
            }
        }
    }

    internal class MigrationDbContext : DbContext
    {
        protected override void OnConfiguring(DbContextOptionsBuilder
```

```
optionsBuilder)
        {
            optionsBuilder.UseSqlServer("Server=tcp:[your
server].database.windows.net,1433;" +
                "Initial Catalog=migrationdb;Persist Security Info=False;"
+
                "User ID=[your username];Password=[your password];" +
"MultipleActiveResultSets=False;Encrypt=True;TrustServerCertificate=False;C
onnection Timeout=30;");
            base.OnConfiguring(optionsBuilder);
        }

        public virtual DbSet<Person> Person { get; set; }
    }
}
```

Again, don't forget to replace your server, username, and password.
`MigrationDbContext` represents our database in code. As you can see, it has a
`DbSet<Person>`, which maps to the `Person` table in our database. We can now query the
database using simple and strongly typed LINQ queries.

Entity Framework migrations

One very awesome feature of EF is **migrations**, which allow you to write your code and
then automatically generate your database accordingly. So, let's add another table to the
database using migrations.

Before we do anything, we need to install the `Microsoft.EntityFrameworkCore.Tools`
package using NuGet. After that, we need to tell EF that we've already created the `Person`
table so that it doesn't try to create it all over again. Go into the package manager console
and run the following command:

Add-Migration InitialCreate

This creates a folder in your project called `migrations` and adds a file named
`[date_and_time]_InitialCreate.cs`. Open this file and empty the `Up` and `Down`
methods. Now, EF won't try to create (or remove) the `Person` table. If it did, it would fail
because we already created it manually. Now, you can update the database using the
`Update-Database` command in the package manager console. This will create the
`dbo.__EFMigrationsHistory` table in your database, which stores which migrations ran
on the database.

Now, let's add the `Address` table to the database and give the `Person` class a foreign key relationship to `Address`. Instead of writing SQL queries or managing the tables using SSMS, we're going to write some code:

```
internal class Person
{
    public int Id { get; set; }
    public string FirstName { get; set; }
    public string LastName { get; set; }

    public int? AddressId { get; set; }
    public Address Address { get; set; }
}

internal class Address
{
    public int Id { get; set; }
    public string Street { get; set; }
    public string Number { get; set; }
    public string Postalcode { get; set; }
    public string City { get; set; }
    public string Country { get; set; }
}
```

Migrations automatically figure out dependencies between classes, so you don't have to add `Address` to `MigrationDbContext` for it to be generated. Run `Add-Migration` and `Update-Database` again to update your database:

```
Add-Migration AddPersonAddress
Update-Database
```

One thing I don't like is how migrations map your tables to `DbSets` in your `DbContext`. We probably want our table to be named `Address` while we want our C# property to be named `Addresses` (depending on your naming conventions in SQL Server). Also, we can see that all of our string properties are created as `nvarchar(max)`, which is also not what we want. We can change this behavior (and a lot more) by overriding `OnModelCreating`:

```
internal class MigrationDbContext : DbContext
{
    protected override void OnConfiguring(DbContextOptionsBuilder
optionsBuilder)
    {
        // ...
    }

    protected override void OnModelCreating(ModelBuilder modelBuilder)
```

```
        {
            modelBuilder.Entity<Person>().ToTable(nameof(Person));
            var addressTable =
    modelBuilder.Entity<Address>().ToTable(nameof(Address));
            addressTable.Property(a =>
    a.Street).HasColumnType("nvarchar(255)");
            // [...]
        }

        public virtual DbSet<Person> Persons { get; set; }
        public virtual DbSet<Address> Addresses { get; set; }
    }
```

Using `ToTable()`, we can explicitly name the table of our entity. With `Property()`, we can set options on the properties of our entity, such as the column type with `HasColumnType()`. These are new changes we're making to our database, so you should run `Add-Migration` again:

Add-Migration ChangeAddressTypes

We're not going to run `Update-Database` this time, though. Instead, we're going to automatically have our software update our database when we run the program. We can do this using `context.Database.Migrate()`:

```
private static void Main(string[] args)
{
    using (var context = new MigrationDbContext())
    {
        context.Database.Migrate();
        var persons = context.Persons.ToList();
        // ...
```

This is a very cool feature that always updates your database to the latest version. However, as you can imagine, this may cause trouble, such as when you try to update the schema of a table with GBs of data or when your change would delete data. So, be careful with this option.

Other than that, you can run the migration commands from the CLI, which also means you can run them during your deployment pipeline. The .NET Core CLI tool has a slightly different syntax, but it's the recommended method for your pipelines:

dotnet ef migrations add MyMigration
dotnet ef database update

There are other options, such as removing a migration, reverting to a previous version, and including data in your migrations. Use the following command to remove or revert to a previous migration:

```
Update-Database SomePreviousMigration
Remove-Migration
```

People tend to have very strong opinions on migrations since they can update your database unattended, and that's a risk. Be aware of the pros and cons and use them wisely. They can be valuable when it comes to managing your database updates.

Connecting to Azure SQL from Java

For developers, connecting to a SQL database in Azure works exactly the same as connecting to an on-premises SQL Server instance. We can use JDBC or JPA. The following two examples assume that you've created the `Person` table and inserted some data, as described in the previous section.

Connecting using JDBC

Let's make a connection and print our data using JDBC. Create a new Gradle project using Eclipse. Gradle simplifies dependency management for our examples. In this case, it will manage the **Microsoft JDBC Driver for SQL**. Update the `build.gradle` file, as shown here:

```
apply plugin: 'java-library'

repositories {
    jcenter()
}

dependencies {
    runtime 'com.microsoft.sqlserver:mssql-jdbc:7.0.0.jre8'
}
```

Now, create a public class called `AzureSqlConsoleApp`, as shown here:

```
package com.packtpub.azure

// [...]

public class AzureSqlConsoleApp {
    public static void main(String args[]) {
```

```
        // [...]
        String url =
String.format("jdbc:sqlserver://%s:1433;database=%s;user=%s;password=%s;enc
rypt=true;hostNameInCertificate=*.database.windows.net;loginTimeout=30;",
hostName, databaseName, userName, password);

        try (Connection con = DriverManager.getConnection(url)) {
            String sql = "SELECT Id, FirstName, LastName FROM Person";

            try (PreparedStatement stmt = con.prepareStatement(sql)) {
                ResultSet rs = stmt.executeQuery();

                while(rs.next()) {
                    System.out.println(String.format("%s - %s %s",
                        rs.getString("Id"), rs.getString("FirstName"),
rs.getString("LastName")));
                }

                System.out.println("Press any key to continue...");
                System.in.read();
            }
        }
         catch(Exception e) {
             e.printStackTrace();
        }

    }
}
```

This code connects to the database, executes the SELECT command, and prints the results to the console window. You can find your connection string in the Azure portal. In your database, find the **connection string's** menu item and copy the JDBC connection string. Next to JDBC, you'll find ADO.NET, ODBC, and PHP connections. Be sure to replace your server, username, and password in the preceding example, or just your username and password in the connection string from the Azure portal.

Connecting using JPA

Another option when it comes to connecting to your Azure SQL Database is using JPA. Create another Gradle project and configure Gradle, as shown here:

```
apply plugin: 'java-library'

repositories {
    jcenter()
```

```
    }

dependencies {
    implementation 'org.hibernate:hibernate-entitymanager:5.3.7.Final'
    runtime 'com.microsoft.sqlserver:mssql-jdbc:7.0.0.jre8'
}
```

Create an `Entity` class to represent a `Person`:

```
package com.packtpub.azure

import javax.persistence.Id;
import javax.persistence.Table;

@Entity
@Table(name = "Person")
public class Person {
    @Id
    @Column(name = "Id")
    private Integer id;

    // [...]

    public Integer getId() {
        return id;
    }

    public Person setId(Integer id) {
        this.id = id;
        return this;
    }

    // [...]
}
```

Now we will recreate the previous example using JPA:

```
package com.packtpub.azure

import java.util.List;

import javax.persistence.EntityManager;
import javax.persistence.EntityManagerFactory;
import javax.persistence.Persistence;
import javax.persistence.TypedQuery;

public class AzureSqlConsoleApp {
    public static void main(String args[]) {
```

```
        EntityManagerFactory factory =
            Persistence.createEntityManagerFactory("jpa-
example");
        EntityManager manager = factory.createEntityManager();

        manager.getTransaction().begin();

        TypedQuery<Person> query =
            manager.createQuery("select p from Person p",
Person.class)

        List<Person> list = query.getResultList();

        for(Person person : list) {
            System.out.println(String.format("%s - %s %s",
                person.getId(),
                person.getFirstName(),
                person.getLastName()));
        }

        manager.getTransaction().commit();
        manager.close();
        factory.close();

        System.out.println("Press any key to continue...");
        try {
            System.in.read();
        }
        catch(Exception e) {
            e.printStackTrace();
        }
    }
}
```

Finally, we will add the JPA configuration to `META-INF/persistence.xml`:

```
<persistence
    xmlns="http://xmlns.jcp.org/xml/ns/persistence"
    xmlns:xsi="http://www.w3.org/2001/XMLSchema-instance"
xsi:schemaLocation="http://xmlns.jcp.org/xml/ns/persistence
http://xmlns.jcp.org/xml/ns/persistence/persistence_2_1.xsd"
    version="2.1">
    <persistence-unit name="jpa-example" transaction-
type="RESOURCE_LOCAL">
<provider>org.hibernate.jpa.HibernatePersistenceProvider</provi
der>
        <properties>
            <property name="javax.persistence.jdbc.url"
```

```
value="jdbc:sqlserver://your_server_name.database.windows.net:1
433;database=your_database;encrypt=true;hostNameInCertificate=*
.database.windows.net;loginTimeOut=30;"/>
        <property name="javax.persistence.jdbc.user"
                value="your_user_name"/>
    <!-- ... -->
</properties>
</persistence-unit>
</persistence>
```

Now that we have set up JPA, we can query and update our database using strongly typed JPA queries.

Understanding Cosmos DB

Besides SQL databases, Azure has some **Not Only SQL** (**NoSQL**) options, with Cosmos DB being Microsoft's very own solution. Cosmos DB is only available in the cloud and no on-premises version currently exists. Like Azure SQL, Cosmos DB is a PaaS solution. The cool thing about Cosmos DB is that it has APIs for all the major NoSQL models out there: the key-value model, the document model, the graph model, and the wide column model.

The Cosmos DB document API matches the popular MongoDB database API and the wide column API matches the Apache Cassandra database API, meaning that you can easily move those databases to Cosmos DB and your software will continue to work. Additionally, Cosmos DB has a SQL API. This doesn't mean your data is stored in a relational model; it simply means that a SQL layer was added over a document database. While Cosmos DB has different APIs available, the underlying database is the same, meaning that no matter what API you pick, you'll always enjoy the benefits of Cosmos DB, which are global distribution, elastic scaling of throughput and storage, extremely low read and write latencies, guaranteed high availability, and 99.9% uptime SLAs. The Cosmos DB engine is **Atom-Record-Sequence** (**ARS**)-based, which allows it to efficiently translate and project data to the different database models: key-value, document, graph, and wide column.

While NoSQL has a few common models, no NoSQL database is the same. With relational databases, you at least had SQL as a shared standard, but NoSQL has no such thing. However, all these databases solve problems that relational SQL databases weren't able to address, most notably speed and flexibility. While SQL databases are well suited for most business needs and have been the default for a few decades now, large SQL databases tend to get a little slow. In certain use cases, SQL isn't even an option; for example, when working with billions of records and finding links between them. Think of contact recommendations by sites such as Facebook and LinkedIn, who know your contacts and the contacts of your contacts, and their contacts too. A graph database, such as Neo4j or Cosmos DB's Gremlin API, is much better suited for such jobs. Also, making schema changes to large tables in SQL databases can be problematic since all the records in that table have to be updated. With a lot of NoSQL databases, this isn't a problem since many are schemaless.

In the upcoming sections, we're going to take a look at the different APIs Cosmos DB has to offer. Because there is no standard for working with NoSQL databases, every API has its own implementation, which is often nothing like the other APIs. Because space in this chapter is limited, we'll only use the MongoDB API in a .NET Core application.

The key-value model/Table API

The key-value model is a pretty simple model. In fact, you've probably used a similar construction countless times. It's really just a dictionary (or map, as it's called in some languages). They have a key and an associated value. In traditional key-value stores, data can only be queried with a key, but it has super performance and is highly scalable. The primary keys when using the Table API are the `PartitionKey` and a `RowKey`; they have to be unique.

The Table API can query on other properties as well and all are automatically indexed as secondary indexes. Next to having a super-fast lookup on all your properties, Cosmos DB guarantees less than 10 milliseconds of latency for reads and less than 15 milliseconds of latency for writes anywhere in the world. So, simply put, the Table API, while not very sophisticated for data storage, is all about performance and super-fast reads and writes.

The document model/MongoDB API

The document model database is probably the most applicable and most popular of the NoSQL databases and closely resembles traditional SQL databases. As the name implies, document databases store documents – not Word or Excel documents, but rather objects, like you would have in your C# code. Each document has a key and properties, such as strings, integers, arrays of values, and even other documents. Thinking in SQL terms, the biggest difference between designing document databases and SQL databases is the lack of foreign key constraints. In document databases, you have to denormalize data.

Imagine modeling a company with employees. In SQL, you'd create a `Company` table and an `Employee` table, perhaps with a table in-between, linking the two. In a document database, you'd have a `companies` collection (the document version of a table) that has a property, `employees`, with a value of an array of documents that resemble employees. Now, if you add a `SalesOrder` table in SQL, `SalesPerson` would be an ID with a foreign key constraint to the `Employee` table. In a document database, a `SalesOrder` document simply has a `salesPerson` property with an employee document as a value. This means you have **the same** employee in your `companies` collection and in your `salesOrders` collection. If that employee has multiple orders, you'll have the same employee multiple times in your `salesOrders` collection.

Your ultimate design may look as follows:

In a document database, this could look a little different. This is actual data, and not so much a diagram:

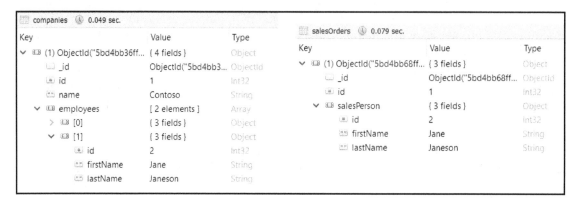

As you can see, Jane Janeson is stored in the `employees` array and in the `salesPerson` property as an object.

The idea behind this is that storing redundant data costs space on your hard disk, which is cheap, while making all those computations to join `Company` with `Employee` and `Order` with `Employee` is much more costly and doesn't scale as well as in GBs. In document stores, the need to **join** collections is minimized.

Another very big difference between SQL and document databases is that document databases are schemaless. In a SQL database, you know that an `Employee` has a `FirstName` and a `LastName`. You also know that every record in the `Employee` table is an actual employee. In a document database, you can have an `Employees` collection and only half of the documents can have a `LastName` because `FirstName` was added at a later time. Not even all the documents would have to be an employee; nothing's stopping you from adding companies to the `Employees` collection. The cons are obvious; the pro, however, is that you never need downtime to update your database schema. Just store an additional property with the new release and everything will work.

In MongoDB, data is stored in Binary JSON, or BSON, and when working with the MongoDB API, you're also working with JSON. Because MongoDB is a popular database that's widely used. We're going to work with this API later in this chapter.

The SQL API

Cosmos DB provides a SQL layer over a document database. The data is stored in collections as JSON, just like they are with MongoDB. However, retrieving that data can be done using SQL queries instead of MongoDB JavaScript objects. That being said, SQL is not entirely what you're used to. While most of it looks the same, some operators, such as LIKE, are not supported. Because we're still dealing with a schemaless JSON database, other functions have been introduced. For example, STARTSWITH, ENDSWITH, and CONTAINS make up for the lack of the LIKE operator, while IS_DEFINED checks whether a property has been defined on a document:

```
1  SELECT * FROM c
2  WHERE STARTSWITH (c.firstName, 'S')
```

Results   Query Stats

1 - 2

```
[
    {
        "id": "2",
        "firstName": "Steve",
        "lastName": "Ballmer",
        "_rid": "+85PALmJuRYGAAAAAAAAAA==",
        "_self": "dbs/+85PAA==/colls/+85PALmJuRY=/docs/+85PALmJuRYGAAAAAAAAAA==/",
        "_etag": "\"0000b2a8-0000-0000-0000-5bd611540000\"",
        "_attachments": "attachments/",
        "_ts": 1540755796
    },
    {
        "id": "3",
        "firstName": "Satya",
        "lastName": "Nadella",
        "company": "Microsoft",
        "_rid": "+85PALmJuRYHAAAAAAAAAA==",
        "_self": "dbs/+85PAA==/colls/+85PALmJuRY=/docs/+85PALmJuRYHAAAAAAAAAA==/",
        "_etag": "\"0000b5a8-0000-0000-0000-5bd612450000\"",
        "_attachments": "attachments/",
        "_ts": 1540756037
    }
]
```

All your documents can be queried through an HTTP-based RESTful API. For example, to get a document, you can use the following C# code:

```
Document document = await
client.ReadDocumentAsync(UriFactory.CreateDocumentUri(DatabaseId,
CollectionId, id));
```

Alternatively, you can use the following Java code:

```
ResourceResponse<Document> response =
    client.readDocument(documentLink, options);

Document document = response.getResource();
```

The best part about this is that Microsoft really put some effort into this. If you create a new Cosmos DB account with the SQL API (see the example in the next section), you can go to the **Quickstart** menu, click **Add a collection**, and then download a sample app that works out of the box with your connection strings and everything. Since we won't be discussing the SQL API in this chapter any further, its recommended that you take a look at it!

The graph model/Gremlin API

In the graph model database, data is stored in graphs, with vertices (or nodes; vertex is the singular term), edges, and properties to represent your data. A graph is a mathematical structure and you probably know of them, even if not formally. While I'm not going to go into graph theory here, you can think of a graph as objects that are connected by certain relationships. For example, John and Mary are two people, or objects, that are connected by a relationship such as *married* or *coworkers*, or maybe both. Social networks such as Facebook and LinkedIn heavily rely on graph theory to model their data.

Let's consider the example from the Microsoft Gremlin API introduction page:

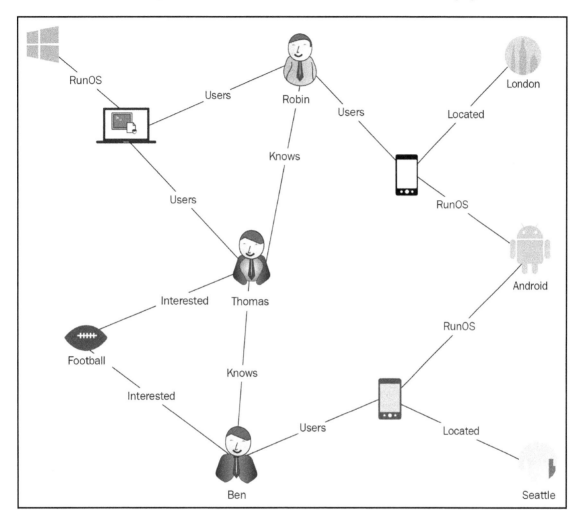

In this graph, the vertices are **Ben**, **Thomas**, **Robin**, their devices, interests, and locations. The edges are the lines between them. They describe the relationship between vertices. For example, **Ben** knows **Thomas** and **Ben** is interested in **Football**. Properties can be anything on a relationship or a vertex. The people and locations have name properties. Other than that, you could store a person's date of birth and a location's coordinates.

Now, let's say you want to know Ben's second-degree contacts. In a SQL database, you'd probably have a `Person` table and a table combining one person with another, so you'd have to query on the combination table, then join on `Person` again, second-degree join on the combination table, and then join the second-degree `Person`. There's no easy way to do this in SQL. What's worse is that this solution doesn't scale at all and when you want to know third- or fourth-degree relations, SQL has serious performance issues (I'm talking minutes here). Now, let's look at the graph; all we need to do is start with Ben and walk along the edges. We quickly find Thomas, so we walk along his edges too and find Robin. This scales really well and even with big datasets, going three or four levels deep takes a matter of seconds.

The wide-column model/Cassandra API

The wide column model has tables, rows, and columns, like a SQL database. They differ from relational systems in that the names and types of columns can differ from row to row in the same table. This last statement is no longer true for Cassandra and tables now have a fixed schema. In that sense, the Table API is more like a wide column model than Cassandra, while Cassandra is more like a key-value store. Cassandra (and Cosmos DB) is still highly scalable and fault-tolerant because it was designed as a distributed system to provide high availability and low latency. The Microsoft documentation for Cassandra is short and the Cassandra documentation is full of to-dos, so unless you have a really good reason to use wide column data stores, there is no real reason to get into it at this point.

Working with the MongoDB API

So, let's get started with the MongoDB API. First, we need to create a Cosmos DB instance in the Azure portal:

1. Either find Azure Cosmos DB in the menu or go to **Create a resource** and find **Cosmos DB**.
2. The blade that opens is a bit different than what we're used to. First, you have to select a subscription.
3. Select or create a resource group.
4. Fill out a name for your account; this has to be unique across all of Azure.
5. Select the API you want to use; in this example, we want to use MongoDB.
6. Pick your location.
7. Leave **Geo-Redundancy** and **Multi-region Writes** disabled.
8. When you have everything filled out, you can click **Review + create**. This will take you to the **Summary** tab. Alternatively, you can click the **Next: Network** button instead, which will take you to the **Network** tab.
9. On the **Network** tab, you can create a virtual network, which allows Azure resources to securely communicate with each other, other (on-premises) networks, and the internet. Chapter 12, *Securing Your Azure Services*, discusses virtual networks in more detail. Creating a virtual network is optional and you can simply click the **Next: Tags** button.
10. On the **Tags** tab, you can assign tags to your resources, which allow you to categorize resources by tag and view billing by category. Again, this is optional and you can continue without it.
11. You'll end up on the **Summary** tab once more.

12. Review the **Summary** tab and hit the **Create** button. This will create a Cosmos DB instance with a MongoDB API. This can take a few minutes, especially if you've also created the virtual network:

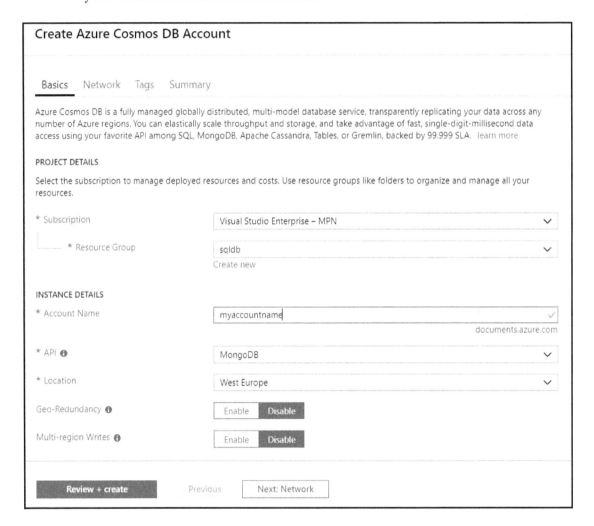

In the next section, we're going to work with MongoDB in the Azure portal.

Working with MongoDB in the Azure portal

Find your Cosmos DB account in the portal. Two menu items are pretty useful when working with Cosmos DB, which are quick start and data explorer. The quick start menu item often lists some code that helps you get started with connecting from C#. Data explorer, as the name implies, allows you to see and edit your data. MongoDB stores its documents in **BSON** format, or **Binary JSON**. Luckily, we get to see regular JSON instead of the binary variant. Fortunately, I still have the companies and salesOrders example, so we can see how data is stored:

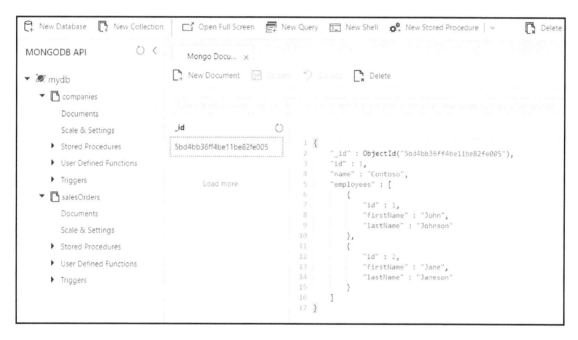

As you can see, each document has a generated _id property. The documents are just JSON objects. It's also possible to query data, although it's not always clear which collection you're querying. Select the salesOrders collection and open a **New Query** window (from the top menu). We can find all the orders where the sales person's first name equals Jane:

```
{ "salesPerson.firstName": { $eq: "Jane" } }
```

MongoDB features rich query capabilities that allow you to filter on any type, query arrays, and use regular expressions and other functions, such as aggregate functions.

There are more sophisticated tools around that you can use to manage your data in MongoDB. Personally, I use Robo 3T (formerly Robomongo), which you can download for free at `https://robomongo.org/`.

Working with MongoDB from C#

Working with MongoDB using .NET Core isn't all that difficult either. Create a new console application and install the `MongoDB.Driver` package using NuGet:

```csharp
using MongoDB.Bson;
using MongoDB.Driver;
using System;
using System.Collections.Generic;

namespace CosmosMongoDbConnection
{
    internal class Program
    {
        private static void Main(string[] args)
        {
            var client = new
MongoClient("mongodb://migrationsdocdb:rdnkUFEE41B6TyRYRnnudmvoDYkPzULclKsT
cJYPsSNNN6R4CyMjB0pKIAvh8oybIT6zDy8ZNqHtpy8j56Gswg==@migrationsdocdb.docume
nts.azure.com:10255/?ssl=true&replicaSet=globaldb");
            IMongoDatabase db = client.GetDatabase("somedb");
            IMongoCollection<Person> collection =
db.GetCollection<Person>("people");
            collection.InsertOne(new Person
            {
                // [...]
            });
            var people = collection.Find(_ => true).ToList();
            foreach (var p in people)
            {
                Console.WriteLine($"{p.Id} - {p.FirstName} {p.LastName} -
{string.Join(',', p.Interests)}");
            }
        }
    }
}
```

I'll explain the code line by line:

1. First, we create a new `MongoClient` and pass our connection string, which you can get from the portal, to the constructor. Be sure to replace the connection string with your own.
2. Next, we get a reference to the database using `client.GetDatabase("somedb")`.
   MongoDB will automatically create the database if it doesn't exist.
3. Then, we do the same for the collection using `db.GetCollection<Person>("people")`.

   Again, the collection is automatically created if it doesn't exist. The documents we are trying to get using this collection will be automatically cast to `Person` objects. However, since MongoDB is schemaless, we can't be sure all the documents have those exact properties.

4. Using `collection.InsertOne`, we can insert a `Person` object. While MongoDB is schemaless, C# isn't, so we have to pass in a `Person` object.
5. The ID on `Person` is of the `MongoDB.Bson.ObjectId` type. This tells MongoDB that this is our ID and that MongoDB can create a value. You can pick another type for the ID, but you'll have to set your own value.
6. Then, we get all our documents from the collection using `collection.Find` and pass in a predicate that always returns true (which means every document passes our search criteria).
7. Finally, we list the results and close the application.

When we insert some extra documents into the database, we can see the actual filter in action. We can use the filter builder to build filters:

```
collection.InsertMany(new[]
{
    new Person
    {
        FirstName = "Steve",
        LastName = "Ballmer",
        // [...]
    },
    // [...]
});

Console.WriteLine();

var builder = new FilterDefinitionBuilder<Person>();
```

```
var definition = builder.AnyEq(p => p.Interests, "Being rich");
people = collection.Find(definition).ToList();
foreach (var p in people)
{
    Console.WriteLine($"{p.Id} - {p.FirstName} {p.LastName} -
{string.Join(',', p.Interests)}");
}
```

With the MongoDB driver for .NET Core, we can do much more, such as filter records, use aggregates, insert bulk data, delete records, create indexes, execute stored procedures, and many other things.

Notice how collections and even databases are generated on the fly. With Azure SQL, we had to define our schema upfront and either run our scripts to update the schema or use migrations (either using the CLI or by auto-updating in code), which risked us locking the database if we changed the schema of large tables. With MongoDB, we don't have to worry about this anymore. You can insert any document into any collection in any database. Of course, you have to make sure your object serializes correctly. Imagine that we're adding two new fields to our `Person` class: `DateOfBirth` and `JoinDate`. Obviously, the documents that already exist don't have these properties, so we need to make sure they get reasonable default values in C#:

```
internal class Person
{
    public ObjectId Id { get; set; }
    public string FirstName { get; set; }
    public string LastName { get; set; }
    public List<string> Interests { get; set; }
    public DateTime? DateOfBirth { get; set; } // Defaults to null
    public DateTime JoinDate { get; set; } // Defaults to 01-01-0001
}
```

Whether you want to default to `null` or to January 1, year 1, is up to you. The same goes for other types, such as `int` and `int?` or `bool` and `bool?`.

Working with MongoDB from Java

Working with MongoDB using Java Core isn't all that difficult either. Create a new Gradle project and install the `mongodb driver` and `mongodb bson` packages, as follows:

```
apply plugin: 'java-library'

  repositories {
      jcenter()
```

```
}

dependencies {
    implementation 'org.mongodb:mongo-java-driver:3.9.0'
    implementation 'org.mongodb:bson:3.0.0'
}
```

Next, create a **Plain Old Java Object** (**POJO**) to represent our JSON document:

```
package com.packtpub.azure
// [...]
public class Person {
 @BsonId
 private ObjectId Id;
 // [...]
public ObjectId getId() {
 return id;
 }
public Person setId(ObjectId id) {
 this.id = id;
 return this;
 }
// [...]
}
```

Now, we can write the application:

```
public com.packtpub.azure;

 // [...]

 public class AzureMongoDBConsoleApp {
     public static void main(String args[]) {
         int port = 10255;
         // [...]
         String url =
String.format("mongodb://%s:%s@%s.documents.azure.com:%s/?ssl=true&replicaS
et=%s", userName, password, host, port, replicaSet);

         MongoClientURI uri = new MongoClientURI(url);
         try (MongoClient client = new MongoClient(uri)) {
             CodecRegistry registry = fromRegistries(
                 MongoClient.getDefaultCodecRegistry(),
                 fromProviders(PojoCodecProvider
                     .builder()
                     .conventions(Arrays.asList(Conventions
                       .USE_GETTERS_FOR_SETTERS)),
                     Conventions.ANNOTATION_CONVENTION))
```

```
                        .automatic(true)
                        .build()));
            MongoDatabase database =
    client.getDatabase(databaseName).withCodecRegistry(registry);
            MongoCollection<Person> collection =
    database.getCollection(collectionName, Person.class);

            collection.insertOne(new Person()
                .setFirstName("Bill")
                // [...]

            FindIterable<Person> it = collection.find();
            try (MongoCursor<Person> cursor = it.iterator()) {
                while(cursor.hasNext()) {
                    Person person = cursor.next();
                    System.out.println(String
                        .format("%s - %s %s - %s",
                            person.getId(),
                            // [...]
                }
                System.out.println("Press any key to continue");
                System.in.read();
            }
            catch(IOException e) {
                e.printStackTrace();
            }
        }
    }
}
```

I'll explain the code line by line:

1. First, we create a new MongoClientURI using our connection string, which you can get from the portal. Then, we create a new MongoClient and pass it to our uri in the constructor.

2. Next, we create a CodecRegistry to enable the automatic mapping of POJOs to documents. Note the conventions setting. This is required for reading lists in our mapped POJOs.

3. Then, we get a reference to the database using client.getDatabase(databaseName) with CodecRegistry(registry). This gets the database and our associated codec to allow POJO mapping. MongoDB will automatically create the database if it doesn't exist.

4. Then, we do the same for the collection using `database.getCollection(collectionName, Person.class)`. Again, the collection is automatically created if it doesn't exist. The documents that we'll try to get using this collection will automatically be cast to `Person` objects. However, since MongoDB is schemaless, we can't be sure that all the documents have those exact properties.

5. Using `collection.insertOne`, we can insert a `Person`. While MongoDB is schemaless, Java isn't, so we have to pass in a `Person`.

6. The ID of `Person` is of the `org.bson.types.ObjectId` type. This tells MongoDB that this is our ID and that MongoDB can create a value. You can pick another type for the ID, but you'll have to set your own value.

7. Then, we get all our documents from the collection using `collection.Find()`.

8. Finally, we list the results and close the application.

When we insert some extra documents into the database, we can see the actual filter in action. We can use the filter builder to build filters:

```
collection.insertMany(Arrays.asList(
    new Person()
        .setFirstName("Steve")
        .setLastName("Ballmer")
        // [...]
    new Person()
        // [...]
));

FindIterable<Person> it = collection.find(eq("interests",
"Being Rich"));
try (MongoCursor<Person> cursor = it.iterator()) {
    while(cursor.hasNext()) {
        Person person = cursor.next();
        System.out.println(String
            .format("%s - %s %s - %s", person.getId(),
                // [...]
    }
    System.out.println("Press any key to continue");
    System.in.read();
}
catch(IOException e) {
    e.printStackTrace();
}
```

With the MongoDB driver for Java, we can do much more, such as filter records, use aggregates, insert bulk data, delete records, create indexes, execute stored procedures, and many other things.

Notice how collections and even databases are generated on the fly. With Azure SQL, we had to define our schema upfront and run our scripts to update the schema, which would risk us locking the database if we changed the schema of large tables. With MongoDB, we don't have to worry about this anymore. You can insert any document in any collection into any database. Of course, you have to make sure that your object serializes correctly. Imagine we're adding two new fields to our `Person` class: `DateOfBirth` and `JoinDate`. Obviously, the documents that already exist don't have these properties, so we need to make sure they get reasonable default values in Java:

```java
public class Person {
    private ObjectId Id;
    private String firstName;
    private String lastName;
    private List<String> interests
    private Date dateOfBirth = null;
    private Date joining = new Date(); // Defaults to today

    // getters and setters follow
}
```

Whether you want to default to `null` or to `today` is up to you. The same goes for other types.

Working with the Redis cache database

Redis is another NoSQL database that is available in Azure. It's a key-value store that's optimized for performance. It achieves this by working with an in-memory dataset. Redis can persist data to disk by either dumping the dataset to disk every once in a while or by appending each command to a log. In contrast to most database systems, persistence is optional. Because of this lightning-fast in-memory approach, Redis is very well suited for caching data. Redis works best on Linux systems, which is no problem for Azure since Microsoft developed a port for 64-bit Windows systems.

Creating a Redis cache

Let's create a Redis Cache in the Azure portal:

1. Either find **Redis Caches** in the menu or go to **Create a resource** and find **Redis Cache**.
2. In the blade that opens, fill out a DNS name that's unique across all of Azure.
3. Select a subscription.
4. Select or create a resource group.
5. Pick your location.
6. Select your pricing tier. You can view the full details by clicking on **View full pricing details**. We'll talk about this in more detail soon.

   For our example, the tier doesn't matter all that much, so go with **C0 Basic**, which is the cheapest tier available.

7. You'll see that the other options in the other pricing tiers aren't available in the Basic tier. Hit **Create** and wait a few minutes for Azure to create your Redis Cache (this took about 30 minutes for me):

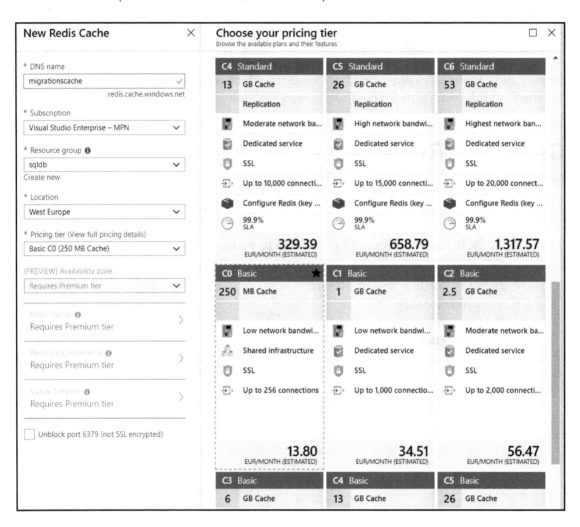

Let's talk about pricing tiers a bit more. A Redis Cache isn't cheap. The cheapest C0 Basic tier is already €13.80 a month and the cheapest after that is over €30. All of the tiers have SSL, and all but the C0 tiers have dedicated services. The C0 tiers have shared infrastructure and therefore are not recommended for production environments. The differences between the other tiers are your RAM (250 MB to 1,200 GB), network bandwidth (low, moderate, or high), number of concurrent connections (256 to 40,000), and features such as replication and a 99.9% SLA. The SLA is especially important since the lack of an SLA in the Basic tier makes it unfit for most production environments.

The Premium tier starts at €348.22 a month and goes up to a staggering €7,566.63 a month. But it doesn't end there. Redis Caches can be clustered, meaning your data is sharded across multiple nodes. This means that you can have even more memory available and you can continue to use Redis if a node fails. Clustering is possible in Azure, but only using the Premium tier. So, go ahead and pick the most expensive Premium tier. Now, configure a Redis cluster and set it to the maximum number of shards, which is 10, with a total size of 1,200 GB. Your estimated monthly costs will now be €75,666.27 for a cache! Let that sink in. Don't hit **Create** now, by the way—you'll have to sell your house to pay for your cache. Some of the other options that are only available on Premium tiers are persistence, which is vital if you plan on using Redis for more than just an in-memory cache, and running on a virtual network.

Working with Redis from C#

Open up Visual Studio 2017 and create a new console application. Install the `Microsoft.Extensions.Caching.Redis` package using `NuGet`. Yes, Microsoft has its own package for working with Redis and it includes MVC Core extensions! However, we're using a console application and not an MVC application:

```
using Microsoft.Extensions.Caching.Distributed;
// [...]

namespace RedisConnection
{
    internal class Program
    {
        private static void Main(string[] args)
        {
            var redisOptions = new RedisCacheOptions
            {
                Configuration = "[your connection string]",
                InstanceName = "[your DNS name]"
            };
            var options = Options.Create(redisOptions);
```

```
            // This would be injected in MVC Core.
            IDistributedCache cache = new RedisCache(options);
            cache.SetString("name", "Bill Gates");
            Console.WriteLine($"Hi, my name is {cache.GetString("name")}");

            cache.SetString("name", "Steve Ballmer", new
DistributedCacheEntryOptions
            {
                AbsoluteExpirationRelativeToNow = new TimeSpan(0, 0, 3)
            });

            Console.WriteLine($"Hi, my name is {cache.GetString("name") ??
"unset"}");
            // [...]
        }
    }
}
```

First, we need to create a `RedisCache` object using `RedisCacheOptions`. In MVC, this is all injected for you, but we're using a console application and we don't have dependency injection. Once we have an `IDistributedCache`, it's just a matter of setting and getting values using keys. First, we'll set the "name" to "Bill Gates". After that, we will overwrite this with "Steve Ballmer", but we'll give this value an expiration of 3 seconds. As we can see, the value is `null` after 3 seconds.

We can only set and get strings, but we can work around this by using `Newtonsoft.Json`, the most popular .NET package for working with JSON, which also comes as standard with MVC applications:

```
// Store object as JSON.
var person = new Person { Name = "Satya Nadella" };
string json = JsonConvert.SerializeObject(person);
cache.SetString("person", json);

// Retrieve object as JSON.
json = cache.GetString("person");
person = JsonConvert.DeserializeObject<Person>(json);
Console.WriteLine($"Hi, my name is {person.Name}");
```

In the next section, we're going to use the ServiceStack Redis API.

Using the ServiceStack Redis API

Unfortunately, the Microsoft extension for a Redis cache is very limited. We can set and get strings and byte arrays (using the `SET` and `GET` methods), but Redis allows us to set all kinds of objects and even to alter them. Another popular package you may encounter is `ServiceStack.Redis`, which is recommended when you're using the full .NET Framework. There's also a .NET Core version of this package called `ServiceStack.Redis.Core`. In this section, we're going to install it and look at some more advanced scenarios.

First, we need to create a connection. The connection string for `ServiceStack` is a little bit different from the Microsoft one:

```
var connectionstring = "redis://[your password]=@[your DNS
name].redis.cache.windows.net:6380?ssl=true";
using (var manager = new RedisManagerPool(connectionstring))
using (var client = manager.GetClient())
{
    // Use the client...
}
```

One of the things Redis supports is atomically incrementing values:

```
client.Set("counter", 1);
Console.WriteLine($"The counter is at {client.Get<int>("counter")}");
client.IncrementValue("counter");
Console.WriteLine($"The counter is now at {client.Get<int>("counter")}");
client.IncrementValueBy("counter", 3);
Console.WriteLine($"The counter is now at {client.Get<int>("counter")}");
```

We can also set and get multiple keys and values using `SetAll` with `Dictionary<string, T>`, `GetAll`, and a list of keys:

```
// Set multiple values at once.
var dict = new Dictionary<string, object>()
{
    { "name", "Bill Gates" },
    { "company", "Microsoft" },
    { "dateofbirth", new DateTime(1955, 10, 28) },
    { "networth", 93800000000 }
};
client.SetAll(dict);

// Get multiple values at once.
var values = client.GetAll<object>(new[] { "name", "company",
"dateofbirth", "networth" });
```

```
foreach (var pair in values)
{
    Console.WriteLine($"{pair.Key} - {pair.Value}");
}

Console.WriteLine($"Hi, my name is {client.Get<string>("name")}");
Console.WriteLine($"I work for {client.Get<string>("company")}");
Console.WriteLine($"I was born on
{client.Get<DateTime>("dateofbirth").ToLongDateString()}");
Console.WriteLine($"And my net worth is {client.Get<long>("networth")}");
```

It's also possible to work with objects and lists of objects, which work the same as other values:

```
var ceos = new List<Person>
{
    new Person { Name = "Bill Gates" },
    new Person { Name = "Steve Ballmer" },
    new Person { Name = "Satya Nadella" }
};
client.Set("ceos", ceos);
ceos = client.Get<List<Person>>("ceos");
foreach (Person p in ceos)
{
    Console.WriteLine($"CEO {p.Name}");
}
```

If you need just the basic functionality, it's fine to use the Microsoft extensions, maybe with a little Newtonsoft.Json wrapper around them, but if you need the full strength of Redis, ServiceStack.Redis(.Core) is a fine alternative.

Working with Redis from Java

Open up Eclipse and create a new Gradle project. Install the Lettuce Redis framework by editing your build.gradle file, as follows:

```
apply plugin: 'java-library'

repositories {
    jcenter()
}

dependencies {
    implementation 'biz.paluch.redis:lettuce:4.5.0.Final'
}
```

Now, we will create the demo application:

```
package com.packtpub.azure

// [...]

public class AzureRedisConsoleApp {
    public static void main(String[] args) {
        String password = "your_password";
        String host = "your_host";
        int port = 6380;

        RedisURI uri = RedisURI.create(host, port);
        uri.setPassword(password);
        uri.setSsl(true);

        RedisClient client = RedisClient.create(uri);
        try (StatefulRedisConnection<String, String>
                connection = client.connect()) {
            RedisCommands<String, String> sync = connection.sync();

            sync.set("count"), Integer.toString(1));
            System.out.println("Count is " + sync.get("count"));

            // [...]
        }
        finally {
            client.shutdown();
        }
    }
}
```

First, we need to create a RedisURI object, remembering to set the password and enable ssl. Then, we use this to create a RedisClient object. Next, we use this to create a StatefulRedisConnection object, and finally, we use this to create a RedisCommands object. This is what we will use to set and get objects in Redis. Now that connectivity has been fully established, we'll set the key count to value 1. After that, we increment it, and then increment it by 3. At this point, we can only work with String objects in the Redis Cache. Next, we will examine working with objects in the Redis Cache. To do this, we will need to implement a codec:

```
package com.packtpub.azure;

import java.io.ByteArrayInputStream;
// [...]

import com.lambdaworks.redis.codec.RedisCodec;
```

```java
public class ObjectCodec implements
        RedisCodec<String, Object> {
    private Charset charset = Charset.forName("UTF-8");

    @Override
    public String decodeKey(ByteBuffer bytes) {
        return charset.decode(bytes).toString();
    }

    @Override
    public Object decodeValue(ByteBuffer bytes) {
        try {
            byte[] array = new byte[bytes.remaining()];
            bytes.get(array);
            ByteArrayInputStream bis = new ByteArrayInputStream(array)
            ObjectInputStream is = new ObjectInputStream(bis);
            return is.readObject();
        }
        catch(IOException | ClassNotFoundException e) {
            return null;
        }
    }

    @Override
    public ByteBuffer encodeKey(String key) {
        return charset.encode(key);
    }

    @Override
    public ByteBuffer encodeValue(Object value) {
        try {
            ByteArrayOutputStream bytes = new ByteArrayOutputStream();
            ObjectOutputStream os = new ObjectOutputStream(bytes)
            os.writeObject(value);
            return ByteBuffer.wrap(bytes.toByteArray());
        }
        catch(IOException e) {
            return null;
        }
    }
}
```

Now that we have a codec to handle serialization and deserialization, we need some serializable objects to work with. Create the following `Person` class:

```java
package com.packtpub.azure;

import java.io.Serializable;
```

```
import java.util.ArrayList;
import java.util.List;

public class Person implements Serializable {
    private static final long serialVersionUUID = 1L;
    private int id;
    // [...]

    public int getId() {
        return id;
    }

    public Person setId(int id) {
        this.id = id;
        return this;
    }

    // [...]
}
```

Now, everything is ready for us to work with objects and the Redis Cache. Add the following code after the `finally` block in `AzureRedisConsoleApp`:

```
client = RedisClient.create(uri);
ObjectCodec codec = new ObjectCodec();
try (StatefulRedisConnection<String, Object> connection =
        client.connect(codec)) {
    RedisCommand<String, Object. Sync.connection.sync();

    Map<String Object> people = new HashMap<String, Object>()
    people.put("1", new Person()
        .setId(1)
        .setFirstName("Bill")
        .setLastName("Gates")
        // [...]
    people.put("2", new Person()
        // [...]
    sync.mset(people);

    sync.set("3", new Person()
        // [...]

    for(Object result : sync.mget("1", "2", "3")) {
        Person person = (Person)result;
        System.out.println(String.format("%s - %s %s - %s",
            person.getId(),
            // [...]
    }
```

```
    }
    finally {
        client.shutdown();
    }
```

There are other Redis frameworks available for Java, but when you have added the codec for serialization for Lettuce, it is full-featured and provides all the necessary features for Redis Cache usage.

Summary

Azure offers plenty of options for all your database needs. In this chapter, we talked about the various databases that can be used to connect to your application.

The PaaS solutions of Azure SQL, CosmosDB, and Redis are easy and convenient. For other databases, you can use an IaaS solution and install your database on a VM. All the big database types, including relational and NoSQL, are available.

Chapter 12, *Securing Your Azure Services*, and Chapter 14, *Designing for High Availability and Disaster Recovery*, will discuss security, high availability, and disaster recovery, which are absolute necessities when you're working with data.

Questions

Answer the following questions to test your knowledge of this chapter. You can find the answers in the *Assessments* section at the end of this book:

1. Which of the following database types are offered in Azure?
    1. Document-based store
    2. Column-based store
    3. Relational database
    4. Graph-based store
    5. Key-value store

2. What APIs are not supported in Cosmos DB?
    1. MongoDB
    2. Cassandra
    3. Gremlin
    4. Redis
    5. Azure Table

3. You need to move your on-premises Oracle database to Azure as quickly as possible; what is your best option?
   1. Create a backup of your database and restore it in Azure SQL
   2. Create a VM and install Oracle on the VM
   3. Use an Azure SQL Database Managed Instance
   4. Rewrite your application so that it uses SQL Server instead
   5. Create an Azure Oracle database account

Further reading

Check out the following links to find out more about the topics that were covered in this chapter:

- **Choosing a cloud SQL Server option**: Azure SQL (PaaS) Database or SQL Server on Azure VMs (IaaS): `https://docs.microsoft.com/en-us/azure/sql-database/sql-database-paas-vs-sql-server-iaas`

- **Azure SQL Database feature comparison**: `https://docs.microsoft.com/en-us/azure/sql-database/sql-database-features`

- **Using a SQL Database Managed Instance with virtual networks and near 100% compatibility**: `https://docs.microsoft.com/en-us/azure/sql-database/sql-database-managed-instance`

- **Overview of Data Migration Assistant**: `https://docs.microsoft.com/en-us/sql/dma/dma-overview?view=sql-server-2017`

- **How to provision a Windows SQL Server virtual machine in the Azure portal**: `https://docs.microsoft.com/en-us/azure/virtual-machines/windows/sql/virtual-machines-windows-portal-sql-server-provision`

- **Create an Azure SQL Database in the Azure portal**: `https://docs.microsoft.com/en-us/azure/sql-database/sql-database-get-started-portal`

- **Elastic pools help you manage and scale multiple Azure SQL Databases**: `https://docs.microsoft.com/en-us/azure/sql-database/sql-database-elastic-pool`

- **Azure SQL Database purchasing models**: `https://docs.microsoft.com/en-us/azure/sql-database/sql-database-service-tiers`

- **DTU-based service tiers**: `https://docs.microsoft.com/en-us/azure/sql-database/sql-database-service-tiers-dtu`

- **Best practices for securing PaaS databases in Azure**: `https://docs.microsoft.com/en-us/azure/security/security-paas-applications-using-sql`

- **Migrations**: https://docs.microsoft.com/en-us/ef/core/managing-schemas/migrations/
- **Azure Database for MySQL**: https://azure.microsoft.com/en-us/services/mysql/
- **Azure Database for MariaDB**: https://azure.microsoft.com/en-us/services/mariadb/
- **Azure Database for PostgreSQL**: https://azure.microsoft.com/en-us/services/postgresql/
- **A technical overview of Azure Cosmos DB**: https://azure.microsoft.com/en-gb/blog/a-technical-overview-of-azure-cosmos-db/
- **Introduction to Azure Cosmos DB**: https://docs.microsoft.com/en-us/azure/cosmos-db/introduction
- **Introduction to Azure Cosmos DB: SQL API**: https://docs.microsoft.com/en-us/azure/cosmos-db/sql-api-introduction
- **Introduction to Azure Cosmos DB: MongoDB API**: https://docs.microsoft.com/en-us/azure/cosmos-db/mongodb-introduction
- **Introduction to Azure Cosmos DB: Gremlin API**: https://docs.microsoft.com/en-us/azure/cosmos-db/graph-introduction
- **Introduction to Azure Cosmos DB: Cassandra API**: https://docs.microsoft.com/en-us/azure/cosmos-db/cassandra-introduction
- **Introduction to Azure Cosmos DB: Table API**: https://docs.microsoft.com/en-us/azure/cosmos-db/table-introduction
- **Azure Redis Cache**: https://azure.microsoft.com/en-us/services/cache/

Managing and Deploying Your Code

11

In the previous chapters, we looked at various Azure services for migrating and modernizing your applications when moving them to the cloud. In this chapter, we're going to focus on the developer's experience regarding how we can manage and deploy our code to Azure using our favorite **Integrated Development Environment** (**IDE**) applications.

We'll be focusing on how some of the popular IDEs among .NET and Java developers integrate with Azure.

The following topics will be covered in this chapter:

- IDEs for Azure
- Using Visual Studio for Azure application development and deployment
- Using Eclipse to manage Java-based application development and deployment
- Visual Studio Code and Azure
- IntelliJ and Azure

IDEs for Azure

Azure is an open cloud, which means there's no restriction on the choice of IDE you want to use or even the choice of programming framework, up to a certain extent. You can write code in a text editor and deploy it to Azure and it should work very well. However, it would definitely be a much smoother experience if you could develop the code that you've designed for Azure, integrate it with Azure DevOps, and deploy to Azure Services directly within the IDEs themselves without any additional heavy lifting.

Let's look at some of the popular IDEs that enable strong integration with Azure natively or using plugins:

- Visual Studio
- Visual Studio Code
- Eclipse
- IntelliJ
- Visual Studio for Mac

Along with integration with popular IDEs, Microsoft provides a vast range of SDKs and plugins for development across .NET, Java, Node, Python, Ruby, PHP, Xamrin, Android, iOS, Swift, and Windows applications. There are also additional tools available, such as Azure Storage Explorer, Azure PowerShell, and CLI, all of which can be used by developers to interact with the Azure platform.

 You can find out more about developer tools for Azure here: `https://azure.microsoft.com/en-in/tools/`.

In the upcoming section, we'll look at how we can use some of these popular IDEs to integrate with Azure DevOps (previously known as Visual Studio Team Services) and the Azure cloud platform.

Using Visual Studio with Azure

Visual Studio has been around for decades now and is one of the most popular IDEs among developers. Microsoft has enabled a strong integration between Visual Studio and Azure at each layer, right from development to publishing. Using Visual Studio brings certain benefits, such as the following:

- **Developing apps for Azure directly from your development box**: With a wide range of templates, plugins, and tools for Azure available, you can directly develop your app for the cloud, write and test locally, and deploy to Azure directly, without changing a single line of code.

- **Deploying faster with DevOps**: Visual Studio integrates very well with Azure DevOps Services, including Azure boards, repositories, pipelines, and so on. You can perform all the DevOps tasks you'd want right from your Visual Studio console, including raising a PR and deploying the application.
- **Enhancing developer productivity**: With a best-in-class development experience, you can write code quickly and find the APIs you need using IntelliSense.

Let's look at how we can use Visual Studio to work with Azure.

Getting Azure tools for Visual Studio

In this section, we'll learn how to set up Visual Studio for Azure development. Note that we'll not be discussing installing Visual Studio in general. Refer to `https://docs.microsoft.com/en-us/visualstudio/install/install-visual-studio?view=vs-2019` to find out more about the general installation of Visual Studio.

Go to the following link for a Visual Studio for Mac installation guide: `https://docs.microsoft.com/en-us/visualstudio/mac/installation`.

Visual Studio in the Azure Marketplace

Microsoft has made plenty of Visual Studio VMs available in the Azure Marketplace, starting from 2015 to the latest 2019 versions, including editions comprising Community and Enterprise. If you choose to deploy these VMs, you'll get Visual Studio preinstalled and ready to use. Note that these images provide you with a preinstalled VM with Visual Studio and don't include Visual Studio licenses. You'll need to have a valid license if you want to use Visual Studio based on the edition you choose. If you don't have a Visual Studio license or subscription, you can use Visual Studio Community, which is free to use.

Let's look at the images that are available:

1. Log in to the Azure portal using a valid account that has access to a subscription.
2. Click on **+ Create a resource.**
3. Search for `visual studio`, as shown here:

4. Here, you can see various Visual Studio and Windows Server version combinations; you can choose the one suits you the most.
5. You can create a VM to use as a development box using this image by following the standard VM creation process.

Installing Azure tools for Visual Studio

If you decide to use a Visual Studio image from Azure Marketplace, Azure tools for Visual Studio will come preinstalled on the VM. For a manually installed version of Visual Studio, you can modify the Visual Studio installation and select **Azure development** under **Workloads** to install all the dependencies and plugins that are required for Azure integration:

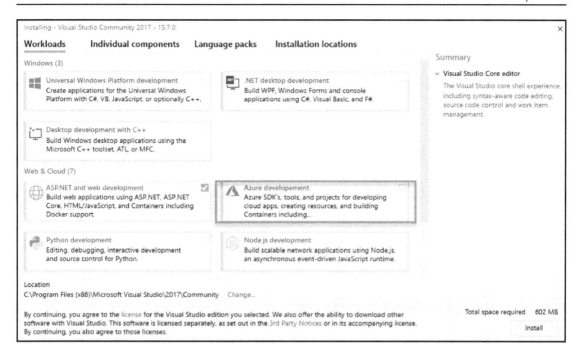

In this section, we learned how to install a variety of Azure tools, as well as how to set up Visual Studio as our IDE for Azure workloads.

Logging in to Visual Studio with Azure credentials

To make the most out of Visual Studio and Azure, you should log in to Visual Studio using an account that also has access to your Azure DevOps/Azure resources. You can have multiple accounts logged in at the same time. Let's see how this works:

1. Launch Visual Studio.
2. If this is your first time launching Visual Studio, you'll be asked to log in. Follow the standard login process and log in with your Azure AD/Microsoft Live account.

3. Once you're logged in, you'll be able to deploy your applications to Azure without leaving Visual Studio. To verify your Azure account or log in with a different account, go to **File | Account Settings**. You can also add additional accounts by going to **Account Settings**:

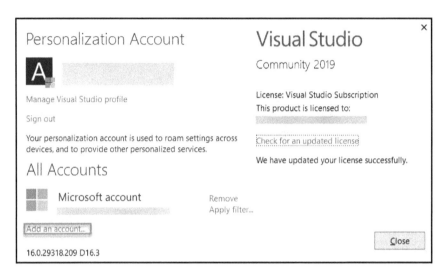

In this section, we learned how to get started by launching Visual Studio 2019 and logging in with our Azure account.

Using Cloud Explorer in Visual Studio

When you install Azure tools in Visual Studio, you also get Cloud Explorer, a plugin inside Visual Studio that helps you explore and manage your cloud resources under your Azure account. Let's learn how to use Cloud Explorer:

1. Launch Visual Studio.
2. Click on **View | Cloud Explorer**:

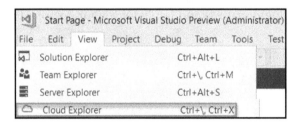

3. You can filter your resources based on the resource's group or type, and browse through your resources hierarchy. Right-clicking on any resources will provide you with the controls that are available for that particular resource. You can also right-click and open that resource in the Azure portal directly:

In this section, we have learned how to use Cloud Explorer in Visual Studio to view and manage Azure resources in the IDE.

Developing and deploying with Visual Studio for Azure

In this section, we'll create a sample ASP.NET-based web application using Visual Studio, store the code using Azure repositories (part of Azure DevOps), and deploy this on Azure without leaving the Visual Studio console.

Connecting Visual Studio to an existing Azure DevOps project

In this section, we'll learn how to connect a Visual Studio workspace to an existing Azure DevOps project; for this, you need to have created an Azure DevOps project. Please refer to Chapter 5, *Modernizing Apps and Infrastructure with DevOps*, to learn more about Azure DevOps. Let's get started:

1. Launch Visual Studio and log in with your Azure DevOps account.
2. Click on **View** and select **Team Explorer**:

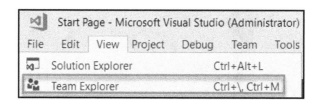

3. Click on **Connect...** under **Azure DevOps** (you might see **Visual Studio Team Services** instead of **Azure DevOps** if you're using an older version of Visual Studio):

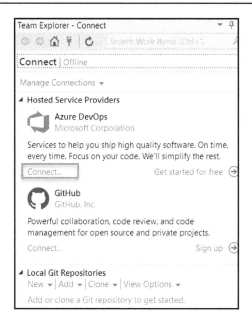

4. If you do not have an Azure DevOps account, you can also sign up using the signup link.

5. The connection will refresh and load up your Azure DevOps account, as well as the projects you have access to. Select the one you want to connect to and click **Connect**:

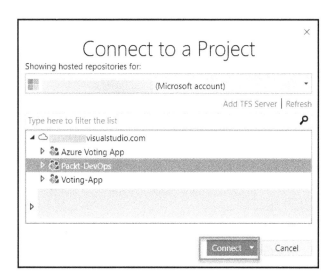

6. Once you're connected, you should **clone** the existing code from your project to your local system to start working. Using Team Explorer, you can also view other Azure DevOps modules, including work items. You may be asked to sign in again to verify your account when cloning the Azure repository to your account:

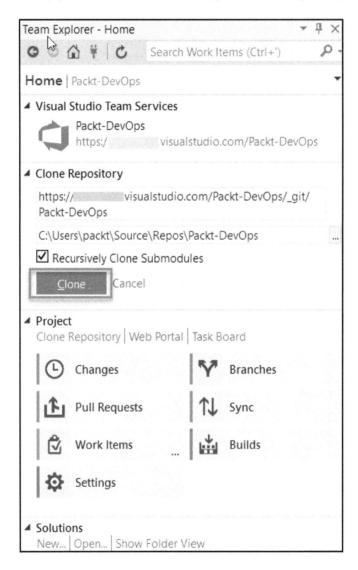

7. You're now connected to Azure DevOps. This means you can now work with your application code cloned within Visual Studio.

Deploying applications to Azure using Visual Studio

In this section, we'll create a new basic ASP.NET application and deploy it to Azure using Visual Studio.

Let's get started by creating the application:

1. Launch Visual Studio and click on **File | New Project.**
2. Search for `web` and select **ASP.NET Core Web Application**. Ensure that you select the **Create new Git repository** checkbox for the project. Checking a new Git repository will allow you to configure this project with an Azure repository:

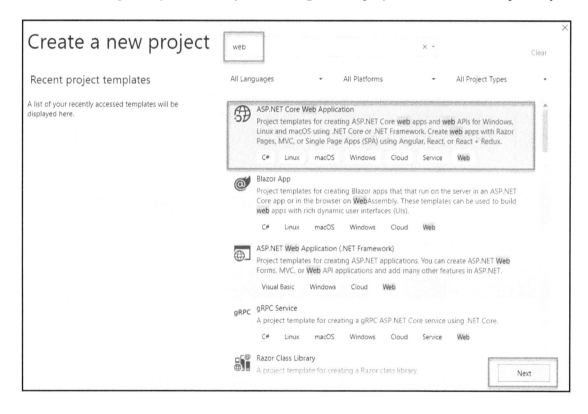

3. Click **Next** and select a **Project name**, **Location**, **Solution**, and **Solution name**, as shown in the following screenshot:

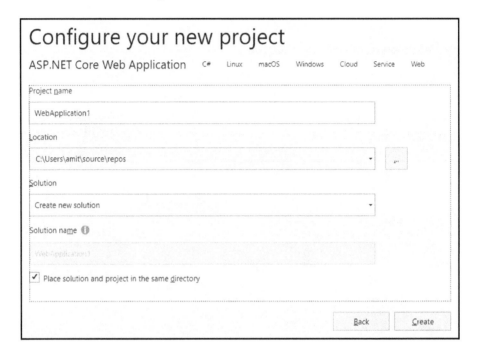

4. Click **Create** to be taken to a new window. From here, select **Web Application** and click **Create**:

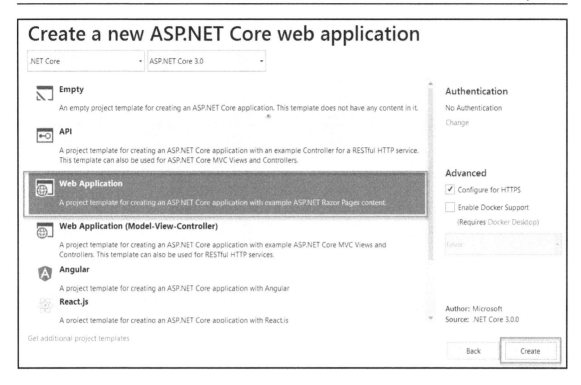

5. You can review the sample application code and modify it if you wish to.

6. Let's build this sample project to ensure it's working well. Right-click on the project's name and click **Build**:

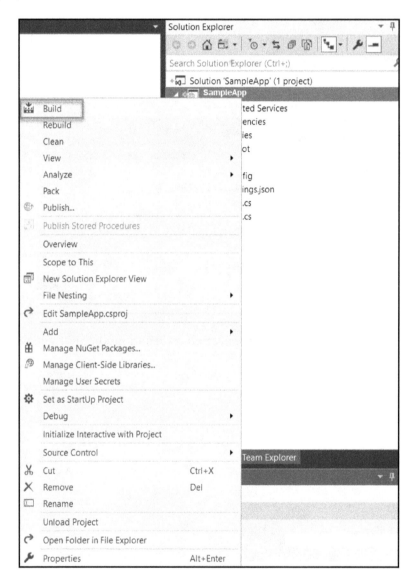

7. Once the build is successful, click on the **Run** button on the ribbon to test the application locally. This should launch IE or another internet browser based on your default application settings; you should be able to see the application running successfully:

8. Now that we've verified that our application is working correctly, we can commit this code to our Azure repository. Right-click on the project and click on **Source Control** | **Commit**. If you don't see this option, right-click on the solution and click **Add to Source Control**.

9. You can commit to the **master** branch directly or create a new branch and go via the **Pull Request** route to commit your code changes. Let's create a new branch; click on the default branch name, that is, **master**:

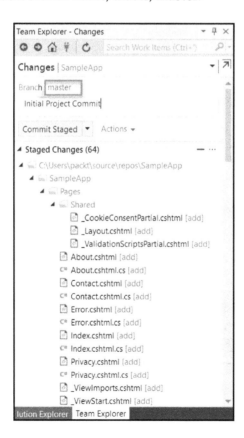

10. Enter a branch name and click **Create Branch**:

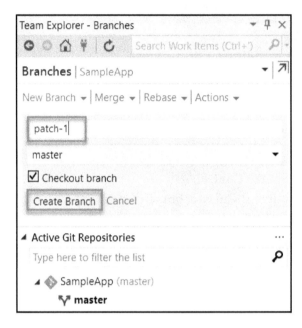

11. Click on the back icon in the Team Explorer window once the branch has been created:

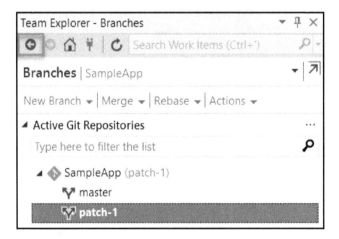

12. Select the patch-1 branch and click **Commit**. Once done, click on **Sync** to replicate these changes to Azure DevOps online:

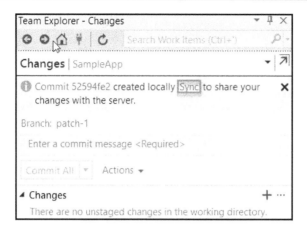

13. Click on **Publish Git Repo** and select your Azure DevOps account and repository. You can choose to create a new repository here:

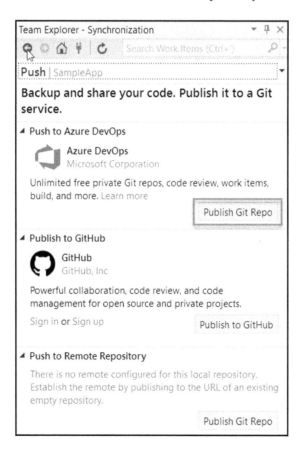

14. Now, we've committed the code for the Azure DevOps repository in a new branch.

15. Similarly, you can make changes to the code and push to new a branch or commit to an existing branch. You can also raise a **Pull request** to merge changes to the master branch.

16. Now that we've integrated the development environment with Azure DevOps, let's deploy the application to Azure using Visual Studio. Right-click on **App** and click **Publish.**

17. Here, you'll see multiple options for deploying your application, such as the following:
    - **App Service**
    - **App Service Linux**
    - **Azure Virtual Machines**
    - **IIS, FTP, etc**
    - **Folder**:

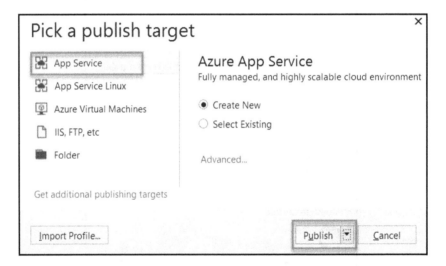

Let's deploy the application to **App Service**. You can choose to upload to an existing App Service or create a new one. Let's create a **new** App Service:

1. Enter an **App Name** and select the Azure subscription, resource group, and hosting plan configuration.

2. Click **Create** to start provisioning; you can also export the configuration so that you can deploy it later:

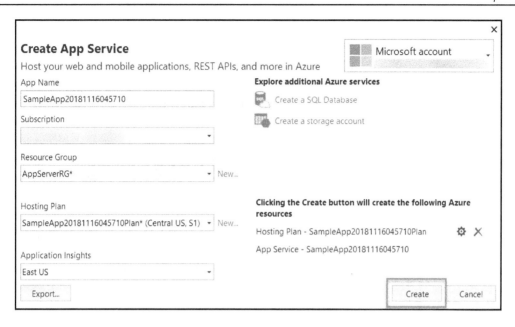

The deployment will now start; you should see your **App Service URL** once the deployment has completed. You can launch the URL in a modern web browser and see our sample app running in the same way it was running locally.

In this section, we looked at how we can use Visual Studio to develop, manage, and deploy applications with Azure without leaving the Visual Studio console.

Using Eclipse with Azure

In this section, we'll take a look at the Azure Toolkit for Eclipse, a very popular IDE among Java developers. You can use Azure tools within an Eclipse IDE for the following reasons:

- For deploying your Java applications to Azure as a container or as an App Service, without leaving Eclipse
- To access Java libraries for Azure development
- To use Azure Explorer to view and manage Azure resources within Eclipse
- To use the Azure Service Fabric toolkit to work with Service Fabric-based applications within Eclipse
- To use the Team Explorer Everywhere so that you can integrate your development environment with Azure DevOps online (also known as Visual Studio Team Services)

Azure Service Fabric and Team Explorer Everywhere are additional tools you need to install so that you can leverage their functionality alongside the core Azure Toolkit.

Let's look at installing and using Azure Toolkit for Eclipse. Note that installing Eclipse is out of scope for this book; go to `http://www3.ntu.edu.sg/home/ehchua/programming/ howto/eclipsejava_howto.html` for more information about how to install Eclipse.

Installing Azure Toolkit for Eclipse

Follow these steps to install Azure Toolkit and the Azure DevOps toolkit for Eclipse:

1. Launch Eclipse.
2. Click on **Help** | **Install New Software**:

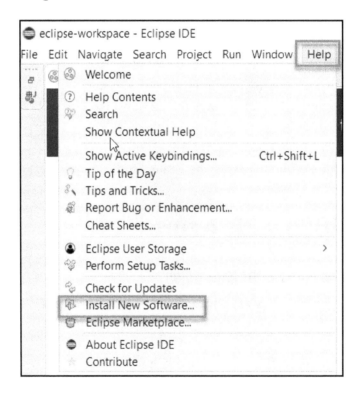

3. Click on **Add** and provide a name for the Azure Eclipse repository and a location URL. Here, we're going to use `http://dl.microsoft.com/eclipse/`:

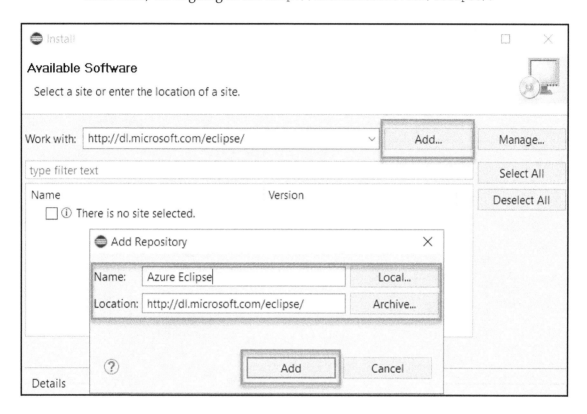

4. Now, you'll be able to see a list of Azure Toolkits available for Eclipse. In **Name**, select both Azure and Team Explorer Toolkit (**Team Explorer Everywhere**) to install them. You can leave Team Explorer unchecked if you don't want to use Azure DevOps within Eclipse. You can check for tools for Service Fabric if you wish to develop applications that can work with **Azure Service Fabric**:

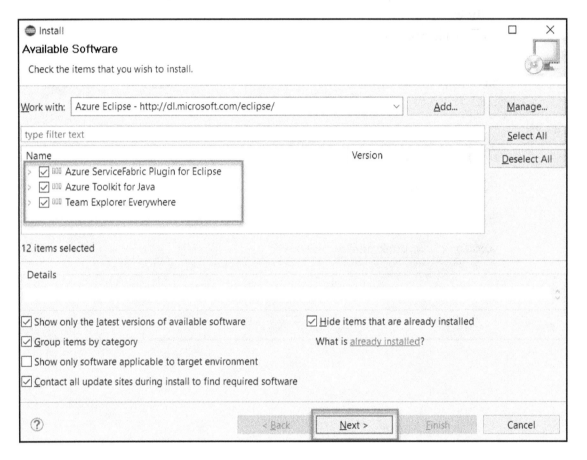

5. Now, you can review a list of components that will be installed as a part of the toolkit; this will give you an idea of the Azure Services offerings that can be integrated within Eclipse:

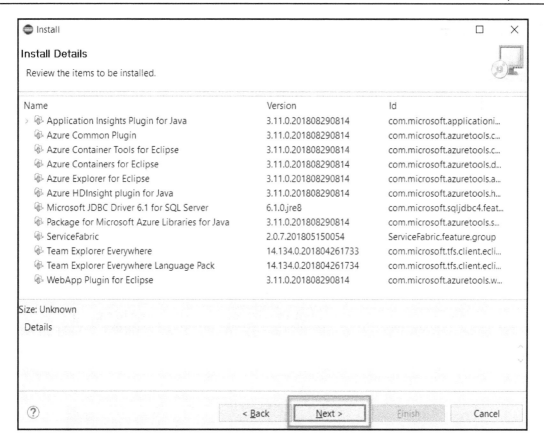

6. **Accept** the terms and conditions and click **Finish.**
7. Now, the Toolkit installation process will start; you can view the progress of the installation by looking at the progress bar at the bottom right-hand corner of Eclipse.
8. You'll be asked to restart the IDE before you can start using the Azure tools you've installed.

Signing in to Azure and using Azure Explorer within Eclipse

Now that your Azure tools have been installed, you can log in to Azure using the Eclipse Azure Toolkit and work with Azure Explorer to manage your cloud resources. Let's get started:

1. Launch Eclipse.
2. Click on **Tools** | **Azure** | **Sign In**:

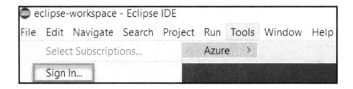

3. This will launch the **Azure Sign In** wizard. You can choose to sign in interactively or use an authentication file. Authentication files will need an **Azure AD SPN** to log in, whereas using the **Interactive** login means that you can use your regular Azure credentials:

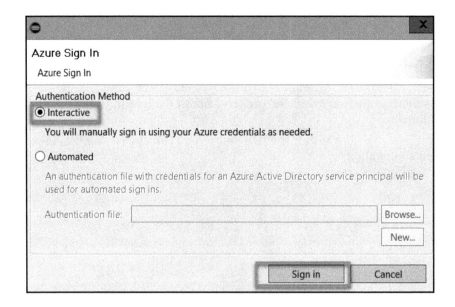

4. Complete the sign-in process and select the **Azure Subscription** you want to use.

5. Once you're logged in, you can use **Azure Explorer** to browse your subscription resources and interact with them. The following screenshot shows you how to launch and use Azure Explorer:

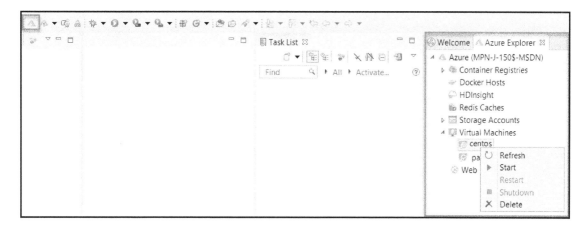

In this section, we learned how to use the Azure plugin inside our Eclipse IDE.

Publishing a Java project to Azure using Eclipse

In this section, we'll create a sample Java application and publish that to Azure App Services without leaving the Eclipse IDE.

Let's get started by creating a Java application:

1. Launch Eclipse and click on **File | New Project**. Select **Dynamic Web Project** as the project type:

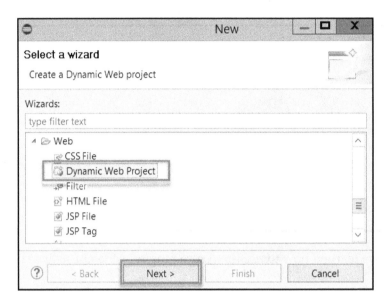

 If you don't see **Dynamic Web Project**, you may need to install the required workload tools within Eclipse. Go to `https://beginnersbook.com/2017/06/how-to-fix-dynamic-web-project-missing-in-eclipse-issue/` for more information.

2. Enter a meaningful project name and click **Finish**.
3. Right-click on the project name and browse the Azure options to find out what you can do with Azure and this project within Eclipse. We will see the following options:
   - **Configure App Insights**: You can add Azure Application Insights code and configurations to your Java project so that you can analyze your app.
   - **Add Docker Support/Docker Run/Publish to Web App for Containers/Publish as Docker Container**: You can use this option if you wish to deploy this app as a container in Azure. You can use ACR to store your Docker images.
   - **Publish as Azure Web App**: You can use this option if you want to deploy this app as a web app on the Azure App Services Engine.

4. For the purposes of this book's demo, we'll deploy this app as an Azure App Service. Let's select that option:

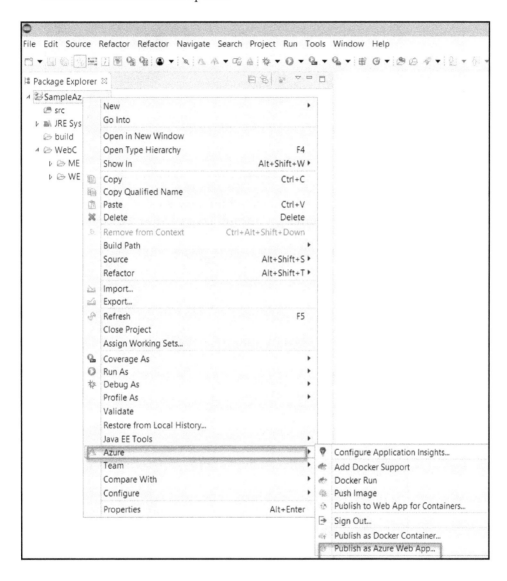

5. You can choose to deploy the app to an existing App Service instance or create a new one. Click on **Create...** to create a new Azure Web App:

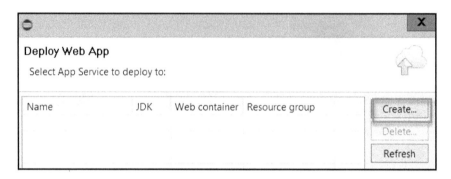

6. Review the App Service settings, including the web app's DNS name, the App Service plan and tier, resource group, and Java version settings, and click **Create:**

7. Clicking on **Deploy** will start the deployment process. It may take a few minutes for the deployment to finish. You can review the deployment progress in the Azure activity log.

8. Once deployed, you can click on **Published** in the activity log to launch the application:

In this section, we looked at Azure Toolkit for Eclipse and learned how to develop and deploy applications for Azure using Eclipse.

Visual Studio Code and Azure

Visual Studio Code is a popular lightweight IDE that's developed and maintained by Microsoft as an open source project. It's a cross-platform IDE that works on Windows, Linux, and Mac.

You can download Visual Studio Code from here: `https://code.visualstudio.com/`.

Visual Studio Code is a very extensible IDE and includes hundreds of extensions to make it easier for developers to develop and manage their code and applications. There are a wide variety of Azure extensions available, such as the following:

- Azure App Services and Azure Functions Tools
- Azure CLI
- Azure Resource Manager
- Azure Cosmos DB
- Azure Storage

 You can find more extensions for Visual Studio Code on the Visual Studio Code Marketplace. You can review the available Azure Extensions here: `https://marketplace.visualstudio.com/search?term=azure target=VSCodecategory=All%20categoriessortBy=Relevance`.

IntelliJ and Azure

IntelliJ is a popular IDE among Java developers. It's developed by Jetbrains and is available as an Apache 2 licensed community edition. Azure Toolkit for IntelliJ provides templates and functionality that you can use to easily create, develop, test, and deploy Azure applications by using the IntelliJ IDE. Along with Azure Toolkit, there are also plugins available so that we can work with Service Fabric applications and develop with Azure DevOps using the Team Explorer Everywhere plugin.

 More information and further reading on IntelliJ is available here: `https:/` `/docs.microsoft.com/en-us/java/azure/intellij/azure-toolkit-for-` `intellij?view=azure-java-stable`.

Summary

In this chapter, we focused on developing and managing applications for Azure and Azure DevOps. We looked at Azure integration with two of the most popular IDEs: Visual Studio and Eclipse. We also covered developing and deploying applications to Azure using IDEs.

In the next chapter, we'll look at some of the interesting security services and features in Azure.

Questions

Answer the following questions to test your knowledge about what was covered in this chapter. You can find the answers in the *Assessments* section at the end of this book:

1. How can you deploy applications to Azure?
    1. Using the Azure portal and Tools
    2. Using the Azure Command Line (PowerShell/CLI)
    3. Using the Azure REST interface
    4. Using your IDEs with Azure plugins
    5. All of the above

2. How can we interact with Azure using Visual Studio?

    1. By installing Azure tools for VS

    2. Azure PowerShell

    3. Azure CLI

    4. You have to use the Azure portal.

Further reading

Check out the following links to find out more about the topics that were covered in this chapter:

- **Azure Developer Tools**: `https://azure.microsoft.com/en-in/tools/`
- **Using Visual Studio with Azure**: `https://visualstudio.microsoft.com/vs/features/azure/`
- **Setting Up Visual Studio and Azure DevOps**: `https://docs.microsoft.com/en-us/azure/devops/organizations/accounts/set-up-vs?view=vsts`
- **Azure Toolkit for Eclipse**: `https://docs.microsoft.com/en-us/java/azure/eclipse/azure-toolkit-for-eclipse`
- **Azure Toolkit for IntelliJ**: `https://plugins.jetbrains.com/plugin/8053-azure-toolkit-for-intellij`

12
Securing Your Azure Services

In this chapter, I'll walk you through some of the security mechanisms to secure your Azure services. You will be introduced to **Azure Key Vault** (**AKV**) and how to utilize it. Then, you will learn how to secure your storage in Azure. Finally, you will learn about some of the storage techniques for Azure SQL databases, Azure Security Center, and securing **Infrastructure as a Service** (**IaaS**).

The following topics will be covered in this chapter:

- Azure Key Vault
- Securing Azure Storage
- Securing Azure SQL databases
- Securing your Azure VMs and network
- Azure Security Center
- Microsoft Trust Center

Understanding Azure Key Vault

AKV is one of the best cloud-hosted management services offering secret storing and management. AKV enables you to store certificates, passwords, tokens, and more. Moreover, it allows applications to access them securely. In the upcoming sections, we will look into some AKV scenarios, advantages, and flavors.

AKV scenarios

AKV is suitable for many scenarios, including the following:

- AKV can be used to secure the storage of your digital secrets.
- AKV can be used in key management solutions, where you can create new encryption keys for your environment and have full control over it.
- Any Azure or on-premises resource connected to the AKV can take advantage of it for creating and managing SSL/TLS certificates.

AKV advantages

There are many compelling reasons to use AKV, such as the following:

- **Centralized administration**: You can store all of your secrets in one place and manage them accordingly. For example, instead of exposing your application database password in the connection string to the application developer, you can store it in the key vault and the app will access it securely.
- **Integration with many Azure services**: AKV can be integrated with many other Azure services, such as OMS log analytics, storage accounts, SQL databases, Azure Web Apps, Always Encrypted SQL Server features, and Azure Disk Encryption.
- **High availability:** AKV is highly available because of the multiple layers of redundancy provided to it in the same region to make sure that it will be up and running whatever happens. In the worst-case scenario, where the whole Azure region is totally destroyed, you do not need to worry because the content of AKV is replicated to a secondary region. So, in the case of a region failure, your data will be available for read-only in the secondary region.
- **Removing the headache of Hardware Security Module (HSM)**: HSM is used to provide strong authentication and cryptoprocessing. However, its cost, installation, management, upgrade, troubleshooting, and so on is a big concern. However, with AKV, you can remove this headache because it is provided as a service as part of AKV.
- **Full auditing for the keys**: You can monitor all of the keys stored in the key vault by knowing how and when the keys were accessed.

AKV flavors

AKV is available in two flavors:

- **Standard**: This flavor offers most of the features besides the high availability and geographic scaling of AKV.
- **Premium**: This flavor offers what the standard flavor offers as well as the supportability of HSM-protected keys.

Now, let's create an AKV.

Creating an Azure Key Vault

You can create an AKV by performing the following steps:

1. Navigate to the Azure portal and search for key vaults, as shown in the following screenshot:

2. Click on **Key vaults**. You will then be navigated to another blade, where you can create a new key vault by clicking on **Add**, as shown in the following screenshot:

3. A new blade will pop up, asking you to specify the following:
   - **Subscription**: Specify the subscription that will be charged for using this service.
   - **Resource group**: Specify the resource group in which this key vault is going to exist as a resource.
   - **Key vault name**: Specify a descriptive name for the vault.
   - **Region**: Select the nearest Azure region to you.

- **Pricing tier**: You can select one of the two available AKV flavors that will fulfill your needs, as shown in the following screenshot:

- **Access policy**: Specify who has access to the key vault, as shown in the following screenshot:

The following options are available:

- **Enable access to Azure Virtual Machines for deployment**: Specify whether Azure VMs are permitted to retrieve certificates stored as secrets from the key vault.
- **Enable access to Azure Resource Manager for template deployment**: Specify whether Azure RM is permitted to retrieve secrets from the key vault.
- **Enable access to Azure Disk Encryption for volume encryption**: Specify whether Azure Disk Encryption is permitted to retrieve secrets from the vault and unwrap secrets.

You can add additional access policies and enable key vault access to other identities.

- **Virtual Network**: Specify whether you want to allow access to the key vault from **All networks** or **Selected networks**.

4. **All networks** will allow access to the services from any network:

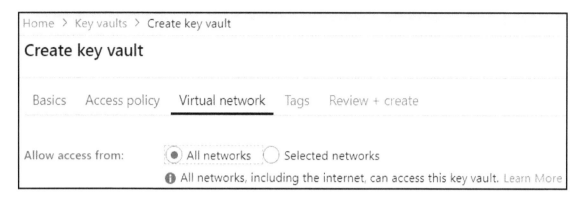

5. The **Selected networks** option will help you to even restrict access to subnets in virtual networks or via service endpoints:

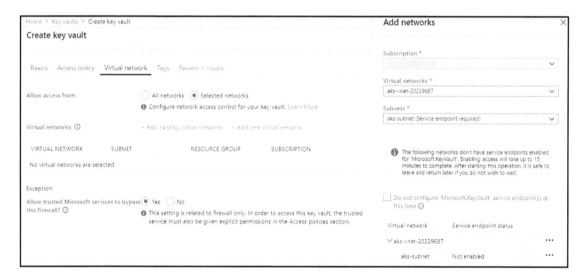

6. Add `Tags` if you want to and, once you are done, click on **Create**:

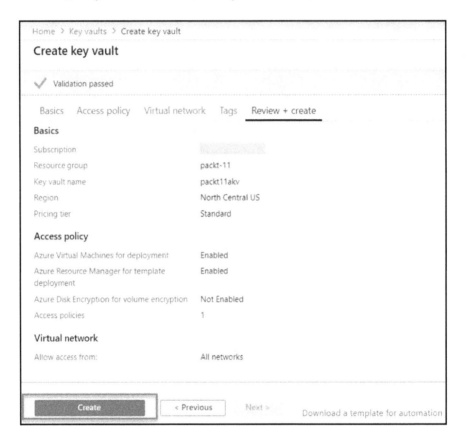

Next, let's look at AKV keys.

AKV keys

You can add your keys in AKV in different ways:

- **Generate**: You can generate the keys you want using AKV.
- **Import**: You can import a file that has the keys.
- **Restore Backup**: If you have a backup of some keys that were stored in AKV and you want to retrieve them now, you can upload the backup file and restore them in this AKV.

To work with keys, perform the following steps:

1. Navigate to the created AKV.
2. Under **Settings**, click on **Keys**.
3. You will be navigated to the **Keys** blade. Click on **Generate/Import**, as shown in the following screenshot:

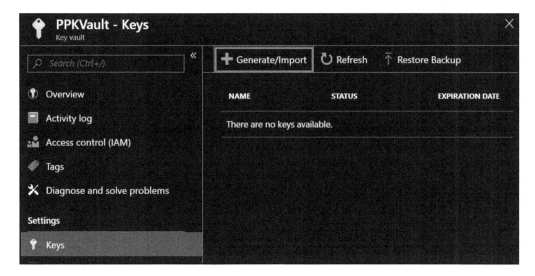

4. A new blade will be opened where you need to specify the following:
   - **Options**: Specify whether you want to generate a new key, import a key, or restore a backup:
     - If you select **Restore Backup**, you will only have to upload the backup file.
     - If you select **Import**, you will be asked to upload the file of the keys and specify the coming settings.
   - **Name**: Specify a descriptive and valid key name.
   - **Key Type**: Select the type of keys you want to generate/import. If you want to import keys, only the options of RSA will be available and if it is premium flavor, RSA-HSM will be available too.
   - **RSA Key Size**: **RSA Key Size** will be available only if you select **Generate**, and it differs from one key type to another.
   - **Set activation date**: You can specify when this key will be activated.

- **Set expiration date**: You can specify when this key will expire.
- **Enabled?**: You can select **Yes** to enable the key once it is created:

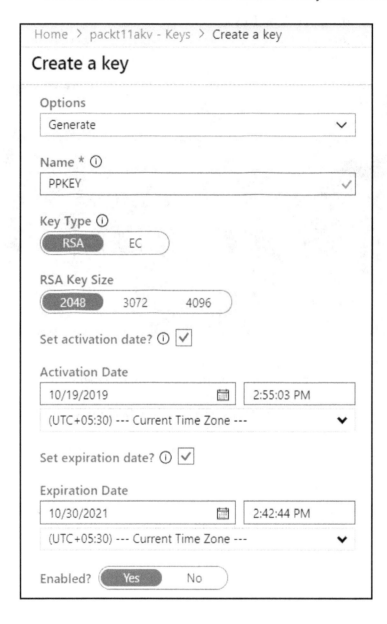

5. Once the key is created, you can click on it and view its properties where you can find the key identifier, the permitted operations, and more, as shown in the following screenshot:

Now, we'll look at AKV secrets.

AKV secrets

Creating secrets is similar to the creating process for keys. To create a secret, perform the following steps:

1. Navigate to the created key vault.
2. Under **Settings**, click on **Secrets**.
3. You will be navigated to the **Secrets** blade. Click **+ Generate/Import**, where you can specify the following:
    - **Upload Options**: We used to have manual and certificate options, but **Certificate** has its own blade and will be discussed in the next section.
    - **Name**: Specify a descriptive and valid secret name.
    - **Value**: Manually enter the secret you wish to store in AKV.
    - **Content-type**: You can specify the content type if you have many secrets to help you in order to remind you what a particular secret is related to.
    - **Set activation date**: You can specify when this key will be activated.
    - **Set expiration date**: You can specify when this key will expire.
    - **Enabled?**: You can select **Yes** to enable the key once it is created.

AKV certificates

AKV can also store certificates and provide certificate generation, or you can import your own certificates in the key vault.

To generate and store a certificate using AKV, you need to perform the following steps:

1. Navigate to the created AKV.
2. Under **Settings**, click on **Certificates**.
3. Then, click on **Generate/Import**.
4. A new blade will open, where you have to specify the following:
    - **Method of certificate creation**: You can select whether you want to generate or import a certificate.
    - **Certificate Name**: Specify a descriptive certificate name.

- **Type of Certificate Authority (CA)**: There are three types available:
  - **Self-signed certificate**
  - **Certificate issued by an integrated CA**: Microsoft recognizes DigiCert, GlobalSign, and WoSign as the integrated CAs. If you select this option, you will be asked to do some configuration to connect to your account on the integrated CA website to the key vault. It is very straightforward.
  - **Certificate issued by a non-integrated CA**: This refers to any CA provider other than the ones mentioned in the previous point.
- **Subject**: This is an X.500 distinguished name, for example, `CN=www.packtpub.com`.
- **DNS Names**: Specify the **Subject Alternative Names** (**SANs**) that can be recognized as DNS names.
- **Validity period**: Specify how long this certificate should last in months.
- **Content-Type**: Specify whether it is PKCS#12 or PEM.
- **Lifetime Action Type**: There are four actions to be done when the certificate reaches a specific lifetime:
  - Automatically renew at a given percentage lifetime.
  - Automatically renew at a given number of days before expiry.
  - Email all contacts at a given percentage lifetime.
  - Email all contacts at a given number of days before expiry.

- **Advanced Policy Configuration**: There are some advanced policy configurations that you can do for the certificate, as shown in the following screenshot:

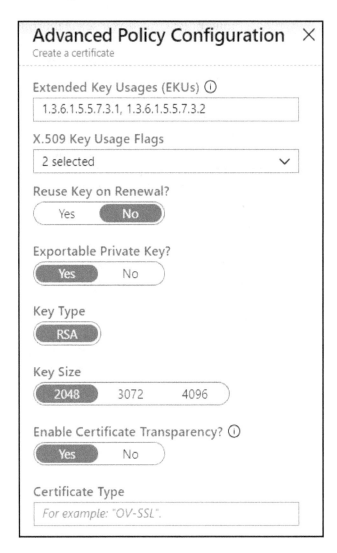

5. After specifying all of the settings, you can click on **Create** and the certificate will be created, which can be used by any of your applications with its URI.

In this section, you've learned about AKV and how to make use of it to secure your super secrets. In the next section, you will learn about some of the methodologies to secure your Azure Storage.

Securing Azure Storage

Azure Storage is the foundation of storing any data in Azure and is one of the most widely used Azure services. Azure Storage provides a comprehensive set of security capabilities, enabling you to build secure applications.

In this section, we'll be covering different ways to secure your Azure Storage, such as the following:

- Securing access to storage accounts
- Securing access to the storage account data
- Azure Storage service encryption
- Advanced Threat Protection for Azure Storage
- Restricting access from public networks

Securing access to storage accounts

Giving every user the exact permissions they need should be your first concern, to avoid exposing a user's credentials, which would be a disaster.

Role-Based Access Control (RBAC) will help you with segregating duties within your team; specifically, everyone is only granted the required permissions to get their job done.

RBAC role assignments are granted based on the following:

- Subscription
- Resource group
- Resource

For example, RBAC can be used to grant permissions for a user to manage the storage accounts within a subscription, or to grant permissions for a user to manage a complete resource group that contains virtual machines, **Network Interfaces** (**NICs**), storage accounts, availability sets, and more, or to grant permissions for a user to manage a specific resource such as a specific storage account. This does not mean the same user can't be granted permissions to another resource, resource group, or even subscription.

Granting the Reader role to a user using RBAC

Throughout this section, we will cover how to grant a user read permissions on a storage account. Let's get started:

1. First, you must have that user in the Azure Active Directory. If not, you can learn how to do it via the following link: `https://docs.microsoft.com/en-us/azure/active-directory/active-directory-users-create-azure-portal`.

2. Open the Azure portal and navigate to **Storage account**, and then select the storage account you want the user to have read permissions on.

3. Navigate to **Access control (IAM)** and click on **Add**, as shown in the following screenshot:

4. Select the **Role**, which, in our case, is the **Reader** role, and select the user you are willing to grant this role to, as shown in the following screenshot:

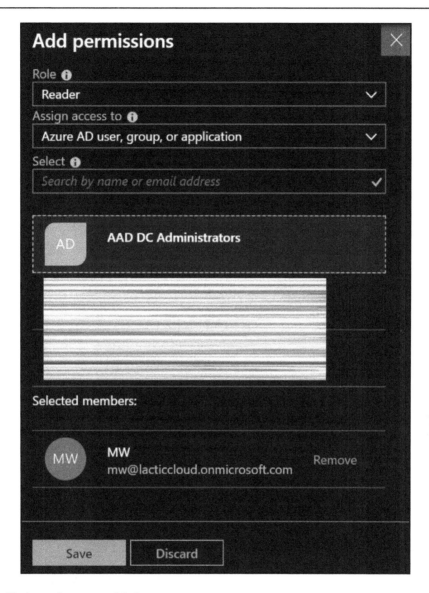

5. Click on **Save** to add the account.

Next, we will learn how to secure data within the storage account.

Securing access to the storage account data

In the previous section, you learned how to secure access to the storage account to make sure that only the right people access storage accounts. In this section, you will learn how to secure the data within this storage account, which can be accessed by other Azure services using access keys.

Storage account access keys are 512-bit strings that are generated once you create a new storage account and get paired with it. These keys are for authenticating Azure services whenever you try to access them.

Fortunately, Azure provides two access keys. So, if the primary key is compromised, you can regenerate the key and use the secondary key in the meantime.

You can store these keys in AKV and you don't have to share them.

To regenerate access keys, you have to navigate to the storage account, and then navigate to **Access keys** under **Settings**, as shown in the following screenshot:

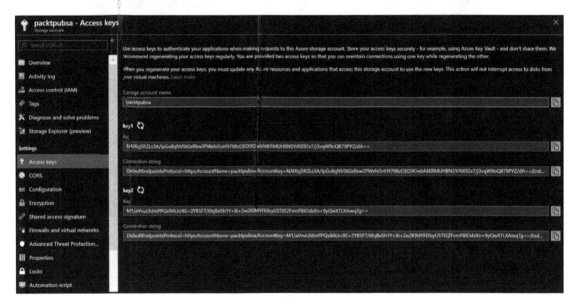

To regenerate the keys, you have to click on the regenerate icon, as shown in the following screenshot:

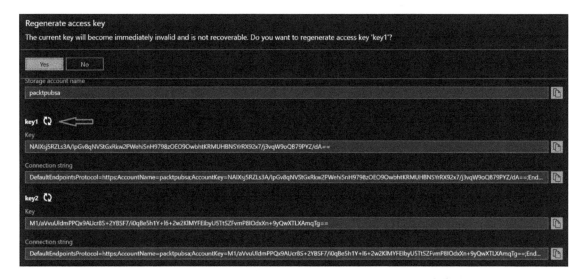

 Whenever you regenerate the access key, you have to update all of the clients who were using the old access key in order to access the storage account. This is to avoid any disruption with your storage services that are based on the storage account for which the access keys were changed.

Azure Storage Service Encryption

Azure Storage provides encryption for data at rest by default using Azure **Storage Service Encryption (SSE)**. Data is secured when it is in transit between the application and Azure using HTTPS, and it gets encrypted when it is written to the storage account using 256-bit AES encryption. You can use SMB 3.0 or a VPN connection for safely transferring the data to Azure as well. Once the data is accessed again, it gets decrypted, and it is sent back over HTTPS. Azure manages the encryption storage keys inside the AKV automatically. SSE is used for table, file, queue, and blob storage, and SSE is available for the Standard and Premium pricing plans, for all redundancy levels and for all regions.

You can set encryption for your storage account in the Azure portal, PowerShell, the CLI, the RESTful API, and the Azure Storage SDK. It is enabled by default, so you don't have to set this in your PowerShell scripts manually.

You can use client-side encryption in your custom code as well. The Azure Storage Client Library for .NET supports this. This also works in conjunction with the AKV. The SDK creates a **Content Encryption Key** (**CEK**), which is used to encrypt the data before it is sent to the storage account. The encryption key is then stored in the AKV by default, but you can use a custom provider as well. Using client-side encryption will encrypt your data before it is sent to Azure and at the same time it is stored inside the storage account.

SSE has one limitation, which is only the data that is created when encryption is turned on will get encrypted. So, if you have disabled encryption for your storage account at some point, then data that is stored inside the storage account is no longer encrypted. When you decide to enable encryption again, the data that was stored earlier does not get encrypted automatically, as data is only encrypted at the time of storing the data. You have to remove and upload this data again to get it encrypted.

Advanced Threat Protection for Azure Storage

Advanced Threat Protection (**ATP**) is an intelligent security capability that detects unusual and potentially harmful attempts to access storage accounts and its data. Once you enable ATP for Azure Storage, it will continuously monitor your storage account access and activity logs and alert you if any anomalies are detected. You can configure alerts to get notified.

To enable ATP, you can access your storage account via **Settings** | **Advanced security** and click on **Enable Advanced Security**. You can learn more about ATP for Azure Storage here: `https://docs.microsoft.com/en-us/azure/storage/common/storage-advanced-threat-protection`.

Azure Storage firewall

Similar to many other Azure services, storage accounts now allow you to restrict access from the public internet and allow only specific virtual networks or specific public IP addresses to be able to access storage account data.

To enable the firewall, open your storage account and browse to the **Firewalls and virtual networks** blade under **Settings**, as shown in the following screenshot:

You can allow access from specific virtual network subnets and specific public IP address ranges with exceptions to allow Microsoft services to access the storage account.

Securing Azure SQL databases

Securing Azure SQL databases is critical to protecting your organization's database server. In this section, we'll be covering different ways to secure your Azure SQL database, such as the following:

- Firewall rules and virtual network access
- Access control
- Transparent data encryption
- **Advanced Data Security** (**ADS**) for Azure SQL Databases

Please note that these are security capabilities specific to Azure SQL Services. Other traditional SQL security best practices such as Always Encryption and Dynamic Data Masking should be considered while planning security for your SQL Databases.

Firewall and virtual network access

You can control the access for each Azure SQL Server by specifying whether you want Azure services to communicate with it or not and which IP addresses are allowed to access this SQL Server and the databases built on it.

Also, you can specify which Azure virtual networks can reach out to this Azure SQL Server.

Controlling access using a firewall

To control access to the Azure SQL Server using a firewall, perform the following steps:

1. Navigate to the Azure portal.
2. In **All services**, search for **SQL servers**.
3. Click on it and a new blade will be opened, where all Azure SQL Servers you have will be displayed.
4. Select the one you want to set firewall rules to.
5. A new blade will be opened. Navigate to **Firewalls and virtual networks**.
6. A new blade will be opened, where you can specify the following:
     - You can specify whether to allow access to all Azure services or not.
     - You can specify the public IP addresses for the clients that are going to connect to this SQL Server. If you wish to add the IP address of the machine you are using, you can click on **Add client IP** and it will be added automatically.
     - Once you are done with the IP addresses you want to add, click on **Save**:

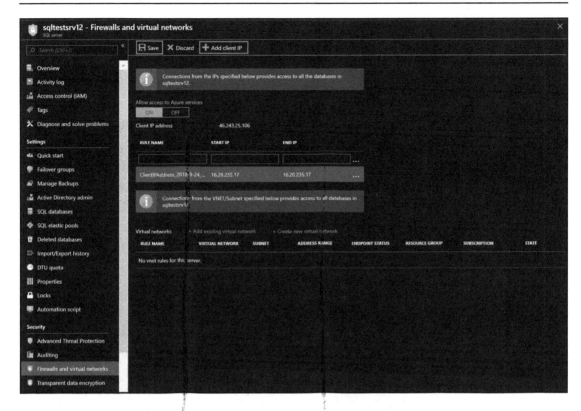

Next, we will be allowing access for services in a virtual network.

Controlling access using virtual networks

You can allow access for the services available in a virtual network to an Azure SQL Server. As a prerequisite, you need to make sure that the `Microsoft.SQL` service endpoint is enabled in this virtual network.

To allow access to the virtual network, perform the following steps:

1. Navigate to **Firewalls and virtual networks**, as indicated in the previous section.
2. In the **Virtual networks** pane, specify whether you want to add an existing virtual network or create a new one.
3. In this case, I selected the option to add an existing one. Once you've clicked on it, you need to specify the following:
   - **Name**: This is a descriptive name for the rule.
   - **Subscription**: Specify which subscription this virtual network exists in.

- **Virtual network**: Specify which virtual network you want to add.
- **Subnet name /Address prefix**: Select which subnet you want to add.

In the end, it will indicate whether the service endpoint is enabled on the virtual network or not:

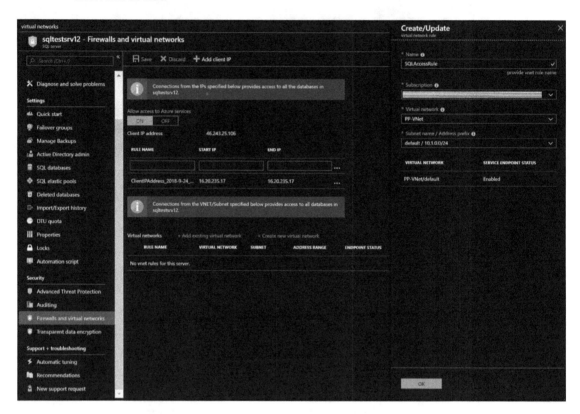

4. Once you are done, click on **OK**, and the subnet will be added.

Next, we will look at access control.

Access control

Like access control in Azure Storage, you can specify which users can access Azure SQL Servers.

You can navigate to the **Access Control** blade of the Azure SQL Server and add the users you wish to add.

Security authentication to Azure SQL

Azure SQL Databases supports two types of authentication:

- SQL authentication
- Azure AD authentication

It is recommended to use Azure AD authentication for all developers/administrators to access Azure SQL Databases; this is done to protect their identities with better security capabilities such as **Multifactor Authentication** (**MFA**) and Azure Active Directory Conditional Access.

You can enable Azure AD Authentication by accessing **SQL Server | Active Directory Admin**.

Transparent data encryption

Transparent data encryption is one of the security features of Azure SQL Databases. It's enabled by default for all newly created databases, but the databases that have been created before May 2017 are not encrypted by default and need this service to be enabled for them.

Transparent data encryption provides the following benefits:

- Protection against malicious activity threats
- Real-time encryption and decryption for the database, its backups, and even the transaction logs with no changes for the application using this database as a backend

How does transparent data encryption work?

This service uses a built-in server certificate to protect the database encryption keys. Each Azure SQL server you create has its own certificate. However, if you have an Azure SQL server working as a replica for another server in another region, it will use the same certificate.

Securing your Azure SQL Databases with your own key

Instead of using the built-in certificates for protection, you can use your own keys to control the process. To do this, the key needs to be stored in Azure and the server must have permission for the key vault. Then, you can perform the following steps:

1. Navigate to the Azure SQL Server you want to configure this service to.
2. Navigate to **transparent data encryption**, and configure the following:
   - **Use your own key**: Select **yes** to enable it.
   - **Specify the key**: You can either choose **Select key** to manually specify the key vault and the key itself or **Enter key identifier** where you need to set the key identifier, which is formatted as `https://{keyvaultname}.vault.azure.net/keys/{keyname}/{versionguid}`.
   - **Key Vault**: If you choose **Select a key**, you need to specify which key vault this key is stored in.
   - **Key**: Select the key you want to secure your Azure SQL Databases.
3. Once you are done, click on **Save**.

Transparent data encryption tips

You need to consider the following tips for a better understanding of transparent data encryption:

- You cannot use transparent data encryption to encrypt a logical master database because the service depends on some objects within this database during the encryption process.
- The built-in certificates used to encrypt the keys are rotated every 90 days.

Advanced data security for Azure SQL services

Azure SQL Databases are designed for security and include various features for you to advance security posture of your databases in the cloud. Advanced data security is a package of multiple capabilities that protects you against database vulnerabilities, detecting anomalous activities, sensitive data privacy, and more.

Let's look at the security capabilities offered by advanced data security for Azure SQL Databases:

- **Data discovery and classification**: This enables you to discover your sensitive and classified data, add confidentiality labels, and track access to sensitive data using them.
- **Vulnerability assessment**: Azure's intelligent security capabilities will continuously monitor and detect whether there are any known vulnerabilities in your database and will help you to remediate them.
- **Advanced Threat Protection**: It continuously monitors your database for any anomalies, harmful attacks and attempts, SQL injections, and other unusual database access patterns. You will receive alerts as soon as any threat is detected.

You can configure advanced data security at a SQL Server and SQL database level. You can refer this link to learn more about ADS and the steps to configure it: `https://docs.microsoft.com/en-us/azure/sql-database/sql-database-advanced-data-security`.

Securing your Azure VMs and network

In this section, we'll discuss various security capabilities and tools to secure Azure IaaS components such as VMs, containers, network, and so on. With that, let's get started. We'll be discussing the following:

- Azure VM security
- Azure network security

Azure VM security

Let's look at some of the security best practices to secure your Azure VMs:

- **Antimalware and virus security**: It is a security best practice to ensure that your VMs are protected from any malware/virus by having an updated antimalware solution. Azure provides a native solution called **Microsoft Antimalware**, however, there are also various third-party antimalware solutions available such as Trend Micro, Symantec, and so on.
- **Encryption**: It is recommended that you encrypt your VM disks using Key Vault. You can use the same BitLocker for Windows and dm-crypt for Linux machines.

- **Access and authorization**: Microsoft provides various roles (Reader, VM contributor, and so on) to enable access to VMs in Azure. It is recommended that you follow the least privileged approach when assigning permissions to team members.
- **Updates and patches**: You can use Azure Update Management to automate and monitor the updates for your VMs.
- **Just-in-Time VM access**: Instead of enabling permanent access to VMs, you can enable VM access to administrators using Azure Security Center's Just-in-Time VM access capabilities.

Azure network security

Let's look at some of the security best practices to secure your Azure network:

- **Perimeter network architecture**: It is recommended that you follow the same network design principle of the traditional world including designing a DMZ zone when designing your Azure virtual network.
- **Network security groups**: Always ensure that you have network security groups configured with minimum needed ports. It is advised that you avoid allowing public access to any management ports.
- **Service endpoints:** Many popular Azure PaaS Services such as Azure SQL Database, and storage accounts, allow configuring access from the specific virtual network only. It is recommended that you create service endpoints for such services and disable public access.
- **Azure Firewall**: Azure Firewall is a fully stateful firewall service and allows you to secure your virtual network with capabilities such as FQDN filtering and network traffic filtering.
- **DDoS protection**: You can create DDoS protection plans in Azure to protect your virtual networks against any denial-of-service attacks.
- **Azure Front Door**: Azure Front Door is a web application firewall service that protects your web applications by detecting and eliminating malicious traffic and attacks and prevents DDoS.
- **Azure Network Watcher**: Network Watcher provides you with tools such as packet capture and security graph view to enable insights during troubleshooting and security reviews.
- **Third-party NVAs**: You can also deploy third-party **Network Virtual Appliances** (**NVAs**) in your Azure virtual network for additional security and configuration choices.

Azure Security Center

In previous sections, we looked at many tools and techniques to secure your Azure resources in a very comprehensive way. Azure Security Center combines them all and gives a holistic view of the security posture of your Azure organization and beyond.

Once you enable Azure Security Center, it examines and continuously monitors your environment, performs a security assessment, and provides you with a number called **secure score**. The secure score is calculated based on various security practices followed in your environment based on their importance; a higher security score would mean that you're following most of the security best practices.

Put simply, the Security Center does the job of a **security analyst** by providing you with an overall security report of your IT environment. You can also use the Security Center to assess security posture on the on-premises environment by installing security agents in your VMs and servers.

The Security Center covers the following scenarios for security assessment and reporting:

- Regulatory Compliance (Azure CIS, PCI DSS, ISO 27001, and SOC TCP)
- Computer and apps:
    - VMs (Azure and on-premises)
    - VM scale sets
    - Azure App Services
    - Containers
- Network security
- IoT solutions
- Data and Storage:
    - Azure SQL Databases
    - Storage Accounts
    - Redis
    - Data Lake Store and analytics
- Identity and Access Security (Azure AD and Key Vault)
- Integration with partner security solutions

Using the Security Center, you can view your overall security alerts, security recommendations, and compliance in one dashboard:

You can visit https://azure.microsoft.com/en-in/services/security-center/ to learn more about Azure Security Center.

Microsoft Trust Center

Microsoft Trust Center is your go-to place for any compliance-related questions around any of Microsoft Cloud Services. It includes resources around security, privacy, compliance, and transparency.

You can access Microsoft Trust Center here: https://www.microsoft.com/en-us/trust-center.

Summary

In this chapter, some of the interesting security services and features in Azure were covered, such as AKV, as well as some techniques to secure Azure Storage and Azure SQL Databases.

In the next chapter, we will be covering application and platform monitoring and alerting strategies by presenting an overview of the available solutions that Azure has to offer.

Questions

Answer the following questions to test your knowledge of the information found in this chapter. You can find the answers in the *Assessments* section at the end of this book:

1. AKV standard provides HSM-backed keys as a feature.
    1. True
    2. False

2. What are the AKV types?
    1. Standard
    2. Premium
    3. HSM
    4. All of them
    5. 1 and 2

3. When you enable Azure Storage Service Encryption, what will happen?
    1. All stored data will be encrypted.
    2. Only data added after enabling the encryption will be encrypted.

Further reading

You can refer to the following links for more information on the topics that were covered in this chapter:

- **Security in Azure App Services and Azure functions**: `https://docs.microsoft.com/en-us/azure/app-service/app-service-security`
- **Azure security best practices and patterns**: `https://docs.microsoft.com/en-us/azure/security/security-best-practices-and-patterns`
- **Tutorial for web applications using AKV**: `https://docs.microsoft.com/en-us/azure/key-vault/tutorial-web-application-keyvault`
- **Azure database security**: `https://docs.microsoft.com/en-us/azure/security/azure-database-security-overview`
- **Azure security guide**: `https://docs.microsoft.com/en-us/azure/storage/common/storage-security-guide`

5
Planning for Security, Availability, and Monitoring

With technologies such as Azure Monitor, Azure Backup, and Azure Site Recovery, you can build an application that is always available and ready to handle any unforeseen disaster scenario.

This section contains the following chapters:

- `Chapter 13`, *Diagnostics and Monitoring*
- `Chapter 14`, *Designing for High Availability and Disaster Recovery*

Diagnostics and Monitoring 13

In the previous chapter, we covered how to design effective messaging solutions by looking at Azure Service Bus and Azure Queue Storage and combining different Azure resources into an effective messaging architecture.

In this chapter, we'll introduce application and platform monitoring and alerting strategies, giving you an overview of the solutions that Azure has to offer. By the end of this chapter, you should know when to use the different types of solutions when issues occur on the Azure platform in general, and within your custom solutions and configurations.

The following topics will be covered in this chapter:

- Azure Log Analytics
- Azure Monitor
- Application Insights
- Azure Service Health
- Azure Advisor
- Azure Network Watcher

Azure Log Analytics

Azure Log Analytics is a service that collects and analyzes log files from various Azure resources and on-premises resources. It can collect all of the data in a single workspace and offers a query language to query data.

You can integrate various resources into Log Analytics, such as data from VMs, by installing an agent on Windows and Linux VMs. Alternatively, you can connect to System Center Operations Manager to collect telemetry from existing agents. Most Azure resources are already integrated into Log Analytics. You only need to create a workspace from the Azure portal to collect the data from them. You can then query the data from the workspace directly using the query language, or you can use analysis tools that can analyze the data. Some examples of analysis tools are Operations Management Suite, Azure Security Center, and Application Insights. You can import the data in Power BI as well to create data visualizations.

After the data is collected, it is organized into data tables that are separated by data type. Azure Log Analytics can collect data from the following resources:

- Data from Azure Monitor can be collected in Log Analytics and searched for using the query language.
- Agents can be installed on Windows and Linux machines to send data to Log Analytics.
- A System Center Operations Manager management group can be connected to Log Analytics to collect data from agents.
- Application Insights and Azure Security Center use Log Analytics by default to store data.
- Log Analytics offers cmdlets that can be used from PowerShell and in Azure Automation runbooks.
- Log Analytics offers the HTTP Data Collector API that can be leveraged in custom applications to send log data to Log Analytics.

Now, let's create a Log Analytics workspace.

Creating a Log Analytics workspace

To create a Log Analytics workspace, follow these steps:

1. Navigate to the Azure portal by opening the following link: `https://portal.azure.com/`.

2. Click on **New** and type in `Log Analytics` in the search bar. Create a new workspace.

3. Enter the following settings:
   - **Log Analytics Workspace**: Type `PacktPubLogAnalytics`.
   - **Subscription**: Pick a subscription.
   - **Resource group**: Create a new one and call it `PacktPubLogAnalyticsGroup`.
   - **Location**: Select **East US**.
   - **Pricing Tier**: Select **Per GB (2018)**, as seen in this screenshot:

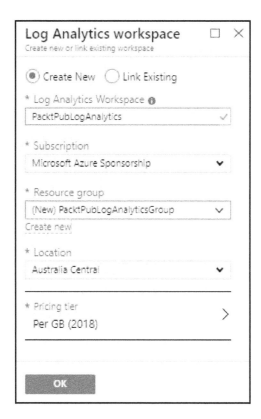

Creating a Log Analytics workspace

   - Click on **OK.**

4. The workspace will now be created.

5. You can now connect the Azure resources to the workspace. Pick a resource group, which we created in one of the previous chapters, and open the settings for the Azure portal. Click on the **Activity log** on the left-hand side menu.

6. The workspace is automatically connected and available for all of the resource groups inside your subscription. The workspace still needs to be associated with the subscriptions, which will be done in the following steps.

7. Logging for this resource group is now possible by clicking the **Logs** button on the top menu:

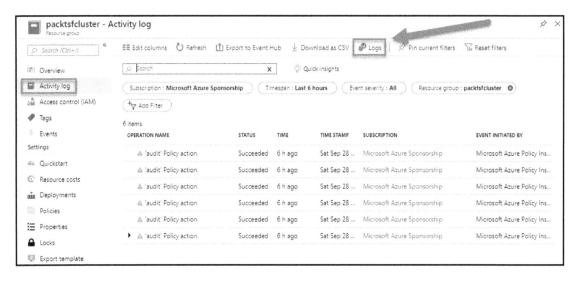

Azure Resource group Activity log blade

8. A new blade will open, where you can add the new activity logs analytics solution to the resource group. Click the **Add** button:

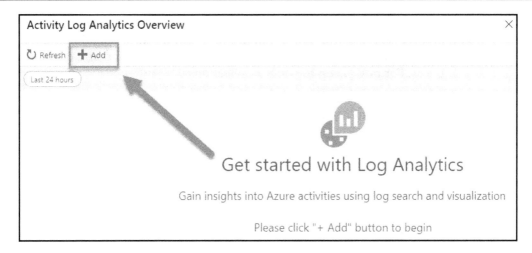

Add a Log Analytics instance

9. A new blade will open, where you can create a new solution or select a solution that is already created. Click the **Select a workspace** button and select the workspace that we created earlier:

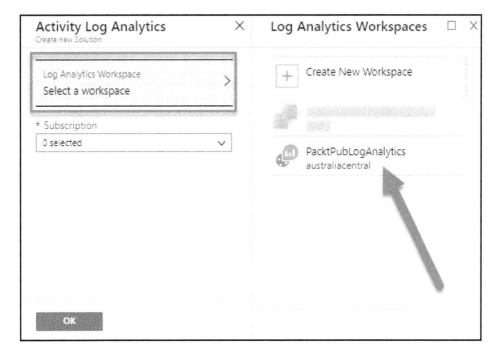

Select the PacktPubLogAnalytics workspace

10. After clicking the **OK** button, all of the available subscriptions are automatically selected to be connected to the workspace. If you want to create additional workspaces for each subscription, you can change the selection and create more workspaces. For now, keep the default selection:

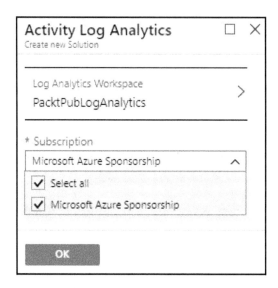

Link PacktPubLogAnalytics to the subscriptions

11. Click **OK**. The workspace will now start to collect all of the data.

12. When you navigate back to the **Activity Log Analytics Overview** blade and click on **Activity Logs**, a new blade will open, where you'll see an overview of all of the activities of your Azure subscription from the last 7 days. This log will give you insights into subscription-level events that have occurred. This includes a range of data, from Azure Resource Manager operational data to updates on Service Health events. The **Activity log** does not include read (GET) operations or operations for resources that use the classic/RDFE model:

Activity log

13. In the left-hand menu, under **Monitoring**, you can also select **Logs**. Here, you can use predefined queries and create custom queries. You can add the following query to retrieve all network-related activities for all of the Azure subscriptions that have been added to the Log Analytics service:

```
AzureActivity
| where ResourceProvider == "Microsoft.Network"
```

The following screenshot shows the output of the preceding command:

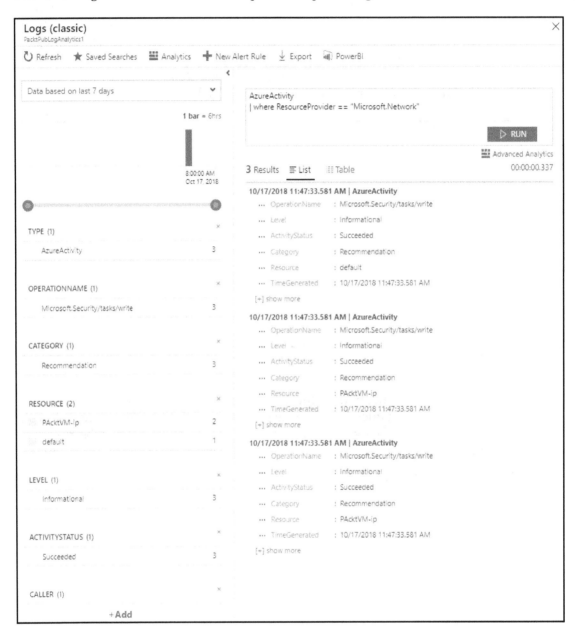

Query result in the Log Analytics portal

In this section, we have covered Azure Log Analytics. In the next section, we are going to learn about Azure Monitor.

Azure Monitor

Azure Monitor is a monitoring solution in the Azure portal that provides infrastructure metrics and logs for most services in Microsoft Azure. Not all Azure resources have been added to Azure Monitor at the time of writing this book, but in the future, more will be added.

Azure Monitor offers the following capabilities:

- **Activity log**: The activity log provides information about every type of event that occurs inside an Azure subscription. These can be activities such as stopping or starting VMs and maintenance activities. It offers different event categories, such as administrative, security, service health, autoscale, alerts, recommendations, policies, and resource health events. The events are stored for a retention period of 90 days. Queries can be saved and pinned to the Azure dashboard, and they can be exported to a storage account so that you can store them for a longer period of time. They can also be exported to an Event Hub for real-time streaming or sent to Log Analytics as well.

- **Diagnostic settings**: These provide information about events that happen inside a particular resource, inside an Azure subscription; for instance, an event for retrieving a secret from Azure Key Vault. These events are not collected by default; they need to be enabled for the resources manually inside the Azure portal, inside an ARM template when the resources are created, or by using PowerShell or calling the RESTful API. These events can be stored inside a storage account or Event Hub or sent to Log Analytics as well, just like the events in the Activity Log.

- **Metrics**: Metrics offer time-based metric points for your resources, just like performance counters in Windows Server. Metrics are available by default, and they have a retention period of 93 days. You can check the performance of an Azure resource and track used and available credits, for instance. They can be sent to Event Hubs or Azure Stream Analytics, and you can retrieve and query data using the RESTful API and PowerShell.

- **Alerts**: The Alerts section offers a single place where you can view and manage all Azure alerts. It displays alerts coming from the Activity Log, Metrics, Application Insights, and Log Analytics. You can create Alert Rules, which can send out an email, SMS, or Webhook; send data to a third-party IT service management application; or call an automation runbook.

The following screenshot shows the Azure Monitor metrics:

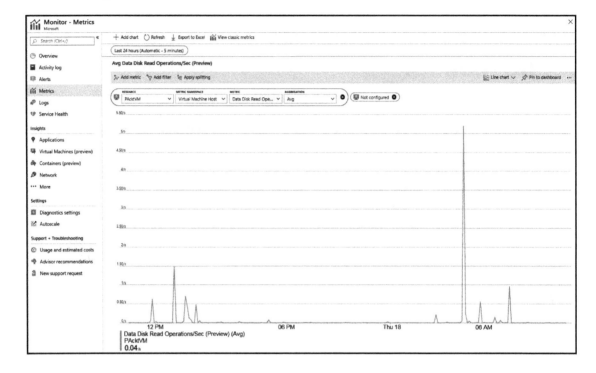

Azure Monitor metrics

In this section, we have covered Azure Monitor metrics. In the next section, we are going to cover Application Insights.

Application Insights

Application Insights offers a monitoring solution for cross-platform apps that are hosted in Azure and for on-premises apps. It is aimed at developers and can be used to monitor performance and detect issues, and it helps to improve the usability of your apps. It can be integrated into DevOps processes and development tools such as Visual Studio.

Developers can set up an Application Insights resource inside Azure and install a package inside their application. This can be an Azure application or an on-premises application; they can both connect to the resource in Azure. This package is responsible for sending telemetry data to Azure. You can add performance counters, Docker logs, and diagnostic logs as well.

Application Insights collects the following types of application events:

- **Rate data**: Different types of rate data can be sent to Application Insights, such as request and dependency rates, and response times and user session counts.
- **Exceptions**: Exceptions that occur inside an application can be sent to Application Insights.
- **Page views and performance**: This can give you information about page views and the load performance of the application.
- **Diagnostic Logs**: This sends Docker Host diagnostic information to Application Insights and traces logging from applications.
- **AJAX calls**: This gives you information about the performance of AJAX calls, failed requests, and response times.
- **Custom events**: You can create custom events in your applications as well.
- **Integration**: You can integrate with Visual Studio App Center and HockeyApp to analyze telemetry data from mobile applications as well.

Once the data has been sent to Azure, it can be viewed in the Azure portal. The Azure portal offers different capabilities so that you can display and analyze data, such as an **Application map** blade, a **Live Metrics Stream**, **Metrics** explorer blades, a **Performance** blade, and more:

Application Insights in the Azure portal

In this section, we have covered Application Insights. In the next section, we are going to cover Azure Service Health.

Azure Service Health

Azure Service Health offers a dashboard in the Azure portal where issues regarding the different Azure resources are displayed. This can give you insights about maintenance schedules, which are platform issues that can affect the availability of resources in Azure.

It offers the following views from the Azure portal:

- **Service issues**: This provides an overview of all of the global issues on Azure that currently occur in all of the different Azure regions. It also offers health history, where you can review or download summaries of historical events.
- **Planned maintenance**: This provides an overview of all of the maintenance events that are scheduled.
- **Resource health**: This provides an overview of the current and historical health of the different resources inside the Azure subscription. When you are having issues, you can run a troubleshooting tool from there as well.
- **Health alerts**: You can create health alerts as well so that you are notified when maintenance activities are scheduled and service issues occur.

The following screenshot shows Azure Service Health in the Azure portal:

Azure Service Health in the Azure portal

In this section, we have covered Azure Service Health. In the next section, we are going to cover Azure Advisor.

Azure Advisor

Azure Advisor is a tool that helps you to follow best practices for deployments in Azure. It analyzes the current configuration of all of the Azure resources, and based on that, it can make recommendations about them. For most recommendations, you can address them from inside the Azure Advisor portal directly.

It offers the following categories:

- **High availability:** This provides several recommendations so that you can improve the continuity of your applications and other Azure resources, such as enabling backups and creating availability sets.
- **Security**: This provides recommendations so that you can improve the security of Azure resources. It integrates with Azure Security Center.
- **Performance**: This provides recommendations for the overall performance of the different Azure resources, such as database performance and App Service performance.
- **Costs**: This section provides recommendations so that you can be more cost-effective, such as resizing or shutting down virtual machines, or reducing costs by eliminating unprovisioned ExpressRoute circuits.

Addressing recommendation from Azure Advisor

To address a recommendation from Azure Advisor directly, follow these steps:

1. Navigate to the Azure portal by opening the following link: `https://portal.azure.com/`.

2. Select Azure Advisor from the left-hand side menu.

3. You will get an overview of all of the different recommendations, categorized into four sections—**High Availability**, **Security**, **Performance**, and **Cost**:

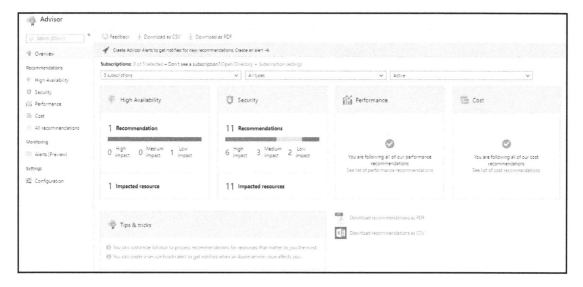

Azure Advisor overview

4. These recommendations are based on all of the different services that are present in your subscription. Select the **Security** section and then pick a high severity recommendation from the overview. For this example, I've selected **Advanced data security should be enabled on your SQL servers**:

Security recommendations

5. A new blade will open, where you will be able to view which SQL servers don't have advanced data security enabled. If you scroll down to the remediation steps, you can select the databases where advanced data security needs to be enabled. After selecting the database, click the **Remediate** button to automatically install it:

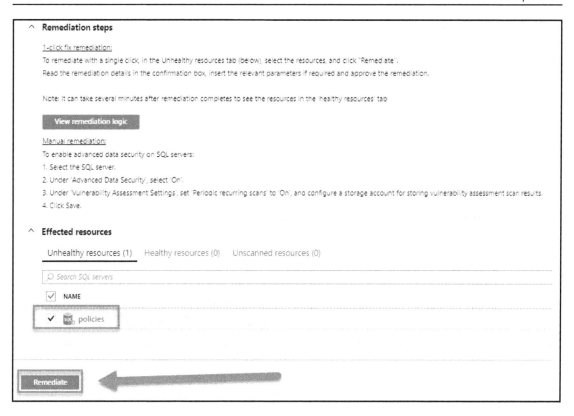

Automatic remediation

In this section, we have covered Azure Advisor. In the next section, we are going to look at Azure Network Watcher.

Azure Network Watcher

Azure Network Watcher offers a network monitoring solution on the Azure resources level for all network communication. This includes VNets, ExpressRoute circuits, application gateway traffic, load balancers, and more. It can be accessed from the Azure portal and offers monitoring tools, diagnostic tools, and logs from the network level.

It offers the following capabilities:

- **Topology**: This provides an overview of all of the network resources in a VNet by offering a graph. From the Azure portal, it provides a subset of all of the network parts. To view a full list of the resources, you can use PowerShell or the RESTful API.
- **IP flow verify**: This offers an overview of the allowed or denied packages for a network interface of a virtual machine. This helps administrators to solve connectivity issues quickly.
- **Next hop**: This provides an overview of the destination routes of packages. This is useful for determining connectivity issues and checking whether packages arrive at the destination, such as on-premises virtual machines.
- **Security group view**: This provides an overview of all of the configured NSGs and rules that are associated with them from two different levels: the network interface level, and the subnet level.
- **VPN diagnostics**: This offers a troubleshooting solution for VPN gateways and connections. Connections and gateways can be called and return the results from the Azure portal, PowerShell, the Azure CLI, or the RESTful API.
- **Packet capture**: From here, you can capture network traffic packets to diagnose network anomalies. It requires an extension that needs to be installed on virtual machines to capture the data packages. Packages can be stored locally on virtual machines or in Azure Blob Storage for further analysis.

- **Connection troubleshoot**: This offers a troubleshooting solution that checks TCP connections from VMs to VMs, IPv4 addresses, URIs, and **Fully Qualified Domain Names** (**FQDNs**). This helps with detecting connectivity issues by collecting all of the configurations. It uses the same extension as the packet capture feature, and connectivity can be checked from PowerShell, the CLI, and the RESTful API as well:

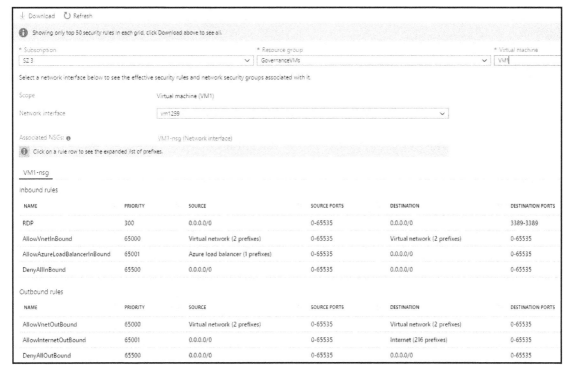

Network Watcher overview

Summary

In this chapter, we covered the different monitoring solutions Azure provides from a platform and application perspective, such as Application Insights, Network Watcher, and Log Analytics.

In the next chapter, we will cover some solutions that will keep your applications highly available so that you can avoid downtime as much as possible.

Questions

Answer the following questions to test your knowledge regarding the information in this chapter. You can find the answers in the *Assessments* section at the end of this book:

1. You are designing an IoT solution and want to provide a real-time monitoring tool for your administrators. Should you use Azure Log Analytics for this?
    1. Yes
    2. No

2. Is Azure Network Watcher a separate application that needs to be installed on your computer?
    1. Yes
    2. No

3. You want to get an overview of all of the maintenance events that are scheduled for the Azure platform. Can you retrieve this information from Azure Service Health?
    1. Yes
    2. No

Further reading

You can check out the following links for more information about the topics that were covered in this chapter:

- **What is Azure Log Analytics?**: https://docs.microsoft.com/en-us/azure/log-analytics/log-analytics-overview
- **Creating custom views using View Designer in Log Analytics**: https://docs.microsoft.com/en-us/azure/log-analytics/log-analytics-view-designer
- **Azure Monitor Documentation**: https://docs.microsoft.com/en-us/azure/monitoring-and-diagnostics/
- **Overview of Azure Monitor**: https://docs.microsoft.com/en-us/azure/monitoring-and-diagnostics/monitoring-overview-azure-monitor
- **Application Insights Documentation**: https://docs.microsoft.com/en-us/azure/application-insights/
- **Azure Service Health Documentation**: https://docs.microsoft.com/en-us/azure/service-health/
- **Introduction to Azure Advisor**: https://docs.microsoft.com/en-us/azure/advisor/advisor-overview
- **Azure Network Watcher Documentation**: https://docs.microsoft.com/en-us/azure/network-watcher/

14
Designing for High Availability and Disaster Recovery

In this chapter, we will cover a number of solutions that will keep your applications highly available so that you can avoid downtime as much as possible. In addition to this, we will also look at how to build a **disaster recovery** solution so that you can ensure business continuity in the unfortunate event of any disaster.

The following topics will be covered in this chapter:

- Introducing high availability and disaster recovery
- App Service
- Azure SQL Database
- Highly available access to apps
- Azure Backup
- Azure Site Recovery

Introducing high availability and disaster recovery

High availability (HA) and **disaster recovery (DR)** may seem like similar terms because they help ensure that the environment is up and running most of the time. Although both of them are business continuity solutions, they are quite different in the way that they work.

High availability is concerned with the uptime of the infrastructure, applications, services, and so on. The goal of high availability is to maintain SLAs for 99.99% of uptime against common outages caused by hardware failures, network failures, and so on.

On the other hand, disaster recovery is concerned with disasters, such as natural disasters, security breaches, and data loss.

Together, high availability and disaster recovery can help you be confident about your business continuity strategy.

Azure provides high availability and disaster recovery solutions to help you ensure the business continuity of your Azure services. Some of these solutions are as follows:

- Azure Load Balancer
- Azure Traffic Manager
- Azure Application Gateway
- Azure CDN
- App Services autoscale
- Azure SQL Database geo-replication
- Azure Storage Geo-Replication
- Availability sets
- Availability zones
- **Virtual Machine Scale Set (VMSS)**
- **Azure Site Recovery (ASR)**
- Azure Backup

Some of these services provide high availability and disaster recovery for applications based on IaaS, such as virtual machine scale sets, Azure Site Recovery, Azure Backup, and so on. On the other hand, there are services that provide high availability and disaster recovery for applications based on PaaS, such as App Service autoscale, Azure SQL Database geo-replication, and so on.

App Service

App Service is one of the most important Azure services out there since it provides PaaS offerings for the following:

- Web apps
- Mobile apps
- API apps
- Logic apps
- Function apps

Because of this, you no longer have to care about the underlying infrastructure that the application is hosted in. You only have to work on developing your applications, provided that Microsoft can provide an SLA of 99.95% availability for your apps.

In the following subsection, you will learn how to provide scalability for your apps.

Scaling up the App Service plan

When you notice that your application is consuming too many App Service plan resources, you can scale up the App Service plan. This gives it more resources so that it can fulfill the application's needs.

> Check out `Chapter 6`, *Designing Web Applications*, for more information about App Service plans.

When you scale up an App Service plan, you get more hardware resources, such as CPU, memory, and storage.

You will also get more support for features such as the following:

- Custom domain/SSL
- The number of instances you can autoscale to
- The number of staging slots you can have
- The number of daily backups for your applications that you can make
- Traffic Manager

To scale up the App Service plan that your application is part of, follow these steps:

1. Navigate to **Azure portal** | **App Services**. Choose the App Service you want to scale up and select **Scale up (App Service plan)**, as shown in the following screenshot:

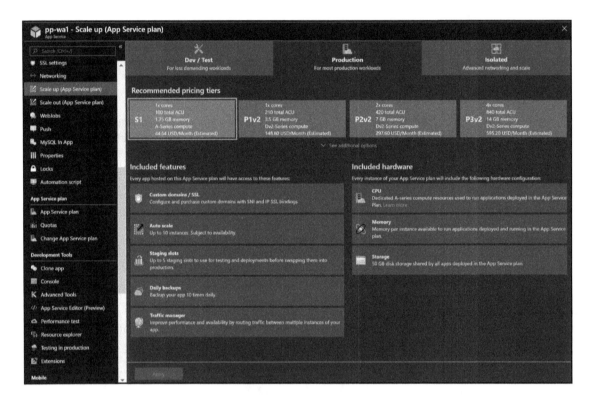

2. Then, select a plan that fits your criteria and click on **Apply**.

3. You can also scale up an App Service plan (if you know which plan your application is part of) by navigating to **App Service plan**. From here, select the App Service plan you want to scale up and click **Scale up (App Service plan)**, as shown in the following screenshot:

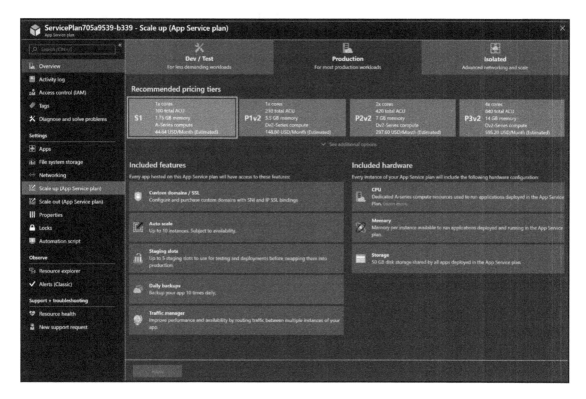

4. Once you're done, click on **Apply**.

Key points regarding scaling up your App Service plan

The following key points will give you more information about App Service plans:

- When you scale up an App Service plan, it affects all of the applications within that plan in a matter of seconds, provided that you don't have to change anything in the code or redeploy the application.
- When you notice that the use of your apps is decreasing, you can scale it down. Otherwise, you will be still charged for the pricing tier you have scaled up to because it has reserved a VM that's running in the background.

Scaling out your App Service plan

Scaling out is a credible solution for applications that have usage peaks from time to time. By scaling out, you can increase the number of instances (VMs) that the App Service is running in instead of increasing its hardware resources. You can also enable auto-scale. By doing this, when a specific threshold is triggered, the App Service plan will be scaled out to handle the load.

There are two ways to scale out your App Service plan, and we will discuss these options in upcoming sections.

Scaling out your App Service plan manually

To scale out your App Service plan manually, you need to follow these steps:

1. Navigate to **Azure portal** | **App Services**. Choose the App Service you want to scale up and click **Scale out (App Service plan)**, as shown in the following screenshot:

2. Then, you can increase the number of instances up to the number you want to scale out to.

3. Once you are done, click **Save**.

You can also perform the same action by navigating to **App Service plan**, selecting the App Service plan you want to scale out, and then choosing **Scale out (App Service plan)**.

Scaling out your App Service plan automatically

To scale out your App Service plan automatically, perform the following steps:

1. Navigate to **Azure portal** | **App Services** and choose the App Service you want to scale out.

2. Click on **Enable autoscale**.

3. Then, you will need to configure autoscale settings by specifying the following:
- **Autoscale setting name**: Specify a descriptive name for the purpose of the autoscale.
- **Resource group**: Specify a resource group for the autoscale setting.
- **Scale conditions**: You can add scale conditions according to your needs by specifying the following:
    - **Scale mode**:
        - **Scale based on a metric**: Specify a metric based on which a scale-out will be performed. For example, when CPU usage exceeds 70%, it will add one more instance.
        - **Scale to a specific instance count**: Specify the number of instances you want to scale to. If you have selected this option, you don't have to proceed with the following settings.

    - **Rules**: Click on **Add a rule** to create a rule that will determine how the App Service plan will scale out/in. A new blade will open, where you have to specify the following:
        - **Metric source**: Specify a source to specify metrics for. These will determine the scale-out/in.
        - **Resource type**: If you have selected **Other resource** as the metric source, you will have to specify the resource type.
        - **Resource**: If you have selected a **metric source** other than the current resource, you will need to specify that source. For example, if you selected **storage queue** as a metric source, you will have to specify which storage account is to be used as a resource.
        - **Time aggregation**: This aggregation method is used to aggregate sampled metrics. For example, *time aggregation = "average"* will aggregate the sampled metrics by taking their average.

- **Metric name**: Specify which metric you want to measure so that the rule can determine whether to scale out/in.
- **Time grain statistic**: This is the aggregation method within the `timeGrain` period. For example, *statistic = average* and *timeGrain = "PT1M"* means that the metrics will be aggregated every 1 minute by taking the average.
- **Operator**: Specify the `measure` operator that will specify when the value of the metric has exceeded the threshold. For example, this operator will specify when the actual value of the resource is greater, less than, equal to, and so on compared to the threshold.
- **Threshold**: This is the threshold that the action will be performed on and specifies whether the plan scales out/in.
- **Duration**: This is the duration of time that's required to look back for metrics. For example, 10 minutes means that every time autoscale runs, it will query metrics for the past 10 minutes. This allows the metrics to stabilize and avoids having to react to transient spikes.
- **Operation**: Specify whether to decrease or increase the instance count/percentage when a threshold is exceeded.
- **Instance count**: The instance count that will be increased/decreased according to the operation you specified in the previous step.

- **Cool down**: The amount of time to wait after a scale operation before scaling again. For example, if the cool-down time is 10 minutes and a scale operation has just occurred, autoscale will not attempt to scale again until after 10 minutes. This allows the metrics to stabilize first. The following screenshot shows the scale rule:

- **Instance limits**:
  - **Minimum**: Specifies the minimum instance count.
  - **Maximum**: Specifies the maximum instance count.
  - **Default**: If there's a problem reading the resource metrics and the current capacity is below the default capacity, to ensure the availability of the resource autoscale will scale out to the default. If the current capacity is already higher than the default capacity, autoscale will not scale in:

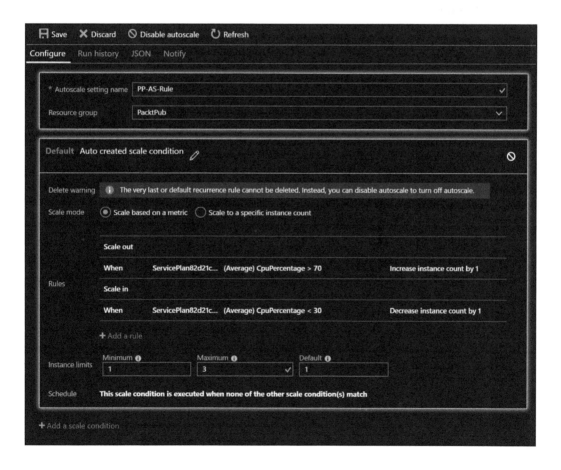

- **Schedule**: By default, the first added rule is executed when none of the other scale conditions match. If you are adding other conditions, you can specify the start/end date or specific days for the rule.
- Once you are done, click on **Save**.

Key points for autoscaling your App Service plan

The following key points will give you more information about App Service plan autoscaling:

- You cannot assign more than one autoscale setting to one resource.
- When you have more than one instance, the threshold will be calculated according to the average of the metric across all of the instances. This is done to decide whether to scale out/in.
- If you want to investigate an autoscale operation failure, you can use the activity log.
- Make sure that you have different values for the minimum and the maximum number of instances with a reasonable margin.
- If you have manually scaled out/in at the same time that you have autoscale rules, the autoscale rules will overwrite the manual scaling you have done.
- Ensure that you have scale-out and scale-in rules so that you can benefit from the usage savings. For example, when the App Service plan scales out after hitting a threshold, it can be scaled in again after going below another threshold that indicates that the resource usage can be scaled in.
- It isn't recommended to set the scale-out/in rules threshold when it goes above or below the same value. For example, do not make the threshold for the scale-out when it is above 70% and scale in when it is below 70%.
- If you have added multiple rules to the same autoscale setting, it will scale out when any scale-out rule is met, but it will not scale in until all of the scale-in rules are met.
- When the metrics are not available, it will use the default number of instances. Therefore, make sure that you have set a reasonable number of instances so that you can get your apps up and running with no negative impact on performance.

App Services deployment slots

Deployment slots are one of Azure App Service's greatest features. With deployment slots in place, you shouldn't be worried if your new release doesn't work appropriately when it is released to production. This is because you can have different slots for dev/test purposes and a different slot for production.

Using deployment slots, you can verify that the application is functioning properly before publishing it. Then, you can swap it with the production slot, which will cause almost no downtime.

If the application doesn't behave as expected, you can swap it with the application that was working in production, right before you swapped the slots.

To add an additional deployment slot, follow these steps:

1. Navigate to the App Service that you want to add another deployment slot to.
2. Under **Deployment**, click on **Deployment slots**, as shown in the following screenshot:

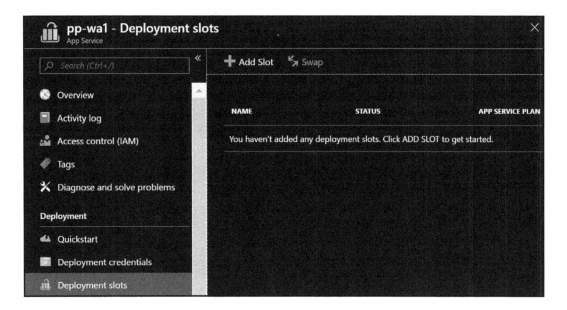

3. Click on **Add Slot**. A new blade will pop up where you have to specify the following:

- **Name**: Specify a descriptive name for the slot.
- **Configuration Source**: Specify whether you want to clone the configuration from another slot or not. Finally, click OK:

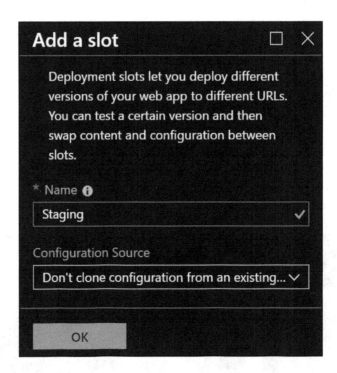

Deployment slots key points

The following key points will give you more information about deployment slots:

- If you have cloned the configuration of a deployment slot, you can edit this configuration later.

- When you swap a deployment slot with another, you will note that some settings will be swapped, while others won't:
    - The following are settings that will be swapped:
        - Handler mappings
        - WebJobs content
        - App settings (unless it is stuck to a slot)
        - General settings, such as WebSockets, framework version, and 32/64-bit
        - Connection strings (unless it is stuck to a slot)
        - Monitoring and diagnostic settings
    - The following are settings that won't be swapped:
        - Custom domain names
        - Scale settings
        - SSL certificates and bindings
        - Publishing endpoints
        - WebJobs scheduler
- Before swapping, make sure that the settings that haven't been swapped are properly configured in the staging slot to avoid any failures after swapping.
- When you swap slots, the traffic will be redirected to the swapped slot and no requests will be dropped. Due to this, you will notice no downtime.

Backing up your App Services

To avoid any unexpected scenarios regarding your apps, it is recommended that you back them up regularly. Then, in the worst-case scenario, you can retrieve your application with minimal data loss.

To configure a backup for your app, follow these steps:

1. Navigate to the App Service you want to back up.
2. Under **Settings**, click on **Backups**, as shown in the following screenshot:

3. When you click on **Configure**, a new blade will open, where you have to specify the following:
   - **Storage settings**: Specify a container in a storage account where the backup will be stored. If you don't have a storage account, you will have to create one.
   - **Backup schedule**: Specify whether you want to run the backup based on a schedule or not. If you enabled scheduling, you will have to specify the following:
     - **Backup every**: Specify the frequency of the backup.
     - **Specify backup schedule from**: Specify when to trigger the backup schedule for the first time.

- **Retention**: Specify how long you want to retain backup files. You can set it to 0 to keep the backup files indefinitely.
- **Keep at least one backup**: Specify whether you want to keep at least one backup or not.

- **Backup database**: If you want to back up a database on the app, tick **INCLUDE IN BACKUP** to back it up too. If you have other backup policies for your databases, you don't have to include this:

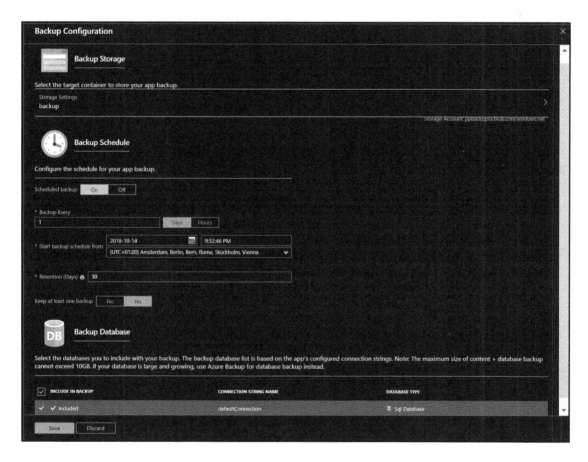

Next, we'll look at some key points for backing up your App Service.

Key points for backing up your App Service

The following key points will give you more information about App Service backup:

- Ensure that the storage account that you are going to store your backup in is in the same subscription as the App Service.
- The backup size should not exceed 10 GB of the application and its database (if the database is backed up too). Otherwise, an error will occur.
- You cannot back up an SSL-enabled Azure MySQL database.
- Don't use firewall-enabled storage accounts to store backups of your apps.
- If you want to back up the database of an application, but you cannot find it displayed under **Backup Database**, ensure that its connection string has been added in the application settings.

In this section, you learned how to apply some HA/DR solutions to Azure App Service. In the next section, you will learn how to do the same with Azure SQL Database.

Azure SQL Database

Azure supports different types of database, such as SQL Server, MySQL, PostgreSQL, Cosmos DB, and so on.

For all of them, Azure provides high availability and disaster recovery solutions. However, in this section, we are going to cover supported solutions for Azure SQL Database. Let's start with active geo-replication first.

Active geo-replication

Active geo-replication is one of the most important business continuity methodologies out there. When using active geo-replication, you can configure up to four secondary databases within the same region or in different regions with reading access. This will help reduce latency for users or applications that need to query the database from a different region.

If a catastrophic disaster occurs, you can fail-over to the other region using a failover group. Failover groups are mainly designed to manage every aspect of geo-replication automatically, such as connectivity, relationships, and failover, provided that it is available for all of the databases in all the service tiers in all the regions.

To implement active geo-replication, follow these steps:

1. Navigate to the desired database on the Azure portal and click on **Geo-Replication** under **Settings**, as shown in the following screenshot:

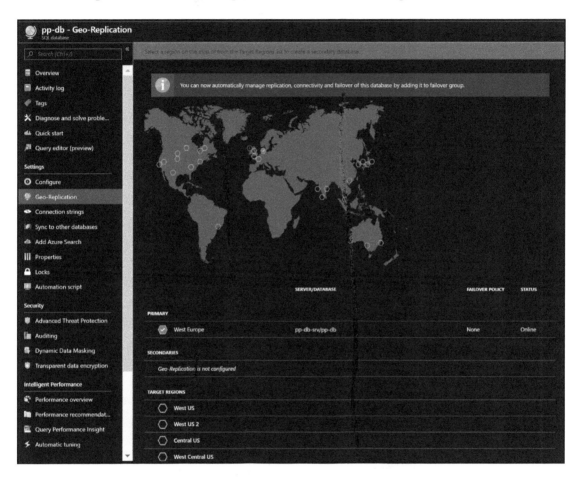

2. Click on the region you want to replicate to.
3. Once you have selected a region, a new blade will pop up, asking you to configure the secondary server that the database will be replicated to. You will have to specify the following:
   - **Target server**: If you haven't created another Azure SQL server in that region to act as a secondary server, you can click on **Target server** and go to the wizard to create a new SQL server. Alternatively, you can select an existing one if you have already created one.

- **Pricing tier**: Select a pricing tier that is not lower than the original one:

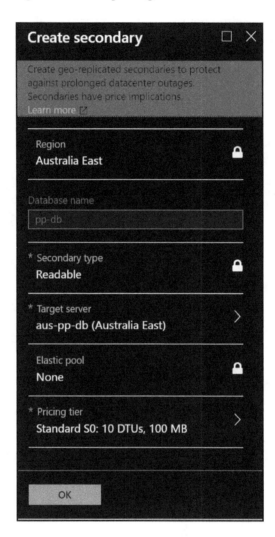

4. Once you are done, click on **OK**.

Auto-failover groups

Auto-failover groups make good use of active geo-replication by providing group-level replication and automatic failover. Moreover, you won't have to change the SQL connection string if a failover occurs.

To create an auto-failover group, follow these steps:

1. Navigate to the SQL server where the databases exist.
2. Under **Settings**, click on **Failover groups**, as shown in the following screenshot:

3. Click on **Add group** to add an auto-failover group.
4. A new blade will pop up, where you have to specify the following:
   - **Failover group name**: Specify a descriptive name for the failover group.
   - **Secondary server**: Specify the secondary server that will host the replicated database.
   - **Read/Write failover policy**: This process can occur automatically, which is the default setting and is recommended. Otherwise, you will have to do it manually.
   - **Read/Write grace period (hours)**: Specify the time between every automatic failover.

- **Database within the group:** Select the databases in the Azure SQL Server to which you would like to add to the auto-failover group:

5. Once you are done, click on **Create**.

Business continuity for Azure SQL Database

Microsoft does its best to address any issues that may occur with Azure SQL Database and it provides a number of solutions for this purpose.

Hardware failures

Hardware failure is something that is expected to happen, but it will not be the cause of database loss.

Just like replication is provided for Azure Storage, there is something similar for Azure databases.

If a hardware failure occurs, don't worry – three copies of your database have been separated across three physical nodes. The three copies consist of one primary replica and two secondary replicas, and in order to avoid any data loss, write operations are not committed in the primary replica until they have been committed in one of the secondary replicas. Therefore, whenever a hardware failure occurs, it will fail-over to the secondary replica.

Point-in-time restore

To avoid any issues that may cause data loss, automatic backups are performed on SQL databases (these include full, differential, and transactional log backups).

Azure SQL Database can be recovered to any point in time within the automatic backup retention period.

The retention period varies from one tier to another: 7 days for the Basic tier, 35 days for the Standard tier, 35 days for the Premium tier, and 35 days for the Premium RS tier. This solution would suit a scenario where your database has been corrupted and you want to restore it to the last healthy point.

To restore your database to the last healthy point, follow these steps:

1. Navigate to the database you want to restore to the last point and click on **Restore**, as shown in the following screenshot:

2. A new blade will pop up, where you can give the restored database a new database name, determine the time that you want to restore to, and change the pricing tier for the restored database, as shown in the following screenshot:

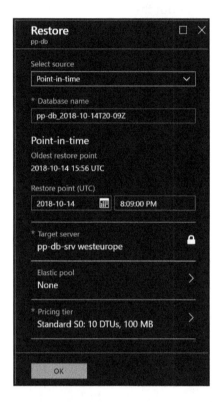

3. Once you click on **OK**, it will start restoring the database.

Key points for point-in-time restore

The following key points will give you more information about point-in-time restore:

- When you restore a database, a new database will be created, which means that you will have to pay for the new database too.
- You cannot give the new database the same name as the original database because the original still exists; to do so, you would have to remove the original one.

- You can choose a restore point between the earliest point and the latest backup time, which is 6 minutes before the current time.
- Database recovery time varies from one database to another according to many factors; the following are some of them:
  - The database's size.
  - The number of transaction logs involved in the operations.
  - The database's performance level.
  - If you are restoring the database from a different region, the network's bandwidth may cause a delay.

In the next section, we will cover Azure Traffic Manager.

Highly available access to apps using Azure Traffic Manager

For end-users, the most interesting thing is being able to access an application as fast as possible with no downtime. That's why Azure provides some services for this, such as Traffic Manager, CDN, and so on.

In this section, we will be covering Azure Traffic Manager.

Azure Traffic Manager is an Azure service that provides users with better and more customizable solutions so that they can control the distributed user traffic of various service endpoints that are located in different data centers around the World. It supports various endpoints, such as cloud services, App Services, and even public IP addresses that can be associated with VMs, load balancers, and so on. It can also be used with non-Azure endpoints, either in other clouds or in your on-premise environment.

Azure Traffic Manager uses intelligent DNS to specify a fulfilling endpoint. In a nutshell, Azure Traffic Manager is Microsoft's global application delivery solution and combines end-to-end application health checks, intelligent DNS, and global load balancing into a single platform.

Azure Traffic Manager benefits

Azure Traffic Manager has many benefits and can help you achieve the following:

- **High availability**: The Traffic Manager ensures that a client request is getting directed to a healthy endpoint. Therefore, in the event that an endpoint goes down, it automatically fails-over to a healthy one.
- **Better responsiveness**: The Traffic Manager can support traffic distribution to a service endpoint that exists in different data centers across the world. As a result, Traffic Managers can direct the traffic to an endpoint that is near the client and will provide better responsiveness.
- **Maintenance with zero downtime**: Whenever you want to maintain endpoints, you can do so because traffic will be directed to the other endpoints; as a result, you will be up and running properly.
- **Distributing across Azure and external endpoints**: You can distribute traffic not only to incorporate Azure services but also to incorporate services that exist on your premises or in other clouds.

Azure Traffic Manager endpoints

Azure Traffic Manager distributes traffic across entities called endpoints. Endpoints can have resources, such as App Service, App Service slots, Cloud Service, and public IP addresses.

Endpoints come in the following three flavors:

- **Azure endpoints**: These endpoints are used for Azure services, such as Cloud Services, App Services (for example, web apps), and public IP addresses that can be associated with a VM or a load balancer.
- **External endpoints**: These endpoints are used for non-Azure services that can be hosted either on-premise or in another cloud.
- **Nested endpoints**: These endpoints can be used for larger and sophisticated environments wherein you have to create endpoints that refer to another Traffic Manager profile.

Azure Traffic Manager routing methods

When the Traffic Manager receives a DNS query from a client, it doesn't directly send it to the service endpoint – it checks which routing method is being used and, based on that method, will determine which service endpoint the request will be directed to.

Azure Traffic Manager supports the following six routing methods:

- **Performance**: This method routes the client's queries to the nearest endpoint based on their geographic location with regard to the client. This provides better performance for the client because it follows the lowest network latency model.
- **Weighted**: This method routes the client's queries based on a weight that you define.
- **Priority**: In this method, queries will be routed to a primary service endpoint, and if they go down, they will be redirected to a backup service endpoint.
- **Geographic**: This method detects the region that the DNS query is originating from and redirects it to a specific endpoint.
- **Multivalue**: This method can only be used if the endpoints are IPv4/IPv6. In this method, when the profile receives a query, all of the healthy endpoints are returned.
- **Subnet**: In this method, sets of IP address ranges are mapped to an endpoint so that when a query is received by the Traffic Manager profile, it is redirected to one of these IP addresses in the address ranges.

Building a Traffic Manager

In this section, you will learn how to create a Traffic Manager via the performance routing method to distribute traffic across multiple App Services. To create a new Traffic Manager, follow these steps:

1. Navigate to the Azure portal and open the **Traffic Manager profiles** blade.
2. To create a new Traffic Manager profile, click on **Add**.
3. A new blade will open where you have to specify the following:
    - **Name**: This will be the name of the Traffic Manager.
    - **Routing method**: This is where you need to specify the routing method that will fulfill your needs.
    - **Subscription**: This is where you need to specify the subscription that you will be using for this service.

- **Resource group**: This is where you need to specify the resource group within which this service will exist as a resource.
- **Resource group location**: This is the location of the resource group in which the Traffic Manager will exist as a resource, but not as a location. This is because Azure Traffic Manager is a global service and not bound to a specific region. However, like all Azure resources, it needs a resource group to be stored logically:

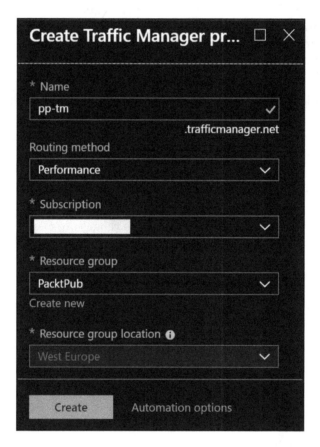

4. Once you click on **Create**, the profile will be created within a minute.

5. Open the blade of the Traffic Manager profile you have created and navigate to **Endpoints**, as shown in the following screenshot:

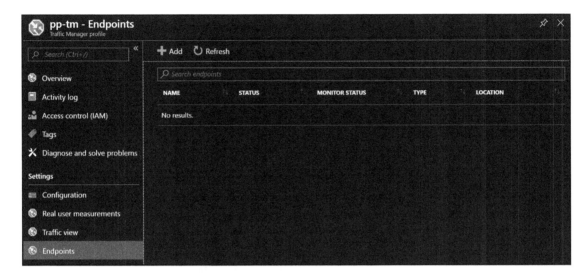

6. Click on **Add** to add an endpoint. A new blade will open where you have to specify the following:

- **Type**: Use Azure Endpoints if you want to distribute traffic across App Services.
- **Name**: Specify a descriptive name for the endpoint.
- **Target resource type**: Select the App Service.
- **Target resource**: Select the App Service resource you want to add to this endpoint.
- **Custom Header settings (Optional)**: You can configure custom headers to the endpoint in the `host:contoso.com,customheader:contoso` format, providing that the maximum supported pair is 8.

- **Add as disabled**: If you want to add this endpoint but disable it, tick this option:

7. Once you are done, click on **OK**. The endpoint will be added.
8. Now, you can repeat this process for other copies of the App Service in other regions.

Azure Traffic Manager key points

The following key points should cover any questions you have regarding Traffic Manager:

- Regarding the performance of Traffic Manager, all of the endpoints located within the same region will receive traffic evenly.
- If the performance of your Traffic Manager endpoints goes down, the client traffic will be sent to the nearest endpoint.
- Since Azure Traffic Manager works at the level of DNS it cannot support sticky sessions, which means binding the user to a specific backend server.

In this section, you learned how to achieve high availability with Traffic Manager. In the next section, you will learn how to make use of Azure Backup to achieve part of the **disaster recovery (DR)**.

Azure Backup

Azure Backup is a cloud-based backup service that allows you to back up, retain, and restore workloads running in Azure and in on-premise environments. Azure Backup uses the highly available Azure Storage in the backend to store your backup data.

The benefits of using Azure Backup include scaling to unlimited workloads without worrying about the underlying infrastructure, keeping them secure by encrypting the data both in transit and in rest, app-consistent backups to ensure your application's integrity, support for a wide range of workloads, retaining data for any duration, and so on.

Supported workloads

Azure Backup supports a wide range of workloads running in Azure and on-premise. Let's take a look at some of the popular workloads supported by Azure Backup:

- Azure Virtual Machines
- SQL databases in Azure Virtual Machines
- SAP Hana Databases in Azure VMs (currently in Preview)
- On-premise workload backups using DPM or Azure Backup Server
- Azure Storage (files)
- File system backup using Azure Backup Agent
- Azure Stack

On-prem workloads support includes Windows Servers, Hyper-V, VMware, Bare Metal, and various other types of workload. Take a look at `https://docs.microsoft.com/en-us/azure/backup/backup-mabs-protection-matrix` to find out more about workloads that are supported by Azure Backup Server for on-premise workloads.

Enabling backups for a virtual machine

In this section, we'll enable backups for a virtual machine running in Azure. Let's start by creating an Azure Recovery Vault.

Azure Recovery Vault stores all our backup and site recovery configurations and is where you manage them. Let's get started:

1. Log in to Azure portal and click **+ Create a resource**. Search for **Backup and Site Recovery** and click **Create.**

2. Select **Subscription** and **Resource group** and provide a name for the vault and region. Note that the region should be the same as where your VMs are running:

3. Click **Review + Create**. This will create a recovery services vault.

4. Open the newly created recovery services vault and click on **Backup** under **Getting started**.

5. Select **Azure** for where your workload is running and **Virtual machine** as the backup type. Click **Backup** once you're ready:

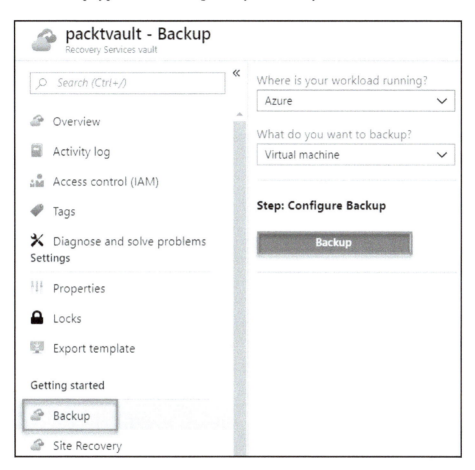

6. Select **Backup policy**. Here, you can choose to use the default policy or create a new one. The backup policy configures the frequency, schedule, and retention of the backup:

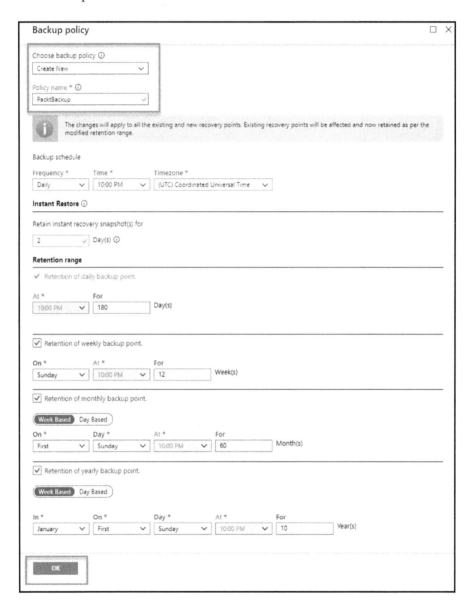

7. Now, you can select the virtual machine you want to backup. You should see all the VMs you have access to that are in the same region as the backup vault. Select the VMs you want to back up and click **OK**. Then, click **Enable backup** to start the backup configuration process.

8. Once the backup is enabled, you will see the VM under **Backup Item** in your recovery service vault. You'll be able to manage all aspects of your backup from here:

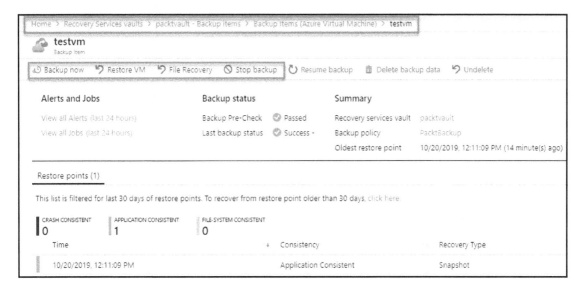

In this section, we learned how to configure backing up a virtual machine in Azure using the Azure Backup service.

Azure Site Recovery

Azure Site Recovery is the disaster recovery service that protects on-premise and Azure workloads against disaster. It is also used to migrate workloads from anywhere to Azure.

Azure Site Recovery (**ASR**) continuously replicates your VMs and physical servers to Azure or your secondary datacenter, which can then be used to fail-over workloads to a secondary location in the event of a disaster at the primary datacenter. Once everything is backed up and normal again at the primary site, you can reverse the replication flow, replicate the changes, and fall back to the primary site.

Supported scenarios – ASR

ASR supports the following topologies:

- **Azure to Azure**: Replicate VMs running in one Azure Region to another Azure Region.
- **On-Premise to Azure**: Replicate VMs and physical servers running in your own datacenters or another cloud to Azure. This includes the following:
    - Hyper-V-based VMs to Azure
    - VMware-based VMs to Azure
    - Physical servers (Windows or Linux) to Azure
- **On-Premise to On-Premise**: Replicates workloads between your primary and secondary datacenters. This includes replication between the following:
    - Hyper-V to Hyper-V
    - VMware to VMware
    - Physical servers (Windows or Linux) to VMware

Please note that support for replication from VMware and physical servers to a secondary datacenter will end on Dec 31, 2020. It is recommended you choose Azure as your secondary site when planning DR for your VMware and/or physical workloads. You can review the Azure documentation for ASR at `https://docs.microsoft.com/en-us/azure/site-recovery/` to find out more about the support matrix around protecting your workload in all of the preceding scenarios.

Summary

In this chapter, we covered some high availability and disaster recovery solutions that are available in Azure so that we can ensure business continuity with a minimal possibility of downtime and data loss.

Here, we covered implementing high availability and disaster recovery in the application and the database and even learned about providing a better client experience by using Traffic Manager, which should provide less load time. We also looked at protecting IaaS workloads using Azure Backup and Azure Site Recovery.

Questions

Answer the following questions to test your knowledge of this chapter. You can find the answers in the *Assessments* section at the end of this book:

1. When you scale up an App Service plan, which hardware resource is increased?
    1. CPU
    2. Memory
    3. Storage
    4. All of them

2. Autoscale only provides a scale-out capability.
    1. True
    2. False

3. When you swap an App Service slot with another one, which of the following settings is not swapped?
    1. Handler mappings
    2. WebJobs content
    3. Scale settings

4. What would happen if you restored an Azure SQL Database from a point-in-time backup?
    1. A new database with a different name will be created
    2. The current database will be overwritten by the restored backup
    3. A new database with the same name will be created

5. If any of the performance Traffic Manager endpoints go down, the client traffic will be sent to the nearest endpoint.
    1. True
    2. False

Further reading

Check out the following links to find out more about the topics covered in this chapter:

- **Learning about Microsoft Azure Storage**: `https://www.packtpub.com/big-data-and-business-intelligence/learning-microsoft-azure-storage`
- **Hands-On Networking with Azure**: `https://www.packtpub.com/virtualization-and-cloud/hands-networking-azure`
- **Azure CDN**: `https://docs.microsoft.com/en-us/azure/cdn/`
- **Azure Site Recovery**: `https://docs.microsoft.com/en-us/azure/site-recovery/site-recovery-overview`
- **Virtual Machine Scale Set**: `https://docs.microsoft.com/en-us/azure/virtual-machine-scale-sets/`

Assessments

Chapter 1: Strategies for Application Modernization Using Azure

The answers to the questions are as follows:

1. 1, 3, and 4: Building cloud-native applications can reduce costs significantly, by using only the compute you need, leveraging serverless applications and containers, and having no need to maintain infrastructure. You can deploy your applications faster and more easily, which will result in a shorter time to market. However, your developers will definitely need to upgrade their development skills to become experienced in building cloud-native applications.

2. 1 and 2: For the rehost migration strategy, no code changes are required. You can just migrate your current VMs or servers to Azure IaaS. This is also the quickest way to migrate your applications to Azure, as they are migrated as is.

3. 2, 3, and 4: By choosing the refactor, rearchitect, or rebuild migration strategy, organizations can start making use of the DevOps capabilities in Azure.

Chapter 2: Building Your Application Migration Roadmap

The answers to the questions are as follows:

1. 1, 3, and 4: Assess, migrate, and optimize are the steps that are part of defining a roadmap for application migration.

2. 3: Azure Migrate can assess both Hyper-V and VMware VMs. For other types of VMs, third-party tooling needs to be used.

3. 2, and 4: Azure Migrate uses Azure Site Recovery and Azure Database Migration Service to migrate workloads to Azure.

Chapter 3: Getting Started with Docker and Kubernetes

The answers to the questions are as follows:

1. 2: You can use many services, such as AKS, ACS, Web Apps for Containers, and ACI, to deploy containers on Azure. It is not required to build your own Docker host.
2. 2: At the time of writing of this book, ACR supports only the private registry type.
3. 5: You can store data in any of the places given as answers. However, it is recommended to use Azure Files or Azure Disks.

Chapter 4: Deploying Highly Scalable Apps with Kubernetes

The answers to the questions are as follows:

1. 1: AKS is the only true managed Kubernetes service on Azure.
2. 2: You can use persistent storage with Kubernetes using Azure Disks and Kubernetes Volumes and Volume Claims.
3. 3: All given options can be used to deploy apps to Azure.

Chapter 5: Modernizing Apps and Infrastructure with DevOps

The answers to the questions are as follows:

1. 2: You can use the Azure DevOps cloud service or Azure DevOps Server (previously known as TFS).
2. 2: Azure Pipelines' release pipelines help you to deploy applications in a CI/CD manner.
3. 1: Azure Boards is meant for overall project planning, management, and tracking.

Chapter 6: Designing Web Applications

The answers to the questions are as follows:

1. 1: Redis Cache is an on-memory key-value data store.
2. 2: You should use Azure Traffic Manager to spread the workload from your web app over different regions.
3. 2: Azure B2C is the one you can leverage in your custom applications, not Azure B2B.

Chapter 7: Scalability and Performance

The answers to the questions are as follows:

1. 2: HPC Pack is used to create HPC clusters in your on-premises environment.
2. 1: The H-series offers VMs that are specifically aimed at high performance.
3. 2: To automate the creation of Azure Batch processes, Azure Batch uses a JSON template.

Chapter 8: Building Microservices with Service Fabric

The answers to the questions are as follows:

1. 2: Azure Service Fabric Mesh is the full PaaS offering from Microsoft.
2. 1: Yes, you can control the full life cycle of your application with Azure Service Fabric.
3. 3 and 4: They are called the Reliable Actor Programming Model and the Reliable Services Programming Model.

Chapter 9: Building Scalable Systems with Azure Functions

The answers to the questions are as follows:

1. 1: While it was possible to write functions in Python in the v1 runtime, it was an experimental language and support was dropped in runtime v2.
2. 3: It is not possible to trigger on files from external providers. Some were supported in v1 but dropped in v2.
3. 4: It is not possible to write any kind of JavaScript in proxies.

Chapter 10: Connecting to the Database

The answers to the questions are as follows:

1. 1, 2, 3, 4, and 5: All types of databases are offered in Azure. Relational databases are covered by Azure SQL, MySQL, and Postgres, while NoSQL databases are available through Cosmos DB and Redis. For other databases, you can spin up a VM and install the database of your choice.
2. 4: Redis is a separate database and is not offered as an API in Cosmos DB.
3. 2: Backups and managed instances are only available for SQL Server; Azure Oracle accounts don't exist, and rewriting the application to use SQL Server instead is not the quickest way possible. Your best option is to use a VM and install Oracle.

Chapter 11: Managing and Deploying Your Code

The answers to the questions are as follows:

1. 5.
2. 1: You have to install Azure Development as a workload to start using integration between Visual Studio and Azure for Azure application development.

Chapter 12: Securing Your Azure Services

The answers to the questions are as follows:

1. 2: Because HSM is supported in the premium flavor, not the standard one.
2. 5: Azure Key Vault has two types—Standard and Premium.
3. 2.

Chapter 13: Diagnostics and Monitoring

The answers to the questions are as follows:

1. Yes.
2. No.
3. Yes.

Chapter 14: Designing for High Availability and Disaster Recovery

The answers to the questions are as follows:

1. 4.
2. 2: You can also scale in.
3. 3.
4. 1.
5. 3: This is how the performance routing mechanism works.

Other Books You May Enjoy

If you enjoyed this book, you may be interested in these other books by Packt:

Azure for Architects - Second Edition
Ritesh Modi

ISBN: 978-1-78961-450-3

- Create an end-to-end integration solution using Azure Serverless Stack
- Learn Big Data solutions and OLTP–based applications on Azure
- Understand DevOps implementations using Azure DevOps
- Architect solutions comprised of multiple resources in Azure
- Develop modular ARM templates
- Develop Governance on Azure using locks, RBAC, policies, tags and cost
- Learn ways to build data solutions on Azure
- Understand the various options related to containers including Azure Kubernetes Services

Azure Networking Cookbook
Mustafa Toroman

ISBN: 978-1-78980-022-7

- Learn to create Azure networking services
- Understand how to create and work on hybrid connections
- Configure and manage Azure network services
- Learn ways to design high availability network solutions in Azure
- Discover how to monitor and troubleshoot Azure network resources
- Learn different methods of connecting local networks to Azure virtual networks

Leave a review - let other readers know what you think

Please share your thoughts on this book with others by leaving a review on the site that you bought it from. If you purchased the book from Amazon, please leave us an honest review on this book's Amazon page. This is vital so that other potential readers can see and use your unbiased opinion to make purchasing decisions, we can understand what our customers think about our products, and our authors can see your feedback on the title that they have worked with Packt to create. It will only take a few minutes of your time, but is valuable to other potential customers, our authors, and Packt. Thank you!

Index

.NET Core
  Azure SQL, connecting from 291
  used, for working with MongoDB API 312, 314

A

ACI, with AKS
  reference link 103
Active Directory Federation Services (ADFS) 176
Active Directory Single Sign-On (AD SSO) 287
active geo-replication
  implementing 437, 438
  using 436
ADO.NET
  used, for connecting Azure SQL 292, 293
Advanced Data Security (ADS) 383
advanced data security
  reference link 389
Advanced Threat Protection (ATP) 382
AKS application
  autoscaling 92
  executing, with ACI 103
AKS cluster, connecting to Kubernetes cluster
  using, kubectl 80
  using, Kubernetes API 80
  using, Kubernetes dashboard 80
AKS cluster
  autoscaling 93, 94
  autoscaling, reference link 94
  connecting to 80, 81
  deploying 74
  deploying, with Azure CLI 79
  deploying, with Azure portal 74, 76, 78, 79
  manually, scaling 93
  scaling 92
  upgrading 95

AKS Kubernetes files
  reference link 97
AKS networking modes 81, 82
app modernization
  about 9, 10
  advantages 10
App Service Environment (ASE)
  about 152, 153
  creating 154, 156, 157
  reference link 157
App Service Migration 32, 33
App Service Plan
  about 150, 151, 152
  key points 424
  key points, for autoscaling 430
  scaling out 424
  scaling out, automatically 425, 426, 427, 428, 429, 430
  scaling out, manually 424, 425
  scaling up 421, 422, 423
App Service
  about 421
  backing up 433, 434, 435
  backing up, key points 436
  deployment slots 431, 432
  deployment slots, key points 432, 433
Application Insights
  about 407, 408
  AJAX calls 407
  custom events 407
  Diagnostic Logs 407
  exceptions 407
  integration 407
  page performance 407
  page views 407
  rata data 407
  types 407

application, exposing outside Kubernetes cluster
  about 96
  Cluster IP 96
  expose, via Azure HTTP routing 97
  expose, via ingress controller 97
  Load Balancer 96
  NodePort 96
applications containerization
  about 45
  Docker host, building in Azure 47, 48, 49
  Docker images, building 54, 55
  Docker images, preparing 49, 50
  Dockerfile, preparing 50, 51
  planning for 46, 47
  sample Dockerfile, preparing for sample app 52,
  53
applications
  deploying 88, 90
  deploying, Helm used 103
  deploying, on AKS 82
  running, with containers 60, 61
  scaling, on AKS 90
  scaling, on AKS manually 91
  upgrading, on AKS 94
Artifacts 265
ASP.NET application
  deploying, to Azure with Visual Studio 341, 342,
  343, 344, 345, 346, 347, 348, 349
  deploying, with Visual Studio for Azure 338
  developing, with Visual Studio for Azure 338
Atom-Record-Sequence (ARS) 301
auto-failover groups
  creating 439, 440
Automatic Scaling Formulas
  reference link 193
Azure Active Directory (Azure AD) 176
Azure Advisor
  about 410
  address recommendation 411, 412, 413
  categories 410
  costs 410
  high availability 410
  performance 410
  security 410
Azure App Service, on Linux

reference link 158
Azure artifacts 116, 117
Azure Backup
  about 449
  benefits 449
  enabling, for virtual machine 450, 451, 452, 453
  supported workloads 449
  supported workloads, reference link 449
Azure Batch service
  creating, reference link 192
Azure Batch, for Containers
  about 42
  reference link 42
Azure Batch
  about 189, 190, 191
  containers on 196
  job, executing from code 196, 197, 198, 199,
  200, 201, 202
  reference link 191
  service, creating 191, 192, 193, 194
  stateless components 195, 196
Azure Blob Storage 186, 188
Azure boards
  about 110, 111
  backlogs 111
  boards 111
  capabilities 110
  queries 111
  sprints 111
  work items 110
Azure Cache, for Redis
  tiers 163
Azure Cache
  using, for Redis 163, 164
Azure CLI
  used, for deploying AKS cluster 79
Azure Container Instances (ACI)
  about 40, 41
  used, for executing AKS application 103
Azure Container Registry (ACR) 56, 124
Azure Container Service (ACS) 68
Azure Cost Management 24
Azure credentials
  used, for logging in to Visual Studio 335, 336
Azure Database Migration Guide

about 31, 32
steps 31
Azure DevOps project
creating 117
voting app code, cloning 118, 119
Azure DevOps services, pricing
reference link 109
Azure DevOps
about 107, 108
obtaining 108
signing up 109, 110
used, for building CI/CD pipeline 117
used, for deploying Azure Functions 263, 265,
266
variants 108, 109
Azure Explorer
using, within Eclipse 354, 355
Azure extensions
reference link 359
Azure Firewall 390
Azure Front Door 390
Azure Functions proxies
about 274
creating 274, 275
using, for testing 275, 276
Azure Functions
best practices 277
creating 249, 250
creating, in Visual Studio 259, 260, 261, 262
deploying 262
deploying, with Azure DevOps 263, 265, 266
deploying, with Visual Studio 262, 263
function, creating 252, 253
HTTP function, consuming 253, 254
management 254, 255
Azure IaaS
Docker 45
Azure Key Vault (AKV)
about 363, 365
advantages 364
certificates 374, 375, 376, 377
creating 365, 366, 367, 368, 370
keys 370, 371, 372, 373
premium 365
scenarios 364

secrets 374
standard 365
Azure Kubernetes Service (AKS), monitoring
capabilities
insights 99, 100, 101
logs 102
metrics 101
Azure Kubernetes Service (AKS), use cases
about 70
IoT 70
lift-and-shift containers 70
machine learning 70
microservices 70
Secure DevOps 70
Azure Kubernetes Service (AKS)
about 41, 68
advantages 69, 70
application, deploying 88, 90
application, scaling manually on 91
application, upgrading 94
applications, deploying 82
applications, scaling 90
deployment YAML file, building 84
logging, Operations Management Suite (OMS)
used 97
monitoring, Operations Management Suite (OMS)
used 97
need for 68
scalable application deployment, planning 82
Azure Log Analytics 398
Azure Marketplace
Docker 42
Visual Studio 333, 334
Azure Migrate
about 28, 29, 30
steps 29
Azure Monitor, for VMs
reference link 185
using 184
Azure Monitor
about 405, 406
activity log 405
alerts 405
capabilities 405
diagnostic settings 405

metrics 405
Azure Network Watcher
    about 390, 413
    capabilities 414
    connection troubleshoot 415
    hop 414
    IP flow, verifying 414
    packet capture 414
    security group view 414
    topology 414
    VPN diagnostics 414
Azure network
    about 389
    security, best practices 390
Azure pipelines
    about 113, 114
    agents 114
    features 113
    reference link 109, 114
    URL 144
    using, with GitHub 144
Azure portal
    bindings, adding 269, 270, 271
    MongoDB API, working 311
    URL 74, 159
    used, for deploying AKS cluster 74, 76, 78, 79
Azure Red Hat Openshift (ARO)
    about 44, 68
    reference link 44
Azure Repos
    about 112, 113
    reference link 113
Azure Security Center
    about 25, 26, 391, 392
    reference link 392
    tools 25
Azure Service Fabric cluster
    creating 213, 215, 217, 218, 219, 220
Azure Service Fabric Mesh 212, 213
Azure Service Fabric, life cycle features
    reference link 212
Azure Service Fabric, programming models
    about 209
    Reliable Actor programming model 211
    Reliable Services programming model 210

Azure Service Fabric
    about 43, 44, 206, 207
    application scenarios 209
    life cycle, management 212
    reference link 44
    roles 212
    stateful microservices 207, 208
    stateless microservices 207, 208
Azure Service Health
    about 409
    views 409
Azure Site Recovery (ASR)
    about 420, 453
    reference link 454
    supported scenarios 454
Azure Site Recovery
    about 30, 31
    features 31
Azure SQL Database
    about 436
    access control 386
    access, controlling with firewall 384
    access, controlling with virtual networks 385,
        386
    active geo-replication 436, 437, 438
    advanced data security 388, 389
    auto-failover groups 439, 440
    auto-failover groups, creating 439
    business continuity 440
    creating 283, 284, 286
    firewall access 384
    securing 383
    securing, with own key 388
    security authentication 387
    transparent data encryption 387
    virtual network access 384
Azure SQL
    connecting, ADO.NET used 292, 293
    connecting, from .NET Core 291
    connecting, from Java 297
    database, using in portal 287, 288
    Entity Framework Core, used for connecting 293
    Entity Framework migrations 294, 295, 297
    JDBC, used for connecting 297
    JPA, used for connecting 298, 300

pricing tiers 286
version, selecting 282, 283
working with 282
Azure Storage firewall 382, 383
Azure Storage Service Encryption (SSE) 381, 382
Azure Storage, ATP
  reference link 382
Azure Storage
  access, securing to storage account data 380, 381
  access, securing to storage accounts 377
  Advanced Threat Protection (ATP) 382
  reader role, granting to user with RBAC 378, 379
  securing 377
Azure test plans
  about 115
  reference link 116
Azure Toolkit
  installing, for Eclipse 350, 352, 353
Azure tools
  installing, for Visual Studio 334, 335
  obtaining, for Visual Studio 333
Azure Traffic Manager, endpoints
  about 444
  Azure endpoints 444
  external endpoints 444
  nested endpoints 444
Azure Traffic Manager
  about 443
  benefits 444
  building 445, 447, 448
  endpoints 444
  key points 448
  routing methods 165, 445
  used, for accessing apps 443
  using 164, 165
Azure VMs
  about 389
  security, best practices 389, 390
Azure Voting App backend 82
Azure Voting App frontend 82
Azure Voting App
  about 82, 117
  application code, pushing 119, 120

Azure repo, setting up 119, 120
build pipeline, setting up 121, 122, 123, 124, 125, 126, 128
end-to-end CI/CD experience, simulating 141, 142, 144
reference link 82
release pipeline, building 129, 130, 131, 132, 134, 135, 137, 139, 140
Azure Web Apps 150
Azure, configuration files
  reference link 84
Azure
  about 61
  ASP.NET application, deploying with Visual Studio 338, 341, 342, 343, 344, 345, 346, 347, 348, 349
  ASP.NET application, developing with Visual Studio 338
  Docker host, building 47, 48, 49
  Eclipse, using with 349, 350
  Integrated Development Environment (IDE) 331, 332
  Java project, publishing with Eclipse 355, 356, 358
  Kubernetes environments, building on 68
  signing in 354, 355
  Visual Studio, using with 332
  with IntelliJ 360
  with Visual Studio Code 359

B

Batch .NET SDK, used for creating Azure Batch solution
  reference link 196
bindings
  about 273
  adding, in Azure portal 269, 270
  adding, in portal 271
  adding, in Visual Studio 272
Bringing Your Own License (BYOL) 286
business continuity, for Azure SQL Database
  about 440
  hardware failures 440
  point-in-time restore 441, 442
Business Critical 286

Business to Consumer (B2C) 176

C

C#
  Redis cache database, working from 321, 322
Cassandra API 308
Certificate Authority (CA)
  types 375
CI/CD pipeline
  building, with Azure DevOps 117
Cloud Explorer
  using, in Visual Studio 336, 337
cloud maturity model
  about 11
  migration strategies 12
  rearchitect 15, 16
  rebuild 16, 17
  refactor 14, 15
  rehost 12, 13
cloud migration plan
  creating 22
cloud-native HPC solutions
  about 185, 186
  ARM templates 186
  Azure Blob Storage 186
  HPC compute nodes 185
  HPC head node 185
  Virtual Machine Scale Set (VMSS) 186
  Virtual network 186
Cluster Autoscaler (CA) 93
containers, on Batch Shipyard
  reference link 196
containers
  used, for running application 60, 61
Content Delivery Network (CDN)
  about 163
  using 163
Content Encryption Key (CEK) 382
continuous delivery (CD) 10
continuous integration (CI) 10
Cosmos DB
  about 301, 302
  document model/MongoDB API 303, 304
  graph model/Gremlin API 306, 308
  key-value model/Table API 302

SQL API 305, 306
  wide column model/Cassandra API 308
Create, Read, Update, and Delete (CRUD) 172
cron 267
cron expressions
  URL 267
cron syntax
  using 267
custom web APIs
  designing 168, 169, 170, 172, 173, 174, 175
  securing 168, 175
  securing, services 176

D

Data Migration Assistant (DMA) 283
deployment YAML file
  backend pod, deploying 84
  building, on AKS 84
  frontend application, deploying 86, 88
  service, for backend pod deployment 86
  service, for frontend application 88
development (Dev) 108
disaster recovery (DR) 420, 449
Docker ecosystem, in Azure
  about 40
  Azure Batch, for Containers 42
  Azure Container Instances (ACI) 40, 41
  Azure Kubernetes Service (AKS) 41
  Azure Red Hat Openshift (ARO) 44
  Azure Service Fabric 43, 44
  Docker, in Azure IaaS 45
  Docker, in Azure Marketplace 42
  Web Apps, for Containers 42
Docker Enterprise Edition
  about 43
  reference link 43
Docker Hub
  URL 159
Docker images
  building 54, 55
  preparing 49, 50
  pushing, to ACR 56, 58, 59
  pushing, to Docker Hub 55, 56
Docker
  in Azure IaaS 45

in Azure Marketplace 42
Dockerfile
  preparing 50, 51
document model 303, 304
dynamic pricing 248, 249
dynamic scaling 248

E

Eclipse
  Azure Explorer, using 354, 355
  Azure Toolkit, installing for 350, 352, 353
  used, for publishing Java project to Azure 355, 356, 358
  using, with Azure 349, 350
Entity Framework (EF) 293
Entity Framework Core
  used, for connecting Azure SQL 293
Entity Framework migrations 294, 295, 297
ExpressRoute 187

F

Fully Qualified Domain Names (FQDNs) 415
function 248
Function as a Service (FaaS) 249

G

General Purpose 286
Git concepts
  reference link 112
graph model 306, 308
Gremlin API 306, 308

H

Hardware Security Module (HSM) 364
Helm-based applications, on AKS
  reference link 103
Helm
  used, for deploying application 103
high availability (HA)
  about 163, 420
  web apps, designing for 162
High-Performance Computing (HPC) 179
high-performance, VMs
  reference link 180

Horizontal Pod Autoscaler (HPA)
  about 92
  reference link 92
HPC Cluster Manager 185
HPC cluster on-premises
  deploying 188, 189
HPC compute nodes 185, 187
HPC head node 185, 187
HPC virtual machines
  scale sets 181, 182, 183, 184
  working with 179, 180
HTTPS, for Content Delivery Network (CDN)
  reference link 163
Hybrid cluster 185
Hybrid HPC architecture
  about 187, 188
  Azure Blob Storage 188
  ExpressRoute 187
  HPC compute nodes 187
  HPC head node 187
  Virtual machine scale sets 187
  Virtual network 187
  VPN Gateway 187
Hyperscale 286

I

Infrastructure as a Service (IaaS) 25, 282
input bindings 269
Integrated Development Environment (IDE)
  for Azure 331, 332
IntelliJ
  reference link 360
  with Azure 360
IO operations per second (IOPS) 286

J

Java project
  publishing, to Azure with Eclipse 355, 356, 358
Java
  Azure SQL, connecting to 297
  Redis cache database, working with 324, 326, 328
  used, for working with MongoDB API 314, 316, 318
JDBC

used, for connecting Azure SQL 297
JPA
  used, for connecting Azure SQL 298, 301

K

key-value model 302
kubectl
  reference link 80
kubenet
  reference link 82
Kubernetes API
  reference link 85
Kubernetes Dashboard, with AKS
  reference link 81
Kubernetes environments
  building, on Azure 68
Kubernetes
  about 61
  architecture 64, 65, 66
  concepts 66, 67
  deploying 74
  extensible 62
  key properties 62
  overview 62
  portable 62
  purpose 63
  recreate 94
  rolling upgrade 94
  self-healing 62

L

local Service Fabric cluster
  setting up 232
Log Analytics workspace
  creating 398, 399, 400, 401, 402, 403, 404,
  405

M

Message Passing Interface (MPI) 190
Microsoft Antimalware 389
Microsoft Assessment and Planning (MAP) Toolkit
  about 28
  URL 28
Microsoft Azure
  URL 332

Microsoft HPC Pack
  about 185
  cloud-native HPC solutions 185, 186
  features 185
  HPC Cluster Manager 185
  HPC cluster on-premises, deploying 188
  Hybrid cluster 185
  Hybrid HPC architecture 187, 188
  PowerShell 185
Microsoft JDBC Driver for SQL 297
Microsoft Trust Center
  about 392
  reference link 392
migration roadmap, assess
  about 22
  apps, discovering 23
  apps, evaluating 23
  cloud migration plan, creating 22
  stakeholders, involving 22
  Total Cost of Ownership (TCO), calculating 23
migration roadmap, optimize
  about 24
  Azure Cost Management 24, 25
  billing 24, 25
migration roadmap, security and management
  features
  about 25
  Azure Security Center 25, 26
  Cloud health monitoring 26, 27
  data protection 27
migration roadmap, tools
  about 27, 32
  App Service Migration 32, 33
  Azure Database Migration Guide 31
  Azure Migrate 28, 29, 30
  Azure Site Recovery 30, 31
  Microsoft Assessment and Planning (MAP)
    Toolkit 28
migration roadmap
  building 22
  migrate 23
migration strategies
  about 24
  rearchitect 24
  rebuilt 24

refactor 24
rehost 24
MongoDB API
  about 303, 304
  working with 309, 310
  working with, from C# 312, 314
  working with, from Java 314, 316, 318
  working with, in Azure portal 311
Multifactor Authentication (MFA) 387

N

N-series virtual machines, hardware specifications
  reference link 180
Network Interfaces (NICs) 378
Network Security Group (NSG) 60
network security groups 390
Not Only SQL (NoSQL) 301

O

operations (Ops) 108
Operations Management Suite (OMS)
  about 69, 78
  used, for logging AKS 97
  used, for monitoring AKS 97
output bindings 269

P

performance
  about 163
  web apps, designing 162
perimeter network architecture 390
Plain Old Java Object (POJO) 315
Platform as a Service (PaaS) 25, 282
point-in-time restore
  about 441
  key points 442, 443
PowerShell 185

Q

Query Explorer, for logs
  reference link 102

R

Redis cache database
  creating 319, 320, 321
  ServiceStack Redis API, using 323, 324
  working with 319
  working with, from C# 321, 322
  working with, from Java 324, 326, 328
Redis
  Azure Cache, using 163, 164
Reliable Actor programming model
  about 211
  reference link 211
Reliable Collections
  using 210
Reliable Services programming model 210
Robo 3T
  download link 311
Role-Based Access Control (RBAC) 377
role-based access control (RBAC) 77
rolling upgrade
  example 94
routing methods, Azure Traffic Manager
  geographic 445
  multivalue 445
  performance 445
  priority 445
  subnet 445
  weighted 445

S

sample Dockerfile
  preparing, for sample app 52, 53
scalability
  about 165
  web apps, designing for 162
scalable application deployment
  backend 83
  frontend 83
  planning, on AKS 82
  solution 83, 84
scale set
  reference link 184
scale sets 181
secure score 391

security analyst 391
serverless computing
  about 248
  dynamic pricing 248, 249
  dynamic scaling 248
  limitations 249
service endpoints 390
Service Fabric .NET application
  creating 220, 221, 222, 223, 224, 225, 226,
    227, 228
  deploying 229, 230
  development environment, setting up 221
Service Fabric Java application
  creating 231, 236, 237, 238, 239, 240
  deploying 241, 242
  development environment, setting up 232
  Eclipse plugin, installing for 233, 234, 235
  local Service Fabric cluster, setting up 232
service principals, with Azure Kubernetes Service
    (AKS)
  reference link 78
ServiceStack Redis API
  using 323, 324
Source Control Management (SCM) 47
SQL API 305, 306
SQL Server Data Tools (SSDT) 289
SQL Server Integration Services (SSIS) 291
SQL Server Management Studio
  connecting 289, 290, 291
stateful microservices 207
stateless microservices 207
Subject Alternative Names (SANs) 375
supported scenarios, ASR
  Azure to Azure 454
  On-Premise to Azure 454
  On-Premise to On-Premise 454
System Center Virtual Machine Manager
    (SCVMM) 114

T

Table API 302
tags
  reference link 78
Team Foundation Server (TFS) 108
Team Foundation Version Control (TFVC) 112

third-party NVAs 390
timer triggered functions
  about 266
  cron syntax, using 267
  second function, writing 267, 268
Total Cost of Ownership (TCO)
  calculating 23
transparent data encryption
  about 387
  tips 388
  working 387
triggered functions
  creating 256, 257, 258
  working with 256

U

Universal Windows Applications (UWP) 113

V

Virtual Actor pattern.
  about 211
  reference link 211
Virtual Machine scale set (VMSS) 186, 187, 420
virtual machines (VMs) 11
Virtual network 186, 187
Visual Studio Code
  about 359
  download link 359
  with Azure 359
Visual Studio Team Services (VSTS) 108
Visual Studio, Mac installation
  reference link 333
Visual Studio
  Azure Functions, creating 259, 260, 261, 262
  Azure tools, installing 334, 335
  Azure tools, obtaining for 333
  bindings, adding 272
  Cloud Explorer, using 336, 337
  connecting, to Azure DevOps project 338, 339,
    340
  in Azure Marketplace 333, 334
  installation link 333
  logging in, with Azure credentials 335, 336
  used, for deploying applications to Azure 341,
    342, 343, 344, 345, 346, 347, 348, 349

used, for deploying ASP.NET application for
  Azure 338
used, for deploying Azure Functions 262, 263
used, for developing ASP.NET application for
  Azure 338
using, with Azure 332
VPN Gateway 187

W

web app, architecture patterns
  reference link 162

Web Apps, for containers
  about 42, 158
  creating 159, 161, 162
  reference link 42
web apps
  designing, for high availability 162
  designing, for performance 162
  designing, for scalability 162
  scaling out 165, 166
  scaling up 168
wide column model 308

www.ingramcontent.com/pod-product-compliance
Lightning Source LLC
Chambersburg PA
CBHW060642060326
40690CB00020B/4484